The Hidden Teachings of Jesus

The Political Meaning of the Kingdom of God

Lance deHaven-Smith

To seek God's will is life's greatest
adventure. To find God's will is life's
greatest discovery. To do God's will is
life's greatest achievement.
"LEMANANDA"

PHANES PRESS

98 97 96 95 94   5 4 3 2 1

Published by Phanes Press, PO Box 6114, Grand Rapids, MI 49516, USA.

Library of Congress Cataloging-in-Publication Data

DeHaven-Smith, Lance.
  The hidden teachings of Jesus : the political meaning of the
kingdom of God / Lance deHaven-Smith
      p.   cm.
  Includes bibliographical references and index.
  ISBN 0-933999-36-4 (pbk. : alk. paper) : $14.95
  1. Jesus Christ--Political and social views.   2. Kingdom of God.
3. Jesus Christ--Prophecies.   I. Title
  BT202.D365   1994
  261.7--dc20   94-10879
                                                          CIP

This book is printed on permanent, acid-free paper.

Printed in the United States of America.

Contents

CONTENTS

Preface

I WROTE this book because I believe that many people are searching for what I have found. I was raised as a Christian, but I became disillusioned with organized religion as I grew to adulthood. I remained uninspired until about five years ago, when circumstances caused me to reexamine my religious beliefs and I began to study the Bible in a new way, using the techniques of my academic discipline.

My method was quite simple and is available to anyone with a Bible and an open mind. I started from the premise, often used in political science to interpret the writings of ancient philosophers,[1] that Jesus was unable to express his beliefs candidly because he was being spied upon and persecuted. This starting point forced me to consider the possibility that Jesus' parables and other sayings had hidden meanings.

Of course, organized Christianity had always said exactly that. The Church taught that many of Jesus' statements were veiled references to his future crucifixion and resurrection. But my method quickly caused me to reject the Church's claims to have decoded Jesus' hidden messages accurately, for, when I read Jesus' words in search of deeper meanings, I found that he was clearly opposed to organized religion itself. He could not say so explicitly, because the priests were always following him and probably would have stoned him to death on the spot (as they did with Stephen), but Jesus made many statements implying his hostility. He told people not to worship in public but rather to pray in secret;[2] he flatly rejected trying to influence God with the kinds of prayers churches use, which he called "vain repetitions";[3] he depicted the inclination to establish organized religion as a temptation presented by Satan;[4] he called for the temple in Jerusalem to be dismantled and replaced by a purely spiritual congregation, a "temple made without hands";[5] and he flatly refused to develop an organized hierarchy among his followers, even though he was requested to do so on more than one occasion.[6] If Jesus was against organized religion, could the organized religion that arose in his name have interpreted his words properly?

This book is a summary of what I believe Jesus intended to convey to us before organized Christianity distorted his meaning. Each chapter focuses on a different teaching, and the teachings are capsulized in the chapter titles.

The book is as much for non-Christians as for Christians, because the true teachings of Jesus are not about creeds and doctrines, but about how to activate spirituality in everyday life. Although I refer to his message as being "political," I am not using this word the way it is usually applied today, that is, in terms of influencing government or public opinion. Rather, by "political" I mean Jesus taught that our basic experience of life depends on the way we organize ourselves collectively and relate to one another interpersonally. Jesus saw that most people are consumed by the constant competition for status, recognition, and control that permeates social and personal relations, and he sought to save us from these self-made webs of "power and glory."

Because this political account of the teachings of Jesus runs counter to traditional Christianity, it has required me to depart from some of the conventional practices of translation and capitalization. For example, I seldom talk of the "Holy Ghost," and I do not capitalize the phrase "holy spirit," because I believe Jesus was referring not to a divine phantom, but to a "spirit of holiness," a detached and defiant attitude emerging whenever one genuinely believes in God. Similarly, I usually do not capitalize the word "messiah," because I do not think that Jesus was (or that he thought himself to be) God incarnate.

I have also drawn on some ancient accounts of Jesus and of his teachings that did not make it into the Bible when the New Testament was codified in Carthage in 397. In particular, I have relied on sources from the Nag Hammadi Library, a set of fourth-century manuscripts unearthed in Egypt in 1945. I have used the Gospels of Thomas, Philip, and Mary Magdalene; the *Gospel of Truth*; the *Treatise on the Resurrection*; *The Book of Thomas the Contender*; and the *Dialogue of the Savior*.[7] These manuscripts contain many of Jesus' most explicit political statements, and presumably this is why they were suppressed by the Church after it was absorbed into the political system of the Roman Empire under the Emperor Constantine. Whenever I have cited these works, I have taken care to distinguish them from the biblical gospels and to indicate how they clarify or amplify the latter.

I would like to thank two people who helped me on the way to writing this book. One is John Champlin, a professor of mine in graduate school at The Ohio State University. He nurtured my interest in classical political philosophy at a time, and in an atmosphere, where it could easily have been extinguished. Without his support during my graduate education, I would never have gone on to make the discoveries contained in this book.

The other person to whom I am especially grateful for help in getting to this point is David Fideler, the Editor and Publisher of Phanes Press and a noted author in the fields of cosmology, philosophy, and early Christianity. In addition to commenting on the manuscript as it was prepared for publication, he introduced me to a whole body of scholarship with which I was not familiar. It has been wonderful to work with someone who shares my conviction that Western civilization needs to resurrect the wisdom of the ancient world.

—LANCE DEHAVEN-SMITH

CHAPTER ONE

The Kingdom of God
is Ours to Create

CHRISTIANITY is commonly thought to be a religion of obedience. Christians believe they should turn the other cheek, render unto Caesar, and bear the cross of adversity.[1]

In this book, I present an entirely different perspective. I argue that Jesus wanted us to join a revolution.

Jesus urged us to abolish all forms of power and glory except those giving power and glory to God. I believe he was talking not about a political order of resurrected souls, but rather about a divine kingdom here on earth, to be established through radical political action inspired by faith in the afterlife. All distinctions of wealth and prestige, all claims of one individual to command the subservience of another, all ranked relations of any sort were to be dissolved.

Jesus could not preach this manifesto openly, because it implied that both the Roman Empire and the glory-demanding priesthood of Judaism should be overthrown. Jesus knew that his anti-establishment ideas made him a target, so he delivered his political message in parables about a "kingdom of God."

Christianity, the organized religion that came later, lost sight of the political meaning of Jesus' teachings. The apostles and Church Fathers became mystical and began to seek salvation, not through divinely inspired *human* action, but from a much hoped-for and prayed-for intervention by God.

My aim in writing this book is to resurrect the political spirit of Jesus. I ask you to examine through your own eyes the gospels and other recently discovered sources of Jesus' teachings. We must shed the preconceptions of organized Christianity and be prepared to see the Jesus of world spiritual revolution, the Jesus who came not to judge us, but to save us.[2]

Still, let me make one thing clear at the start. Although I am

13

convinced that Jesus preached revolution, and that he meant a real revolution and not merely a spiritual transformation, I do have faith that he brought a message of divine salvation. Jesus was not simply a political revolutionary in prophet's clothing. He taught about a political revolution with a spiritual end. Jesus explained to us how to bring God—the God described in the Bible, the God who created us and who at times intervenes into human life—down from heaven and into our own world.

1. New Meanings for Ancient Prophecies

I recognize the apparent arrogance of claiming to have seen for the first time something supposedly missed by all previous generations of Christians, even by those who knew Jesus or his disciples personally. But I believe my willingness to read the gospels in new ways actually shows more humility than those who insist that the only true Christianity is traditional Christianity.

The meanings of revelations have often been misunderstood, even by those who have listened to the prophet who brought them. Until Jesus preached and was crucified, the prophecy of Isaiah—that someone would take on the sins of the world and be wrongfully persecuted—was misunderstood for over 700 years to mean not a single individual or messiah, but the people of Israel as a whole. Jesus himself appears to have been amazed and appreciative that the meaning of earlier biblical revelations had not been perceived by others before him. "I thank thee, O Father, Lord of heaven and earth," he said, "because thou hath hid these things from the wise and prudent, and hath revealed them unto babes."[3] The coming of Jesus had been prophesied, but the meaning of the prophecy was not recognized until Jesus actually arrived.

For that matter, many things Jesus said to his disciples did not make sense to them before Jesus had been crucified. When he spoke, for example, of the "sign of Jonas,"[4] no one seems to have understood at the time that he was referring to his own death and resurrection. Similarly, the disciples completely failed to notice some of the first miracles Jesus performed;[5] the disciples recognized them only later when they came to accept Jesus' divinity. Even Mary and Joseph, who had been told before Jesus' birth that he had a divine mission,[6] did not understand all of their son's prophetic statements. For example, they were completely baffled when, after being lost from them for three days because he had tarried at the temple, the young Jesus shook off their concerns by saying, "How is it that you sought me? Wist ye not that I must be about my Father's business?"[7] Many of Jesus' deeds and remarks went right over the heads of those who knew him best, for events had not yet revealed his purpose.

By the same token, it is certainly possible that many of the teachings of Jesus, and not just his veiled references to the resurrection, have been misunderstood even up to our own times because important events have not yet taken place that will make their intent clear. Indeed, viewed in this light, it is presumptuous to conclude, as most Christians do today, that Jesus has been fully or at least essentially comprehended. As the great theologian Karl Barth has pointed out, when we approach the word of God, whether it is the Old Testament or the gospels or some other source of revelation, we must decipher the message anew in light of our own era.[8] The meaning of revelation is itself revealed as history unfolds.

2. Why the Kingdom Has Not Come

We must be open to a new Christianity. Many things have happened in the current era to suggest a different interpretation of Jesus' teachings. Jesus came preaching the kingdom of God; he said God's will would be done on earth, but first there would be a protracted conflict between good and evil, with evil becoming increasingly concentrated and visible, and good suffering great outrages, until eventually goodness would triumph and a heavenly kingdom would be established.

The great question of earlier eras has been why this kingdom has not come. Almost all of Christian theology for the past two millennia can be understood as an effort to account for what appears to have been this failure of prophecy. The disciples and apostles said the kingdom would arrive in the future when Jesus returned from heaven. The theologians who wrote after Christianity had gained dominance in the Roman Empire claimed the Church itself was the kingdom, and that eventually Jesus would arrive to stand at its head. When the Church became corrupt in the fifteenth century, the Reformation erupted, and the Protestants asserted that the kingdom was not the Church but the spiritual body of true believers who would be resurrected at the second coming. In each instance as these new versions of Christianity were formulated, faith was rekindled; but still the kingdom did not come.

Today, the same quest to explain the kingdom's detainment continues. Like the Christians of old, some say the kingdom is just around the corner and that signs of the apocalypse are everywhere.

Of course, many have concluded from the failure of the kingdom to materialize, that Jesus was simply deluded. They say he mistook the Roman occupation of Israel for the end of the world because he was consumed by the apocalyptic tradition of Judaism. From this perspective, Jesus may have offered some wise sayings, but at heart he was only a wild-eyed doomsayer, and those who think he spoke for God are naive.

But in my opinion the Bible tells us something entirely different. It calls on us neither to pray for a kingdom from heaven nor to reject the prophecy of the messiah. The kingdom of God has not come, because we have not yet accepted our responsibility for establishing it.

If we rid ourselves of prior interpretations and look at the gospels in light of our own times, the kingdom Jesus spoke of, and the day of judgement he said he anticipated, no longer appear so distant, nor does it seem they must come on clouds descending from heaven. Today we can see a global conflict emerging between power and love.

As Jesus predicted, evil has indeed come out of the shadows and penetrated virtually all human relations. It is now visible that not just certain individuals or institutions are evil, but that evil is woven through the whole human world. The best courts in the land deliver only a partial justice. The most democratic governments are rife with corruption and deceit. Economies founded on free enterprise and individual initiative give incredible advantages to those born wealthy, while leaving the mass of humanity in a dead-end life of toil. We strive for a world of goodness, but we find ourselves embedded in cultural, political, and economic muck. No one can live a single day in the modern era and be part of the modern world without feeling countless times the struggle between doing what is right on the one hand, and doing what law, position, or advantage requires on the other.

At the same time, though, a breakthrough seems increasingly possible. Acts of charity on a huge scale are common, from humanitarian relief for starving Africans to benefit concerts for victims of AIDS. Numerous philanthropic organizations have worldwide missions. Through mass communications, the possibility for a global public opinion or spirit has been born. We can see today the potential for peace on earth and goodwill among all people. The contrast could not be more dramatic between the evil imbuing the world and the sudden possibility for spiritual salvation.

This book is about the real kingdom of God, the divine order Jesus envisioned and called on us to establish. Jesus was not talking about a kingdom up in the sky or a kingdom to be wrought by God at some distant or even not-so-distant time; he called for a true kingdom here on earth, a kingdom governed by divine law. This is a difficult message to acknowledge because it puts the responsibility for creating the kingdom on us rather than on Jesus or God, but once we accept it, we can stop waiting on God to save us from ourselves, and we can proceed with the real cross that Jesus handed us, which is to perfect ourselves. As we do this, Jesus promised, God will enter our world.

3. A Politics to End All Politics

The idea that Jesus had real-world political aims is not new, but generally the political principles of Jesus have been seen as falling into one or another of the established camps of his or later days. In my view, the effort by Christians from the third century up to our own era to define Christianity in particular partisan forms is totally misguided. We can see the absurdity of such partisanship in the conflicting Christianities proposed: the Christianity of the Roman Empire, which said civil authority existed and should be respected because it was intended to punish sinners; the Christianity of medieval monarchies, which claimed that the powers of kings were granted from heaven; the brand of Christianity that somehow allowed believers to condone Nazi Germany and Fascist Italy;[9] and the so-called "liberation theology" of today, which depicts Jesus as a revolutionary in the struggle between rich and poor.[10] In these theo-political ideologies, the message of Jesus has been distorted to accommodate the demands of power, which Jesus actually opposed at all levels.

The politics preached by Jesus is political only in the sense that it is *anti*-political. It is opposed to all forms of government that we know. Jesus preached the kingdom of God, but the kingdom of God is not a monarchy, or a benevolent dictatorship, or a socialist republic, or even a democracy.

True, most people both now and in the past would reject the whole idea of government without power. They would say that it is totally impractical, that political power is necessary because people are selfish and violent.

But it is equally arguable that the kingdom we now have, the kingdom of nations governed according to the economic interests and narrow preferences of human beings defined as workers and consumers, is itself impractical. Increasingly, we see that society cannot be held together by carrots and sticks. To the extent that faith and spirituality are cast aside and replaced by collectively enforced incentives and sanctions, the social order crumbles. Just look at our cities and our children! A social order based on the negative coercion of force and the positive coercion of recognition—a society organized, in other words, on power and glory rather than on love and faith—is a society built on sand.

We know this, and yet we doubt our ability to live any other way. We believe that if our cages of fear and social ranking were to be dismantled, lust and rage would blow in whirlwinds through our streets, scattering us like the dry, red leaves of autumn.

Our fear of doing without collective force and of not making dignity contingent on conformity has been woven into Western civilization for three millennia. The first to articulate and defend this fear scientifically were the ancient Greek philosophers. They said that society is inevitably conflictual and that government must be arranged so as to manage and balance the conflict and maintain social order. On this premise, the Greeks and later the Romans developed systems of mixed government that included monarchical, democratic, and judicial elements. Each element was intended to represent a different social class, and the government as a whole was structured so that all classes had to cooperate for any decisions to be made at all. The Founding Fathers of American democracy drew on this tradition to formulate a governmental system of checks and balances. We have long believed that society is divided and fractious, and that therefore political power and social restrictions are necessary evils.

Although almost forgotten in our own day and age, the alternative view of political organization, the view Jesus presented under the very nose of the Roman Empire, that the only peaceful and enduring social order is one ruled by divine law and grounded in the consciences of spiritually activated human beings, has deep roots also. Jesus did not invent it; he found it and sought to bring it back to life. The ancient Jews as well as Jesus gave sound reasons for believing that the rulership of princes and other powers is doomed to failure. They also provided our civilization with detailed explanations and practical advice for establishing a peaceful, divinely ordered society.

The great role of the Judeo-Christian tradition in Western civilization has been combatting the demonic powers of the state, powers defended by Greco-Roman rationalism and its heir, modern science. Abraham defied the Canaanites. Moses overcame the totalitarian Pharaohs of Egypt. Isaiah prophesied against the king of Assyria. Amos insisted that all nations are subject to the rule of God. John the Baptist and Jesus stood up to the imperial power of Rome.

And so it can and must go today. The world has arrived at a critical moment. Great technologies have been developed; a world culture is emerging that transcends the perspectives of individual nations; petty tyrannies of all sorts are being exposed and dismantled. But, at the same time, an unparalleled oppression is taking shape, a dominion that is neither black nor white but grey: the arms-length despotism of the impersonal bureaucrat, the giant corporation, and the blank-faced public, all of which demand conformity in thought, appearance, and action. If we are to save ourselves from this new manifestation of a perennial threat and take advantage of the potential for world salvation which can be seen behind the new oppression, we must understand the true message of Jesus, for the lessons Jesus taught about worldly power and glory were meant for our own times.

4. Jesus Spoke "Between the Lines"

In the past century, numerous attempts have been made to find the real Jesus, but the search has been woefully misdirected. Scholars have correctly targeted the kingdom of God as the central element in Jesus' message, but in seeking to unlock the mystery of the kingdom, they have merely kept trying, first one, and then the other, of two wrong keys. They have said that Jesus meant by the kingdom either a spiritual bond, such as the Church, or a future world-order to be established and governed directly by God.[11] In neither case has Jesus been thought to have counseled revolutionary political action. He has been seen as either a prophet of love or a prophet of doom.

But biblical scholars have missed the political message of Jesus because they have failed to see that the key to the kingdom resides, not *inside* Jesus' words, but *behind* them. In trying to decipher the meaning of Jesus' sayings about the kingdom of God, they appear to have been blind to the fact that he often spoke, not simply figuratively or in symbols, but specifically with the aim of not being understood by the political and religious authorities. For two thousand years, those who have tried to understand Jesus have mistaken his subtle messages about politics for theological claims about God.

This misinterpretation of Jesus is understandable, because Jesus intended for his teachings to be misperceived in exactly that way. Jesus lived in an occupied land. The Romans had appointed Herod as a puppet ruler. All of the many Roman soldiers and government officials in Israel had the power of *aggareia*, that is, the power to compel any of the Jews to serve them in any way the Romans liked, from carrying their bags to giving them their horses and livestock.[12] The soldiers had merely to command them, and the Jews were required to respond like slaves, just as Simon of Cyrene did when he was told to carry the cross used to crucify Jesus.[13] The only real freedom the Jews had was to practice their own religion. Hence Jesus could speak against the

Romans only in religious metaphors.

Jesus was known for having a remarkable way of speaking. I believe that what was remarkable about it was that he was able, through his entertaining parables and aphorisms, to present a revolutionary political message "between the lines."[14] Jesus spoke in code. He was like a prisoner who is allowed by his captors to send a message home; he had to choose words that his captors would allow him to speak but that at the same time would have a deeper meaning for those who were looking for an alternative interpretation of the words. To understand Jesus' message, we must recognize that he was preaching in a situation of extreme oppression and persecution, and that he therefore had to present his teachings with great subtlety—with such subtlety that even his disciples had difficulty understanding him.

Jesus knew well the risks of speaking too freely in his captive kingdom. He had been a disciple of John the Baptist, who Herod beheaded. The gospels contain numerous stories about plots against Jesus. Because of his popularity as a healer, the Pharisees "held a council against him, how they might destroy him."[15] The priests, scribes, and elders plotted to kill him.[16] The Pharisees sought out the Herodians, the Jewish supporters of Herod and Rome, and tried to find "how they might destroy him."[17] The chief priests and the scribes "sought how they might take him by craft, and put him to death."[18] Clearly, Jesus was a marked man, and he knew it.

Furthermore, he was not indifferent to the danger. When he learned that the Pharisees were plotting against him, "he withdrew himself from thence."[19] When he was urged by his disciples to go to the feast of the tabernacle in Judea, he initially declined, saying that he would be persecuted, but later he did attend, "not openly, but as it were in secret."[20] On the day that he sent his two disciples to prepare the room for the last supper, he had made prior arrangements to have them met discreetly, like secret agents, by "a man bearing a pitcher of water."[21] On the night when he was arrested, he had withdrawn into a garden and had posted Peter, James, and John to watch over him, and Peter, if not the others, was armed.[22] Clearly, Jesus wanted to avoid being apprehended.

And yet he could not keep his message to himself. He had a light to bring to the world, and he could not put it under a basket.

So Jesus offered two teachings. To his disciples he preached a new faith that would bring about an entirely new political order, but to the multitudes, he told parables seemingly about a heavenly kingdom that would eventually descend to earth, righting all wrongs and rewarding the meek, the loving, and the faithful. What a wonderful messenger of God! In the heart of occupied Jerusalem—at the center of the temple, watched carefully by the Roman troops, spied on by Herod's agents, surrounded by the puppet priesthood—he could tell the crowds his stories, and many could understand his hidden meanings, but the authorities could never convict him of sedition.

And how they tried to force him to reveal himself! "They watched him, and sent forth spies, which should feign themselves just men, that they might take hold of his words, that so they might deliver him unto the power and authority of the governor."[23] Should we pay taxes, they asked? Look on the coin, he said. Is it not Caesar? Then render unto Caesar what is Caesar's, and unto God what is God's.[24] (But is not everything God's?) By what authority do you forgive sins, they asked? Well, he inquired in reply, by what authority did John baptize? They could not answer, for to challenge John was by then already a sacrilege.[25] The spies were repeatedly stymied.

Jesus was a master at delivering his message in public. Indeed, he was not arrested until he was betrayed by one of his disciples. Judas was a paid informer; he revealed Jesus' hidden meanings.

We can see the effectiveness of Jesus' ambiguity in the problems the authorities experienced at his trial. After Jesus was arrested, Judas was overcome with remorse, and he killed himself rather than testify against his master. Without Judas, the high priests were unable to find witnesses who could provide credible testimony. The worst thing they could corroborate Jesus having said was that the temple would be destroyed and he would raise it again in three days.[26] But apparently, and for obvious reasons, this did not make much sense to the authorities.

If Jesus' own disciples had trouble following his teachings, and if the high priests could not find witnesses who understood his words, we should be very cautious about taking Jesus' statements at face value.

The New Testament contains glimpses of Jesus' secret philosophy, but most of his mysteries are deeply encoded. To understand Jesus, we must read as carefully as Jesus spoke. Furthermore, we must recognize that the statements by Jesus quoted in the New Testament are like messages passed from one person to another; in some instances, part of the meaning may have been lost in the transmission, because the underlying ideas were not understood by those who passed them along.

If the duality of Jesus' teachings were not enough, our uncertainty about what Jesus actually said is further compounded by the nature of the gospels themselves. Not only were they written fairly long after Jesus' crucifixion, perhaps as long as a generation, they were written originally in Greek.[27] Although enormous importance and attention have been given to the words in the New Testament, the fact is that we do not have a single quote from Jesus using his actual words, which were Aramaic.

We should accept as a precaution what Jesus said to his disciples after he delivered his sermon on the mount. His disciples asked him to explain one of his parables, the parable about the seeds falling on different terrains, some on rocks, some amidst thorns, and some in good soil. If Jesus' disciples did not understand this allegory, which is a message about how his new faith would take root, how were they to decipher his more difficult lessons, and how were they to deliver Jesus' tidings to the disciples who followed after them?

5. The Secret Gospels of Thomas, Philip, and Mary Magdalene

That Jesus had both an esoteric or secret teaching for his disciples, and an exoteric or public teaching for others, was well known in the ancient world. We can catch glimpses of this in the gospels. After Jesus preached to the crowd from a boat by the shore where they thronged, his disciples asked him why he spoke to the multitudes in parables rather than directly, as he did with the disciples. Jesus explained that he had to speak in code. "Unto you it is given to know the mystery of the kingdom of God: but unto them that are without, all these things are done in parables, that seeing they may see, and not perceive, and hearing they may hear, and not understand."[28] Outsiders were given parables because if the true message of Jesus, the political message, had been understood, Jesus would have been executed immediately, as eventually he was.

In addition to such statements in the gospels that have come down to the current era in the New Testament canon, writings have survived from several ancient Jewish and Egyptian sects which were founded specifically for the purpose of developing and transmitting the esoteric tradition. These sects came to be referred to as "gnostic," which is the Greek word for "knowing," because they believed salvation depended not on faith but on knowledge. Perhaps best known in this tradition, the Dead Sea scrolls and the Nag Hammadi library, both of which were exhumed in the middle of the twentieth century, present an image of Jesus as having a message shrouded in secrecy. The writings from these sects, which include gospels by Thomas, Philip, and Mary Magdalene, cannot be counted as any more accurate than the texts in the New Testament canon; the influence of Greek philosophy on the gnostic tradition is particularly evident, just as the influence of Jewish apocalyptic ideas is evident in the Gospels of Matthew, Mark, Luke, and John. But the mere existence of the gnostic tradition points to the fact that there was more to what Jesus said than met the ear.

Both the gnostic gospels and the gospels in the New Testament canon contain many statements from Jesus indicating that he had secret teachings. The canon gospels are replete with numerous anecdotes about the disciples needing to have Jesus' analogies and stories explained to them. The disciples asked about the parables of the tares in the field;[29] the "leaven" of the Pharisees;[30] the seeds that fell in different soils;[31] the words that defileth;[32] and the blind leading the blind.[33] The canon gospels also say that Jesus took care never to speak straightforwardly to the multitudes. "But without a parable spake he not unto them: and when they were alone, he expounded all things to his disciples."[34] That Jesus spoke so often in parables is an indication in itself of the fact he was delivering an encoded message.

The gnostic gospels say this directly. According to the *Gospel of*

Thomas, Jesus explained that "it is to those who are worthy of my mysteries that I tell my mysteries. Do not let your left hand know what your right hand is doing."[35] Similarly, the *Gospel of Philip* includes a parable about a sensible householder. "He served the children bread. He served the slaves meal. And he threw barley and chaff and grass to the cattle. He threw bones to the dogs and to the pigs he threw acorns and slop."[36] This parable recalls Jesus' injunction in the Gospel of Matthew not to give what is holy to dogs, and not to cast pearls before swine, "lest they trample them under their feet, and turn again and rend you."[37] Jesus knew that the crowds would turn on him if they understood his revelations, so he placed his holy gems in boxes that the multitudes and even the priests could not open.[38]

Some of the first disciples thought they had opened the lock to Jesus' treasure once Jesus was crucified.[39] The key, they thought, was the prophecy of Isaiah, who had said that a lamb would die for the sins of Israel. Jesus had quoted Isaiah often, and the first words Jesus preached were from Isaiah's book.[40]

And yet this was obviously not the secret. Several of the gospels indicate that Jesus was not averse to saying, either in public or in private, that he was the messiah. He openly told the sick and maimed they were forgiven for their sins, as if he spoke for God himself. Indeed, he said as much to the Sanhedrin, the priestly rulers of Israel, when he was being interrogated prior to his crucifixion. To assume that Jesus' message was that he was the messiah is to believe that the message from the telephone is the ringing bell.

6. The New Judaism of Jesus

To understand Jesus' message, we must ask why he changed the Judaic tradition so radically in his teachings. Up to this time, the prophets had revealed to the Jewish people only that God is one and that the Jews had a historic role to play in educating the world about him. Maimonides, the great Jewish scholar who lived in the twelfth century, has shown that all of the teachings of Abraham and the laws of Moses were designed to break the people from their idolatrous ways and to inculcate self-restraint.[41] Speaking about the nature-worshiping beliefs of the surrounding peoples, Maimonides says, "it is the principle object of the [Old Testament] Law and the axis around which it turns, to blot out these opinions from man's heart and make the existence of idolatry impossible." When Jesus came into the world, the Judaic tradition was not centered on love, equality, and nonviolent resistance to oppression, but monotheism and opposition to graven images.

We can see this thrust in Judaism from the conflict it sparked between the Jews and the Romans. During the same century in which Jesus lived, the Jews rebelled against the Roman occupation. "The Jewish War," as it was termed by Josephus Flavius, a military commander and historian of the era, was provoked by the Romans' insistence that their insignia and statues be allowed into Jerusalem and the holy temple.[42] At this the Jews revolted because of their prohibition against idolatry. Even after being defeated and surrounded at the fortress at Masada, almost a thousand Jews took their own lives rather than accept Roman symbols in the holy places.

Jesus presented, if not a different account of humanity's relation to God, at least a more fully developed one. He preached about a coming "kingdom of God." The world, he said, is ruled by evil forces which flow from a single fountainhead named "Satan." Those who accept distinctions of power and status between people are bowing to Satan because they are putting human perspectives ahead of God's. They should understand, though, Jesus said, that there is a life after death where they are rewarded or punished according to their actions on earth. Those who have power and glory in life will have none in the afterlife. Further, in announcing this invisible reality, Jesus said he was bringing God into the world like a tiny but insuppressible spirit that would eventually overturn Satan's kingdom and establish a divine order, an order governed not by power and glory, but by love and mercy. Eventually, Jesus prophesied, the meek would inherit the earth, and there would be universal peace and love.

These ideas—of the afterlife, Satan, and the kingdom of God—were not foreign to Judaism, but neither were they central. There is nothing at all in the Old Testament describing the afterlife in Christian terms. Even the premise that the soul lives on after death is mentioned only a few times. One is when Saul used a medium to contact the dead priest Samuel, but Samuel did not provide any clues as to the nature of heaven.[43] Just about all that is learned about heaven from the Old Testament is that it is where God resides.

A similar situation holds with the case of Satan. Much of the Old Testament attributes the suffering of the Jews to their own poor judgement, not to an evil force. God is depicted as having selected a particular people to communicate his unity and singularity to the world. The history of the Jews is described as one where this people falls in and out of faith and experiences all sorts of calamities when they turn away from God and worship idols. The only book in the Old Testament that devotes much attention at all to Satan is the Book of Job, which is a story about a man, Job, whose faith is tested by an evil angel.

For that matter, Jesus himself pointed out that the idea of the kingdom of God had been mentioned and then quickly forgotten in the Judaic literature. In one of his parables that is related in both the biblical accounts and the gnostic *Gospel of Thomas*, Jesus said the idea of the kingdom of God is like a treasure, presumably a cultural treasure, that a man had buried unknowingly in a field. After this man died, he left the field to his son:

> The son did not know about the treasure. He inherited the field and sold it. And the one who bought it went plowing and found the treasure. He began to lend money at interest to whomever he wished.[44]

When Jesus said the idea of the kingdom of God was like a buried treasure, he meant that it was not obvious or central to the biblical heritage. There are only a few references to either a kingdom of God or a kingdom of heaven in the Old Testament. Books attributed to Solomon refer to these ideas once and Isaiah uses one of the phrases as well.[45] Jesus implied that he stumbled upon this treasure while plowing through the biblical fields.

Certainly the Jews of his day understood that Jesus was teaching something new and different. This is why Jesus was asked by the scribe to explain what was the highest commandment.[46] In traditional Judaism, as everyone was aware, the highest commandment was the commandment against idolatry. But Jesus changed the commandments given by God to Moses; Jesus said the highest commandments are to love God and neighbor. Jesus did not simply spiritualize the law or make it more demanding. He transformed it. He said that God sees into each of our hearts, that we are placed in a world of temptation, and that we will be judged in the afterlife according to our choices. Our salvation is not a matter of obeying a slew of rigid rules. In fact, rules are foolish and wrong; they cause us to judge and condemn. Salvation comes from replacing laws with love.

We can see the stark contrast between the Old Testament and the New. We must ask, then, why did Jesus develop—or why did God present through Jesus—an entirely new account of heaven and earth? Why did Jesus not just elaborate or stress the importance of traditional Judaism? The Jewish War shows that Judaism could inspire opposition to the Romans. Jesus could have reminded his countrymen of the laws against idolatry. He could have taught that paying tribute, accepting the Roman power of *aggareia*, and yielding to Herod and the other Roman puppets were forms of idolatry. But Jesus did exactly the opposite. He rejected the Judaism of the past, he chided the Pharisees for their preoccupation with the Mosaic law, and he counseled, or seemed to have counseled, obedience to the Romans' demands.

7. Why Jesus Rejected the Old Testament

The traditional explanation offered by organized Christianity for the marked difference between the teachings of the Old and New Testaments is that God's attitude toward humanity changed. After ejecting Adam and Eve from the Garden of Eden, God is said to have gradually come to forgive mankind. He first offered Abraham and his descedants a land of their own if they would worship him and turn from idolatry, then punished them when they veered from faith, and finally sent his own son to be subjected to mistreatment at human hands so that mankind would recognize the sinfulness of its nature. In the Christianity of the churches, God is thought of as a teacher, and each stage in history is seen as a lesson.

There is much to commend this account of the New Testament's break from the Old. Jesus did indeed speak of himself as a sacrificial lamb who was bringing forgiveness of sins.

But organized Christianity's explanation of the meaning of Jesus fails to account for the new things Jesus said about good and evil. Jesus taught not only about God's forgiveness, but also about the struggle between the holy spirit and Satan. He never depicted God as a teacher; he described him as a father, who, like all parents, watches from a distance as his children deal with their own difficulties. If Jesus brought a new message, it was that a change had occurred, not in God, but in the challenges faced by humanity.

I believe God or the spirit of God sent Jesus with a different teaching, a teaching directed at power and glory generally rather than just at graven images, because evil had shown itself to be resilient and changeable, and humanity needed deeper insights to deal with the expanding cloud of temptation. In fact, one of the central points in the revelations of Jesus is that evil is not a static phenomenon; it appears in new forms as it is confronted by faith and holiness. This is why Jesus spoke of evil as a personality, as "Satan." It is a spirit that constantly threatens to take over humanity and push it toward a hellish end. When it is defeated in one configuration, it reappears in another.

Jesus described the world as conflicting "kingdoms," because the many guises of Satan are forms of social organization. The idolatrous empires of Egypt and Babylon were one form, but there would be many others. Jesus said that humanity would remain snared in the clutches of evil until it establishes a kingdom of God. All other kingdoms are just variations on the same basic iniquity.

Jesus was brought forth in the Roman Empire, because the Empire was founded on a new doctrine that the old Judaism, the Judaism focusing on graven images, could not defeat. Jesus said this outright; he prophesied correctly that the temple of the Jews, the historic home of their faith, would be destroyed, and that only the new faith of Jesus could rebuild it.

The soul-anesthetizing oppression of the Romans was unlike what the Jews had experienced under the Egyptians and the Babylonians. In the latter instances, the dominion had a geographical limit, and the Jews were able to break free of it by leaving the land of their oppressors. It was for this reason that the prophecies of the Old Testament centered around a promised *land* rather than a promised *day of judgement*. The evil confronting the Old Testament prophets was localized in graven images and bordered regions. In such a context, God's spirit revealed to the holy people among the Jews that salvation lay in securing their own territory and worshiping the God whose only image is humankind.

But the Roman Empire was not an isolated place any more than modern society is a nation. The Empire embodied an entirely new form of evil. Rome did not demand that its subjects worship Roman gods or idols; to the contrary, it treated all religions as superstitions. As Edward Gibbon observed in *The Decline and Fall of the Roman Empire*, "The various modes of worship which prevailed in the Roman world were all considered by the people as equally true; by the philosopher as equally false; and by the magistrate as equally useful."[47] The only things the Empire expected people to revere were its laws, which ignored religion and dealt almost exclusively with rights concerning property, political participation, and the like. Prior to Christianity, the Empire practiced a distinct separation between church and state, at least in the sense that it prescribed no religious creed for its citizens or its vassal states.

The purely secular orientation of Roman law was evident at the trial of Jesus. Initially, Pontius Pilate would not authorize the crucifixion requested by the Jewish priests because at first the priests charged Jesus solely with breaking the Jewish religious laws against blasphemy and against working on the sabbath.[48] Pilate refused to order the execution until he was convinced by the priests that Jesus was in some way seeking to undermine the laws of the Empire. The question Pilate asked was not whether Jesus professed to be a prophet or a messiah, but whether he was claiming to be the true monarch of his people.[49] Although Jesus replied that his kingdom was "not of this world,"[50] his accusers, shifting their complaints to apply to Roman law rather than to their own religious codes, said "whosoever maketh himself a king speaketh against Caesar."[51] The sign Pilate ordered to be placed on the cross—"THE KING OF THE JEWS"[52]—at once mocked Jesus and stated that his crime was against the Empire, not against Judaism.

The new form of evil stalking humanity was an evil we are beginning to know very well in the modern era, as Jesus implied we would. It was a faith not in idols but in human beings, in the commandments of men and women.

Of course, in Jesus' day as in our own, those who worshiped at the altar of this new creed saw it as urbane and tolerant. In their view, it was a philosophy rather than a religion. Just as today science and government are depicted as eminently reasonable, so were the beliefs and laws of Rome.

The political philosophy of the Empire had been developed several centuries earlier in Athens by Socrates, Plato, Aristotle, and their later followers.[53] In a profound break from all prior thinking, they unleashed political power and social ranking from religious moorings and made possible what we are seeing today, that is, the emergence of huge political formations that are totally devoid of religious convictions and constraints. The Greek philosophers rejected religion as a foundation for social order and argued that society should be structured instead around the abstract aim of justice. From this principle came the possibility of, first, the empire of Alexander the Great, who had been educated by Aristotle himself, and then the empire of the Romans, who took over the Greek empire after Alexander's successors began to fight among themselves. The whole framework of Roman law was based on Greek philosophy; Roman law was supposed to be higher than any particular nation's religious law. This was the justification for Roman troops to occupy other countries. They enforced Roman law and, in so doing, were thought to be securing a higher justice for numerous sub-states which had previously been governed only by parochial legal codes based on dubious religious traditions.

The most famous book of the era was titled *The Republic*. Written by Plato, it was like a Greek and Roman Bible. It claimed that the aim of society is justice; that justice is giving all persons what they deserve on the basis of effort and ability; that the most just society is ruled by the people who deserve to rule, that is, by the best people, the *aristoi*; that the force which threatens social order and drags society into oppression is the greed of the common people, the *demos*, who support tyrants in order to take from the better people; and that therefore the *aristoi*, the aristocrats, should rule, and the common people, the *demos*, should be encouraged to adhere to their native religions so that they would more willingly accept the dominion of the aristocracy.[54]

The vision of Plato still lives today in the aspirations of the modern era. We may not advocate rule by aristocrats, but we certainly believe in the need for experts and professionals, and we continue to aim for a social order where goods are distributed on the basis of merit rather than need, where the best people govern rather than serve, and where laws are designed to achieve fairness rather than love or mercy. Just as in the Roman Empire, law and government are seen, not as a religion in themselves, but as a framework in which various faiths may reside.

But Jesus came to tell us that a kingdom based on law, no matter how much it tolerates various beliefs and regardless of whether it is ruled by the best people, is a kingdom of hell. When Jesus preached about the kingdom of God, he was directing our gaze to the kingdoms of human beings. The problem we face, he said, is not merely the temptation to deify images, but our willingness to worship ourselves. The pit to be circumvented is not just idolatry, but earthly power and glory generally.

We are only now beginning to see the full implications of legal and social systems that are devoid of respect for God. Jesus warned us that the Roman Empire was merely the beginning. When he was being led to his crucifixion and many women were sobbing for him, he said,

> Daughters of Jerusalem, weep not for me, but weep for yourselves, and for your children. For, behold, the days are coming in which they shall say, blessed are the barren, and the wombs that never bare, and the paps which never gave suck. Then shall they begin to say to the mountains, Fall on us; and to the hills, Cover us. For if they do these things in a green tree, what shall be done in the dry?[55]

Raw power was just coming into existence during the days of the Roman Empire, and the culture, the tree in which the Roman eagle[56] perched, was still green because it was still nourished by the living water of faith. At this early point in the growth of power, the evil spirit that haunts humankind could cause the people of Israel only a few thousand crucifixions. But behold where we are now; in the twentieth century, we have efforts, almost successful, to exterminate entire peoples. Human beings are shot by the hundreds of thousands and bulldozed into trenches, or gassed in groups and cremated, or killed indiscriminately with bombs of poison. What were Caesar and his legions when compared to Joseph Stalin, Adolf Hitler, Idi Amin, Pol Pot, the Shah of Iran, and other tyrants? The tree of our culture is withered, and vultures sit in its branches.

Totalitarian terrors continually appear in our era like a recurring nightmare because the modern state does not acknowledge God and therefore does not accept ultimate limits to its power. Although modern political constitutions restrict the exercise of authority, these restrictions are considered not to be final and immovable, but based on an agreement among the citizenry. Hence, in emergencies, constitutional limits are routinely ignored; people suspected of being dangerous to the regime are rounded up and incarcerated, as the Japanese were in the United States during World War II, and as Jews, Catholics, and Communists were in Nazi Germany. In twentieth-century America, whenever the state has been threatened, whether it has been by anarchists, labor organizers, communists, civil rights leaders, students, war veterans, or hippies, the government has *always* violated the very rights it claimed to be protecting. The Constitution is obeyed only so long as it is convenient.

This attitude toward power, and not the exigencies of national security, is at the root of all modern tyranny. Oppression, aggression, and organized cruelty originate in the atheism of the age. As Friedrich Nietzsche predicted fifty years before the Third Reich, if God is dead then everything is permitted.[57] To the extent that values and laws are believed to flow only from human beings and not from God, each person is free to choose his or her own standards, and the highest values are merely the values of the strongest people or the most brutal nation.

And the horrifying truth is that the new evil, which was seen first in the Roman Empire but which is now a thousand times more savage and more pervasive, has not even completed its development. Indeed, it may still be in its infancy. Drugs, genetic engineering, mass media, and other modern technologies that can take possession of people's minds are only just now being deployed, and no state has had time to fully integrate them into its systems of social control. The use of computers, which provide the means to track and direct enormous numbers of people, is at the same stage. Clearly, we have not yet arrived at the real totalitarianism that is possible.

8. Jesus Poured New Wine into Old Bottles

Jesus did not merely warn us about the threat we face, he also explained to us how to defeat it. He flatly rejected the tactics that have been used historically to combat oppression. His strategy was not to *fight* power and glory, but to *subvert* it.

He explained that we cannot overthrow our earthly kingdoms with violence or rebellion. No matter how well intended it is, any war of liberation leads back to the very oppression it seeks to conquer, because, in relying on force, it brings coercion into whatever new institutions it establishes, and one kind of master is merely replaced by another. In the words of Jesus, "all they that take the sword shall perish with the sword."[58]

In addition, Jesus said we cannot escape earthly kingdoms by establishing spiritual enclaves that leave the social order unreformed. This was the tack taken by the Pharisees, whom Jesus never missed an opportunity to deride. They called for their countrymen to follow strict religious rules regarding diet, cleanliness, the celebration of the sabbath, and so on, because they wanted to preserve Judaism against the influence of Roman rule and Greek and Roman culture. We should take special note of what Jesus concluded about this spiritual isolationism, for it is also the stance of the modern era, which has institutionalized a separation between church and state. Jesus foresaw the unworkability of such arrangements. When he was baited in public by the Pharisees, he may have said that we should "render unto Caesar what is Caesar's, and unto God what is God's." But when he was speaking privately to his disciples, he warned against any division of loyalties: "No man can serve two masters: for either he will hate the one, and love the other; or else he will hold to the one, and despise the other."[59]

Jesus taught that power and glory can neither be defeated militarily nor fended off culturally; they must be attacked *spiritually* at their origin in the human heart. With his usual subtlety, he made this point with an analogy that is contained in both the canon gospels and in the gnostic *Gospel of Thomas*: "It is not possible for anyone to enter the house of a strong man and take it by force unless he binds his hands; then he will be able to ransack his house."[60]

Jesus implied that the strongman is the whole idea that power and glory should be granted to anyone or anything besides God. The idolaters gave power and glory to graven images and to the priests and rulers who claimed to speak for them. The philosophers of Greece proclaimed that power and glory should be conferred to the people who are wisest and bravest. We in the modern era extend power and glory to the wealthy, the beautiful, and the smart. In rejecting the Judaism of the Old Testament, Jesus was saying that it is not enough to combat evil in each of its successive forms, first overthrowing idolatry, then repulsing the influence of Rome with strict codes of religious conduct, then taking on the next social formation and so on down the line as the evil reconstitutes itself. This is merely living in the house of the powerful, rather than owning it for one's self.

By urging us to tie the strong man's hands, Jesus was telling us to subdue oppression with a faith that binds power itself, regardless of the form it happens to take. He explained that even the most vicious system can be overthrown if only people will use their spirituality against its ideological defenses, for no justification of earthly kingdoms can withstand the scrutiny of spiritual discernment.

The spirit of God had already revealed the ability of spirituality to explode an ideology when the Jews overturned the idolatrous religion of the Canaanites after coming into the promised land. The prophets of the Old Testament had taught the ancient Jews how to subvert the

Canaanites' religion *from the inside*. The Canaanites called every force of nature "Baal" or "Lord." They said that every part of nature has its lord, its own Baal. Sculpt me a bird with a man's head, they said, and it is the wind, the Baal of air. Look upon the mountain and worship its glory, the Baal of high places. Bow down to Baal and to images of Baal; humble yourself before nature. But the prophets of Israel listened well and understood. They saw the stupidity of the Canaanites' idea. If your god is nature, then every part of nature is your lord, and you worship not only the stars and the mountains, but also the maggots and the dung. So the Israelites made the true God laugh. They mocked Baal. They joked that the Canaanites worshiped Baal ze Bubb or, as we say today, Beelzebub, "the lord of flies."

Jesus knew this lesson, even though the Pharisees did not. According to the gnostic *Gospel of Thomas*,

Jesus said, "If those who lead you say to you, 'See, the kingdom is in the sky,' then the birds of the sky will precede you. If they say to you, 'it is in the sea,' then the fish will precede you. Rather, the kingdom is inside you, and it is outside of you. When you come to know yourselves, then you will become known, and you will realize that it is you who are the sons of the living father. But if you will not know yourselves, you dwell in poverty and it is you who are that poverty."[61]

Jesus taught that we should apply the tactic of subversion not just to idolatry, but to power and glory generally. We must understand that we are all children of God, and that none of us should claim the right to command others or to be exalted. All earthly kingdoms put some thing or some value ahead of God and humanity and thereby reveal their own spiritual poverty.

In preaching the kingdom of God, Jesus went to the heart of the matter, just as the Old Testament prophets had done with their epigram about the lord of flies. The Greek philosophers had advocated a society aimed at a merciless fairness they called "justice," governed by laws that give each person what he or she deserves, and administered by the best people. Jesus took their idea, which he prophesied would threaten humanity's very soul, and he embedded within it a revelation that would blow apart the whole system it supported. If you want to have the best kingdom, as Plato advocated earlier and we still call for today, then seek a kingdom ruled by God.

The idea of subverting earthly power and glory was the deeper meaning in Jesus' aphorism about pouring new wine into old bottles. Early in his ministry, Jesus was asked by the disciples of John the Baptist why Jesus did not expect his followers to fast, as John did. Jesus replied that people normally avoid putting new wine into old bottles, "else the bottles break, and the wine runneth out, and the bottles perish."[62] The disciples seem to have thought that Jesus was simply indicating that, since his teachings were new, so were his religious practices. But Jesus was really saying that he was changing the teachings of Judaism, or creating a new wine, in order to break the bottles of political power and social status that hold people's souls. That this was his meaning can be seen in the fact that the aphorism shows no concern about the loss of the wine but instead stresses that the bottles will both "break" and "perish." Similarly, Jesus suggested that he was going to tear the social fabric, into which people had been woven, by sewing onto it a new cloth, for "no man also seweth a piece of new cloth on an old garment: else the new piece that filled it up taketh away from the old, and the rent is made worse."[63]

Jesus was careful in how he said it, but those who knew his intentions could easily understand his analogies and parables. He brought a new faith to destroy the new or deeper evil that had appeared with the Roman Empire.

9. The Subversion of Christianity

At this point I must be blunt. The political teachings of Jesus were lost and remained unrecognized until now because of organized Christianity. In the formative years of the political movement initiated by Jesus, the Church accommodated itself to the Roman Empire, and vice versa. Jacques Ellul, one of the most free-thinking biblical scholars of the twentieth century, has referred to this development as "the subversion of Christianity."[64] Necessarily, as the Church embraced the very Roman state that Jesus had opposed and by which he had been crucified, Jesus' radical political revelations became increasingly problematic, and eventually they were quite literally suppressed. The gnostic tradition was driven underground and was lost for over a millennium. The good news brought by Jesus about the kingdom of God became identified, totally and exclusively, with the Church. Consequently, to this day, those who would unearth the political message of Jesus must go against almost all of what Jesus has come to stand for.

By reading the Acts of the Apostles, which contain not the history of the Jesus movement as a whole but rather only that of the organized Church, we can see how quickly the Church Fathers lost sight of the fact that the teachings of Jesus sought to tie the hands of Rome by subverting Greek philosophy. When Paul went to Athens and addressed an audience of Greek philosophers, he was totally unable to explain how the Christian religion differed from the philosophy of Plato and Aristotle, a philosophy which had been the preeminent worldview of the Empire for over three hundred years and which Jesus was clearly addressing with his revelations about the kingdom of God. Although Paul was speaking to educated aristocrats who did not believe at all in the Greek and Roman gods worshiped by the common people, he talked to them as if they were simple pagans. He told them that they were too superstitious, that they should not worship idols, and that the true God, while he had "winked at" these beliefs in the past, was unwilling to tolerate them any longer.[65] Paul does not seem to have realized that the Greek philosophers, much like scientists today, thought that the world was governed by abstract principles laid down by a Prime Mover who did not interfere in human affairs. Paul did not tell them that, with their philosophy about justice and law, they were searching for the kingdom in the wrong place. He did not explain to them that the highest value is love, not the merciless fairness they called justice. He did not even tell them that their so-called "republic," which they glorified and obeyed, had brutally executed the holiest person who had ever lived. No, in perhaps the most direct encounter between secular philosophy and Judeo-Christian faith in all of Western civilization, the advocate for Christianity showed little understanding of the issues, and the philosophers mocked him.

Already by Paul's time, the organized Church was preaching, not a spiritual *revolution*, but rather a spiritual *patience*. The Church Fathers had thrown open the gates of their organized kingdom to all comers. Those who wanted to join had only to profess their belief in the divinity of Jesus and in the second coming. The Church was then and is now an organization built around the ideas of the afterlife and a future Armageddon. The priests minister to the people by handing them sacraments, and the people file by, taking morsels of hope while they live in the world as it is, the world of earthly power and glory.

But in truth Jesus never intended to start an organized religion, at least nothing like the one created by Peter, Paul, and the other Church Fathers. Rather than a universal church, he expected his movement to involve only a relatively small group of believers who would possess a profound faith. Many would be called, but few would be chosen.[66] His plan was to scatter this very exclusive but inflammatory faith throughout the social order, where it would eventually transform power and status. As an analogy, the canonical gospels point to the way a small amount of leaven, concealed in bread dough, makes the whole loaf rise.[67] Similarly, according to the gnostic *Gospel of Thomas*, Jesus said, "I have cast fire upon the world, and see, I am guarding it until it blazes."[68] Jesus did not intend to create a large institution open to everyone. He guarded the embers by speaking cryptically until the fire could spread.

Even the gospels that have been transmitted to us by the Church itself indicate that Jesus was totally opposed to joining the power structure. One of the temptations Jesus faced in the desert was Satan's offer of the power and glory of all earthly kingdoms, but Jesus flatly refused Satan's bargain.[69] Jesus was opposed to all forms of hierarchy except that of the prophet or messiah and his or her people. When Jesus sought to spread the good news about the kingdom of God, he did not do so by creating any sort of structured organization. Rather, he sent disciples two by two, from city to city, having them display their faith through their actions.[70]

No doubt, Jesus' opposition to power and glory is why the social order of early Christianity was nothing at all like the later Church or the monasteries, which were male dominated, hierarchical, and ritualistic. The early Christians lived as a community of believers united by love, sharing their property equally, and focusing on friendship. Luke says,

> And all that believed were together, and had all things common; and sold their possessions and goods, and parted them to all men, as every man had need. And they, continuing daily with one accord in the temple, and breaking bread from house to house, did eat their meat with gladness and singleness of heart, praising God, and having favor with all the people. And the Lord added to the church daily such as should be saved.[71]

The family-like community of the early believers followed directly from Jesus' preachings.[72] The kingdom of God described by Jesus was inconsistent with all forms of authority and status. To enter the kingdom, one needed to be like a child: forgiving and non-judgmental.[73] Distinctions of wealth were prohibited; those with riches were no more able to enter the kingdom than a camel was capable of passing through the eye of a needle.[74] Political leadership did not give one power but instead required service:

> Ye know that the princes of the Gentiles exercise dominion over them, and they that are great exercise authority over them.
>
> But it shall not be so among you: but whosoever will be great among you, let him be your minister; and whosoever will be chief among you, let him be your servant.
>
> Even as the Son of man came not to be ministered unto, but to minister, and to give his life as a ransom for many.[75]

The unavoidable conflict between, on the one hand, the Roman Empire, and, on the other hand, those who declared their allegiance to God, appears at least initially to have taken the explosive form Jesus anticipated. By the end of the second century, those who declared themselves to be Christians faced a horrible death, usually by being taken to the arena or some other public place, being beaten, being mauled by wild animals, and then having their throats slit.[76] To avoid this torture and escape punishment entirely, the faithful had only to deny their Christianity and vow allegiance to the Emperor; and yet, as time passed, more and more stood their ground, willing to endure a terrible death rather than renounce their convictions. Jesus had indeed cast a fire upon the earth, and by the third century it had begun to blaze.

However, in the fourth century the flames were brought under control. The Emperor Constantine adopted the cross as his battle insignia, and in 325 he called the first Nicene Council, which, by declaring that Jesus was God incarnate, assured that his aphorisms and parables would be interpreted mystically rather than politically. By 380, mass Christianity was the official religion of the Empire. Predictably, in 397 many of the works that expressed Jesus' secret teachings were omitted from the Bible when the canon of New Testament texts was selected by the Church from among the many gospels that were circulating at the time.[77] Not much later, the writings in the Nag Hammadi library were buried because they were outlawed books.

The new Christianity, the orthodox Christianity of the Holy Roman Empire, was a tame Christianity. To seek to understand the subtle political message in Jesus' teachings became socially and legally prohibited. The veil Jesus had placed over his message to keep it from being seen by the Roman authorities of his day became a screen that allowed the Church to avoid recognizing the radical ideas Jesus had preached.

10. Resurrecting the Spirit of Jesus

I believe that all of this is as it should be, or at least that it could not have been avoided. We had to experience the subversion of Christianity to truly understand Jesus' teachings, to understand that there can be no compromise with power and glory. We went into the desert with our faith, and we were offered the power and glory of earthly kingdoms. Although we had been warned that earthly power corrupts, that it requires us to prostrate ourselves before Satan, we took the bargain, and the Jesus movement became Christianity. From this point forward, the liberating spirit Jesus brought to us began to be choked and tied down. The Church at one point became as oppressive and murderous as the Roman Empire. Today it struggles to regain its vitality, but still, as Jesus said of the Pharisees, it "teaches for doctrines the commandments of men."[78]

If Christians are to put Jesus back at the head of their movement, they must return to his aims. He said that we must establish a godly kingdom on earth. This does not mean prayer on the Sabbath and business as usual during the rest of the week. Nor does it allow wealthy churches that pay homage to the power and glory of their host nations, or even being a good citizen and a good worker.

It requires a radical change of heart, mind, and spirit, a change so profound that it will awaken the spirit in others and spread a fire across the land!

I know, of course, that to most Christians the idea of trying to establish the kingdom of God through human action would appear profoundly sacrilegious, for the prevailing belief within Christianity since shortly after the crucifixion of Jesus has been that the kingdom and the second coming are dependent upon the will of God, not the actions of men and women. People *await* the return of Jesus; they do not *cause* the return to occur.

But a wait-for-the-coming attitude is actually contrary to the real Judeo-Christian tradition and misses the essential point Jesus made in his teachings about the kingdom of God and the kingdom of heaven. The entire history of the ancient Jews up to the time of Jesus clearly shows that God appears only *after* humanity first takes a step in God's direction. God did not enter into a covenant with Abraham and his descendants until Abraham had left his homeland and his family,[79] nor did God appear to Moses until after Moses had first departed Egypt.[80] Likewise, the messiah did not come until John the Baptist, acting on Isaiah's prophecy, had preached in the desert, and God did not voice his pleasure with Jesus until Jesus was baptized.[81] It seems that God does not merely help those who help themselves; he speaks only to those who act on their faith before seeing Him.

Jesus said, "Seek and ye shall find; knock and it shall be opened unto you."[82] He did not say, "Wait, and I shall return." In fact, the gnostic *Gospel of Thomas* reports that Jesus opposed this very idea. "His disciples said to him, 'When will the kingdom come.' Jesus said, 'It will not come by waiting for it. It will not be a matter of saying, Here it is or there it is. Rather, the kingdom of the father is spread out upon the earth, and men do not see it.' "[83]

The same is true today. The kingdom of God exists as a spiritual potential in our souls; all we must do is realize it. Jesus will return, or there will be a new Jesus, or the spirit of Jesus will be resurrected, if only we will stop waiting and will begin bringing the kingdom to life.

CHAPTER TWO

The Holy Spirit
is a State of Mind

EARLIER, I asserted that Jesus was more than a revolutionary in prophet's clothing, that he brought divine salvation. Before going further in explicating Jesus' political message, we should examine the connection between his teachings about government and his revelations about God. This connection can be seen most clearly in what Jesus said about the holy spirit.

In my view, when Jesus spoke of spirits, holy or otherwise, he was not talking about phantoms or ghosts, but rather about tendencies or motivations which arise within and around all worldly systems of power and status. "Satan" was the name Jesus gave to the spirit that tempts us to accept worldly kingdoms aimed at security and fairness, while the "spirit of holiness" was what he called our impulse to seek a divine kingdom of love and mercy. Although Jesus said that both of these spirits have supernatural origins, he did not see them as separate from humanity, but rather as arising from within humankind, as forces or inclinations.

Jesus prophesied that the spirit of holiness would stir in people as they sought to establish a kingdom of God, and that the satanic tendencies of those who clung to worldly power and glory would become stronger and more visible in reaction. The result would eventually be what we have today, that is, an escalating contradiction between, on the one hand, our potential for world peace and universal love, and, on the other hand, expanding systems of political power and social status. Jesus implied that this spiritual conflict would culminate in a decisive showdown, or day of judgement.

Unfortunately, the founders of organized Christianity misunderstood this message. They came to think of the holy spirit as a Holy Ghost—not an inspiration, but a phantom that could be controlled by human beings through certain rituals. This view of the holy spirit was not coincidental; it gave the new Church its ability to claim to control access to God through the priesthood and the sacraments. If the Church Fathers had preached that the holy spirit is an innate inclination to reject authority and status, they would have had nothing to offer to the multitudes being recruited, for the populace would have been told precisely what Jesus had told his disciples: that the kingdom of God was already within them, and that they had only to release it to bring the kingdom into the world.

1. Why the Trinity is a Mistaken Idea

I understand that many people may find what I am saying offensive, but I believe my account of the holy spirit is evident in the Scriptures, whereas the traditional account offered by the Christian churches is not. Please recognize that I draw a sharp distinction between, on the one hand, what Jesus said (or is said to have said), and on the other hand the doctrines developed later by the apostles and other Church Fathers. Most people educated in the Christian faith lump together the teachings of Jesus and the subsequent ideas of his disciples and of his disciples' disciples, because this is what the Church did. But if the Scriptures are read carefully, it can be seen that the apostles departed radically from Jesus' prescriptions.

Keeping clear the distinction between Jesus' teachings and those of the apostles is especially important when it comes to the subject of the holy spirit, because the Church developed its view of the holy spirit, and more generally of the trinitarian character of God, primarily on the basis of what was said by the apostles in the Acts, not what was preached by Jesus himself. Indeed, the doctrine of organized Christianity, that both Jesus and the holy spirit are coequal aspects of God the Father, was not propounded until roughly *three hundred years after the crucifixion*. To treat the Church's thesis of the "Trinity" as if it were a direct teaching of Jesus, rather than merely a speculation of Christian theoreticians, is to do exactly what Jesus criticized the Pharisees for, that is, claiming divine authority for what are merely the doctrines of fallible human beings.

The view that I am proposing—that Jesus was simply a man endowed with the holy spirit, which he sought to awaken in others so that they would reject worldly systems of command and status—is not at all a recent idea, or a view that only someone from the modern era would develop. Actually, it was widely accepted by many Christians in the second and third centuries. It was first stated formally around 190 in Rome by Theodotus of Byzantium, and subsequently elaborated by Artemon.[1] The view became established well enough to be given a name by the theologian Tertullian; he referred to it as "monarchianism" because it aimed at protecting the "monarchy" of the one God—God the Father.[2]

In fact, the doctrine of the Trinity might never have been propounded by the Church and adopted as dogma if a huge controversy had not erupted around a particular "monarchian" cleric. Arius, a priest of the church in Alexandria, was excommunicated by his bishop for preaching that Jesus was not divine.[3] After the excommunication, the churches in Egypt, Palestine, and Syria went into an uproar, presumably because many Christians agreed with Arius. Further, Arius gained important support from a renowned church historian, Eusebius, who was from Caesarea in Israel. By 324, the controversy had reached Rome and was apparent even to the Emperor Constantine.

Clearly indicating just how serious the dispute had become, Constantine felt compelled to call a meeting of bishops in 325 to settle the matter. He wanted the Church to have a single, dogmatic position on the question of the divinity of Jesus and of the spirit of holiness, because he believed that a uniform opinion was important to the Empire, which might become fragmented if internal, religious disputes were left unresolved. Constantine had good political reasons to be concerned; in 295, the Roman Empire had been divided between eastern and western kingdoms, and Constantine's great accomplishment had been, first, to gain control over the western territories and then, in 324, to defeat the Emperor of the East and become sole ruler of the reunited polity. Hence one of the first things Constantine did after achieving victory over the East was to require that the Church support the political unity of his kingdom by squelching debate and formulating unequivocal doctrines.

The meeting in 325, which produced the doctrine of the Trinity, became known as the Council of Nicaea, named after the city where it was held. Arius presented his own views, while the trinitarian theory of God was argued by Arius' great enemy, Athanasius. The council ruled in favor of Athanasius and adopted what is now called the "Nicene Creed":

> We believe in one God, the Father Almighty, maker of all things, both visible and invisible; and in one Lord, Jesus Christ, the Son of God, Only begotten of the Father, that is to say, of the substance of the Father, God of God and Light of Light, very God of very God, begotten, not made, being of one substance with the Father, by whom all things were made, both things in heaven and things on earth; who, for us men and for our salvation, came down and was made flesh, was made man, suffered, and rose again on the third day, went up into the heavens, and is to come again to judge both the quick and the dead; and in the Holy Ghost.

Two bishops, including Eusebius, refused to sign this statement, but Arius was condemned nevertheless, and banished.

An invention of men, the Nicene Creed became the core belief of organized Christianity. It is shared today by Catholics and Protestants alike. Although most Christians are not really aware of its history and of the controversy that surrounded its adoption, they hold the creed to be the defining statement of their faith.

I do not enjoy being the one who says the emperor has no clothes, and frankly I would not mention specific points of doctrine if I could avoid it, for I am neither a theologian nor a minister. But since the official students of the Bible are silent on this issue, someone else—a theological child, as it were—must ask the obvious question, which is whether the Nicene Creed is actually consistent with the gospels.

I feel that the spirit of Jesus would lead us to examine this creed very critically. We should be at least suspicious of a doctrine spawned by the same political system that crucified the man the doctrine is trying to describe. Would Jesus have wanted us to attend a meeting called by the Emperor to develop a code which would be required opinion throughout the realm? It seems preposterous to suggest that Jesus would have gone with his disciples to a council called by Herod or Pontius Pilate for the purpose of formulating dogma, yet this is precisely what the Christian bishops did in the fourth century. The Emperor demanded a uniform opinion, the bishops complied, and to this very day Christians adhere to the decision as if the words had come directly from the mouth of God.

Imagine how different the faith might be if the Emperor had never called the Council of Nicaea and instead had allowed differing ideas about Jesus and the holy spirit to coexist. Rather than being directed for resolution to an elite class of priests, questions of doctrine would have remained open to all, and the deciding factor would have been, as it has become under Protestantism, not the statements of the Pope and his bishops, but the words of Jesus in the gospels as interpreted by every thinking individual.

In this context, those who opposed the trinitarian theory would surely have asked why, if Jesus actually held a set of doctrines to which he wanted everyone to adhere, he did not state them himself? But of course, for dogmatists likes Constantine and the bishops at Nicaea, this was the problem!

The reason the Emperor had to require the Church to formulate a clear doctrine is that the gospels are thoroughly ambiguous. Jesus never used the word "trinity," or anything like it. Never did he say that he was, to quote the creed, "of one substance with the Father"; to the contrary, when someone called him "good master," Jesus rebuked him, saying, "Why callest thou me good? There is none good but one, that is, God."[4] Jesus spoke of himself as God's "son" and as having been "sent" by God, not as being God incarnate.

In fact, the whole idea of the Trinity is loaded with problems. The central message of the entire Old Testament is that God is one. Jesus reaffirmed this revelation when he was asked what is the highest commandment. Jesus began his answer by saying, "The first of all the commandments is, Hear, O Israel; The Lord our God is one Lord."[5] To the extent that God is assumed to be divided into parts or personalities—to be, in some sense, more than one—the whole idea of God becomes in jeopardy of dissolving into paganism.

But the Trinity requires us to believe, clearly, in three gods: the Father, the Son, and the Holy Ghost. Although theologians may speak of them as being all "of one substance," they are each separate and distinct. Either trinitarianism is polytheism, or it is very close to it.

Why, then, did the bishops use a tortured logic to arrive at a doctrine that was, at best, dubious in light of the Scriptures? No doubt, there were many reasons, but one was certainly the underlying interest of the Empire's political and religious authorities in avoiding the political implications of Jesus' teachings. By equating Jesus and the holy spirit with God, the Church Fathers were able to put the burden of creating the divine kingdom on Jesus in a future "second coming." They did not have to create the kingdom themselves, because they had a God to depend on rather than an inspired man to emulate, and they did not have to consider what type of inspiration Jesus was talking about when he spoke of the spirit of holiness, because they had a spirit that was a ghost rather than a motivation.

The bishops could also find support for their trinitarian theory in the Acts of the Apostles, a history of the early church written by Luke. Jesus' teachings about humanity's defiant spirit of holiness was already being depoliticized as soon as he was crucified, and both Jesus and the holy spirit were depicted in the Acts very differently than in the gospels. Later in this chapter, we will examine the shift from the teachings of Jesus to those of Peter and some of the other disciples. Suffice it to say for now that the Nicene Creed was a fairly late step in the Church's long retreat from Jesus' political message.

2. Spirit of Holiness, or Holy Ghost?

There is very clear evidence in the canon gospels that Jesus meant by the "holy spirit" a natural human tendency to stand up to authority. For reasons discussed below, Jesus fully expected his followers to be persecuted, and not merely by bigots in traditional sects and other religions, but by the highest authorities in the land. In the Gospels of Matthew, Mark, and Luke, Jesus is reported to have told his disciples,

"Ye shall be brought before governors and kings."[6] He explained that it was precisely in this circumstance that the spirit of holiness could be activated; all the disciples had to do was to focus totally on the moment and to speak directly from their hearts rather than from their minds. "Take no thought of how or what ye shall speak: for it shall be given you in the same hour what ye shall speak. For it is not ye that speak, but the Spirit of the Father which speaketh in you."[7] The holy spirit is the attitude we possess in the face of power when we do not think ahead about consequences or punishments.

Unlike the account of the holy spirit in the theory of the Trinity, an account which borders on polytheism and creates all kinds of theological problems, the thesis that the holy spirit is an attitude or state of mind engendered by faith explains many of Jesus' most important ideas—ideas which, from a trinitarian point of view, seem baffling and bizarre. For example, it clears up why, in the Gospel of John, Jesus referred to the holy spirit as the "Spirit of Truth."[8] The trinitarian theory causes us to wonder whether—and, if so, how—God manifests himself as some sort of truthful angel, or some force that reveals reality to the faithful. But, if we adopt the more straightforward premise that Jesus was speaking of an inspiration rather than a facet of the Creator himself, there is no need to puzzle over the significance of this frequently used phrase: Jesus simply meant that the holy spirit is an attitude of conviction that takes hold of people when they accept the truth, that is, the teachings of Jesus about heaven, Satan, the afterlife, and the potential for a kingdom of God on earth.

Faith brings about an attitude of conviction, truth, and defiance, because it takes away our worldly fears and concerns. In a fair description of what we in the modern era call "anxiety" and "depression," one of the gnostic texts says that life without God is like a nightmare. Those who are without God experience "terror and disturbance and instability and doubt and division," for their fixation on the world has their thoughts racing from one thing to the next, as the mind does in disturbing dreams. But when those who have been experiencing these swirling fears and panicky emotions finally find God, "they leave [these emotions] behind like a dream in the night."[9] They do not fear punishment, loss, or even death, because they believe that they are watched over by the Creator, who will reward their good acts in the afterlife.

Another teaching of Jesus that this psychological account of the holy spirit helps us to understand is the particular symbols Jesus told his disciples to use in the ceremony of communion. One question that generally goes unasked and unanswered by Christians is why Jesus instructed his followers to employ both bread and wine in the ceremony reminding us that he gave his life so that we might be saved. From a trinitarian point of view, one would have expected Jesus just to have used wine. After all, the ceremony was about his blood being shed for the remission of sins, and Jesus had frequently spoken about how the Pharisees and scribes were "the children of them which killed the prophets" and were "partakers with them in the blood of the prophets."[10] If the ceremony was simply about Jesus being wrongly condemned, why the need for bread?

Two symbols were used, rather than just wine alone, because Jesus was bringing not one, but two things into the world: both his teachings, and the spirit they would inspire. The Gospel of John tells us that Jesus said, "Except ye eat the flesh of the Son of man, and drink his blood, ye have no life in you."[11] The *Gospel of Philip* explains: "His flesh is the word, and his blood is the holy spirit."[12] The good news of Jesus, the flesh, brings with it his blood, a spiritual transformation. The trinitarian theory is wrong in thinking that Jesus and the holy spirit are separate emanations of God. Jesus and the spirit of holiness go together like flesh and blood; the body, the teachings of Jesus, carry the blood, the spirit these teachings inspire, and neither of them can survive without the other.

Still a third puzzle solved by this view of the holy spirit is why Jesus cautioned us that it is worse to raise questions about the spirit than about anything else. Jesus said, "All manner of sin and blasphemy shall be forgiven unto men: but the blasphemy against the Holy Ghost shall not be forgiven . . . neither in this world, neither in the world to come."[13] Why did Jesus single out the spirit of holiness? Why did he not say that people would also be condemned if they blasphemed against Jesus or against God?[14] The trinitarian theory provides no explanation, for it treats Jesus, the spirit of holiness, and the Father, all as manifestations of God and therefore as equally important.

But once we accept that the holy spirit is an inspiration, Jesus' warning about not maligning it makes sense. It is one thing to commit sins, even the worst sins; they are wrong, but they have limited effects; they harm one or a few people, and usually only their bodies or their dignity, not their souls. To ridicule people's sense of God's presence is something entirely different; it is to strike at humanity's only real hope against power and glory, against people's inclination to set themselves up to be obeyed and exalted. The spirit of holiness, the attitude that comes from faith in God, the afterlife, and divine judgement, is the only thing that gives people the motivation and courage to defy authority and to withstand social pressure. If this spirit is lost, then humanity is lost.

Jesus was surely speaking to the modern era when he warned us about blasphemy against the holy spirit. Has there ever been an epoch when the spirit of holiness was more mocked and denied? We have gone far beyond discussing, philosophically, whether God exists. In the secular universities of the Western world, which have become the pinnacles of culture for the entire planet, a religious spirit is considered to be childish and foolish, an indication of "soft" thinking. Students are taught to evaluate everything in terms of costs and benefits, underlying interests, short and long term advantage. The idea that people should try to live in a state of inspiration, detached from the power and glory of the world because they anticipate an appointment with God, is treated as a ridiculous.

3. The Resurrection is for the Living

Much of what Jesus revealed about the holy spirit has been misunderstood because he did indeed say that the spirit is "given" or "sent by" God,[15] but he did not intend by this that the holy spirit is God himself. Rather, he meant that the holy spirit is a divine spark God planted in humanity at creation. Jesus' teachings about politics hinged on his belief that this spirit—this sense of God's presence and the attitudes this conviction engenders—was emerging inexorably within humanity. When Jesus prophesied that the holy spirit would become increasingly visible, or that it would be a "comforter" after he was crucified,[16] he was not saying that a divine ghost would come and reveal the secrets of heaven, but that his death would accelerate the holy spirit's development. The resurrection that Jesus spoke of referred to the birth of this attitude in a single individual as well as to its recurring return in human history.

Jesus saw himself as the voice of this growing inspiration. He referred to himself as the "son of *anthropos*," that is, *not* the son of God or the son of a single man and woman, but the son of *humankind*. Jesus was the product, the son, of the spirit of holiness in humanity, but he was not the only son, nor did he expect to be the last.

Once, Jesus tried to make this clear; it was when he was about to be stoned after speaking from Solomon's porch on the east side of the temple in Jerusalem. He had enraged his listeners to the point that they were about to kill him, because he had said, "I and my father are one."[17] When he saw the people in the audience begin to pick up rocks, he asked why they were going to slay him, and the crowd responded, "for blasphemy."[18] At this point, Jesus argued them down by showing that the scriptures said the same thing. He quoted God's words in Psalm 82 (verse 6), "I said, ye are gods."[19] Those who knew the psalm understood that the verse went on, "and all of you are children of the most high." Jesus asked how they could stone him for saying he was the son of God, when the Scriptures showed that God called everyone gods "unto whom the word of God came."[20] The implication was that Jesus was the son of God *only in the sense that he had been inspired by God's revelations*.

Jesus may have given the impression to the crowds following him that the holy spirit is a thinking and willing personality, but he explained himself to his disciples, or at least to some of them. His favorite was Mary Magdalene, and with her he shared his most secret teachings.[21] He is quoted in the gnostic *Gospel of Mary* as saying that "the Son of Man is within you."[22] Given that he also referred to himself as the Son of Man, this statement implied that the spirit moving in him existed in everyone. The holy spirit emerges in humanity and produces outspoken sons and daughters. Although many of these offspring of the spirit are killed, Jesus taught that the attitude of holiness will be repeatedly reborn until eventually it prevails over the world.

The doctrines developed by organized Christianity about the resurrection of souls and the "second coming" of Jesus were merely distortions of his revelations about the holy spirit. Although Jesus probably did speak of his future resurrection and of his ability to give people life, he did not mean he personally would return or that people's disembodied minds would roam the earth. Rather, he was talking about the spirit of holiness and each person's ability to experience it.

To understand his revelations about eternal life, we must recognize that Jesus thought of the world as dead. As he is quoted in the gnostic *Gospel of Philip*, "This world is a corpse-eater. All the things eaten in it themselves die also."[23] Those who lack faith in God remain captivated by the world and in a sense are dead, for they are totally caught up in the pursuit of pleasure and security. They are the slaves of their fears and impulses, because they have no spiritual orientation to lift them above the cares of earthly life. They become just other corpse-eaters.

The resurrection of which Jesus spoke occurs not at some "second coming" of the Messiah, but through participation in this spirit, which is the spirit that "anointed" Jesus because he was the bearer of the gospel, the "good news."[24] As one of the gnostic texts says, "flee from the divisions and the fetters" of the world, "and already you have the resurrection."[25] The same thought is expressed in the *Gospel of Philip*: "Those who say you will die first and then rise are in error. If they do not receive the resurrection while they live, when they die they will receive nothing."[26] Without faith and the spirit it brings, Jesus said, "your thoughts are filled with the smoke and fire that is in you," and you "surrender your freedom for servitude" to your burning desires.[27] When you believe in God, the afterlife, and the judgement of heaven, you participate immediately in the spirit of God, which has existed since the foundation of the world.

This explains why each person's resurrection depends on faith. You must believe in God and in his ultimate justice before you can extricate yourself from the grip of the world. Until you believe in God and the afterlife, the worries of the world are a personal hell.

The New Testament words for holy spirit are *pneuma hagion*. Spirit or *pneuma* means "wind," while holy or *hagion* comes from a word that literally means "separated."[28] The holy spirit is thus a force that divides people from their normal circumstance. Faith causes a person to be filled with a new spirit, a spirit that separates the mind from the world like a wind lifting a leaf toward the sky.

The summary Jesus gave for this revelation is reported in *The Dialogue of the Savior*. Jesus was asked by Matthew, "How does the small join itself to the big?" The question was about the small spirit in each person, the "breath" or "wind" of life that God blew into Adam's nostrils to make him a "living soul."[29] How does this small spirit unite with the larger Spirit of God above, the spirit that "moved upon the face of the waters" when God created heaven and earth?[30] Jesus replied, "When you abandon the works which will not be able to follow you, then you will rest."[31] In other words, you will unite with the Spirit of God when you turn your thoughts and actions from the world to heaven and the afterlife.

I think this is also what Jesus meant when he spoke of himself and others as being "not born of woman." Whoever is inspired by the spirit of holiness is not subject to the same desires, fears, and anxieties experienced by most children of the flesh. Hence Jesus said, "When you see one who was not born of woman, prostrate yourselves on your faces and worship him. That is your father."[32]

Whenever any person accepts the teachings of Jesus, the spirit of Jesus is born again, and the soul of this person becomes eternal because of its participation in the eternal spirit of holiness. The flesh of the body becomes like a garment for the spiritually activated soul. This idea of eternal life underlies one of the aphorisms in the *Gospel of Philip*: "The Lord said, 'Blessed is he who is before he came into being. For he who is, has been and shall be.'"[33] Those are blessed who understand their connection to the Spirit of God. Similarly, in the *Gospel of Thomas*, the disciples ask Jesus, "When will the repose of the dead come about, and when will the new world come?" He answered, "What you look forward to has already come, but you do not recognize it."[34] The resurrection is a spiritual resurrection, an uplifting of the soul from its dwelling in the fires and fears of the mind. Eternal life is the conjunction of each resurrected soul with the larger spirit, the strong wind of holiness that has always blown and always will. As Jesus said in the Gospel of John, "I am in my Father, and ye in me, and I in you."[35]

4. The Inevitable Conflict Between Faith and Power

Jesus expected his followers to be persecuted, because he knew that faith in God, or the spirit of holiness that faith inspires, strikes at the heart of worldly systems of power and glory. In the modern era, we are inclined to think that faith and power can exist side by side; we have even enshrined this coexistence into law, in the constitutional division between church and state. God has the Sabbath, the churches, and the synagogues. The world, on the other hand, has the six days of creation and the bulk of our thoughts and actions. The modern era has put faith in a box and has put the box on a shelf, taking it out only on special occasions.

But the condition of faith and power in the modern era is simply an indication of just how threatening the spirit of holiness is. Faith has been cordoned off and boxed in precisely because, if unleashed, it would dissolve power and glory *instantly*.

Coercive authority and social rankings are respected only to the extent that one's awareness of God is kept out of mind. People accept injustice from those who have power over them because they are afraid of pain and death. They worry about acquiring and keeping possessions because they want to be protected against scarcity in the future. They pursue recognition and honor from others because they see this as the highest form of glory.

If people truly believed in God, even slightly, they would have entirely different priorities. They would neither fear death nor desire glory, because they would have confidence in God's ultimate protection and justice, and they would be less concerned with accumulating riches than with displaying their righteousness to heaven.

People who survive a close call with death are noted for changing their priorities. They realize they have been caught up in their daily routines and in the pursuit of pleasure and gain, and that the really important things in life have been, as they say, "passing them by." Faced with death, they see there is no second chance. If they do not share in life now, experiencing love and community, they never will.

A similar transformation of perspective occurs as people mature. In the years of adolescence and young adulthood, what matters to most people is finding pleasure, accumulating possessions, and establishing a secure trade, career, or business. But as middle age arrives, the emphasis moves to spouses, children, and friends. Again, the reason for this change is that pleasure, possessions, and security seem relatively unimportant in the face of life's inevitable end.

Still, these shifts in perspective are trivial in comparison to the transformation wrought by faith in heaven, the afterlife, and God's judgement. Anyone who believes, even slightly, in what Jesus preached about God judging each soul, would do exactly what the disciples did when they heard Jesus' message, which was to drop everything and take up a life of righteousness. That people instead put up with the world the way it is—working at jobs they hate, obeying corrupt rulers and bosses, striving with incredible intensity for fleeting moments of fame—is an obvious statement of their lack of faith. They may go to church, follow all the commandments and the laws, and generally be good neighbors and good citizens, but their lives are testaments to their disbelief.

Jesus prophesied that the kingdom of God would come as soon as we lived our faith. Already then as now, faith was spread across the land; millions of people, even most people, profess to believe in a supreme being. But we do not see the meaning of this faith, for if we saw it, or if we opened our eyes for a moment to its implications, the power and glory of the world would dry up and wither away like a vine cut at the root.

If we lived for the judgement of God in the afterlife, how much would the glory of the wealthy matter to us? Would we be awed by stylish clothes, expensive cars, manicured nails, and coiffured hair? Surely not. Indeed, displays of wealth would strike us as signs of spiritual depravity!

If we believed in a personal day of reckoning, just imagine how we would respond to the powerful. We would neither ignore injustice nor participate in oppression.

This is the reason Jesus repeatedly expressed his amazement at everyone's lack of faith. He did not expect us to go around moving mountains through sheer willpower. He merely thought we should live according to our professed belief in God, and that if we did, the entire social and political landscape would shift. When Jesus, who had faith, looked at us, he was shocked, and rightly so.

But Jesus said that our faith would grow. He prophesied that his teachings would launch a protracted, even millennial, conflict between our holy spirit and the world. He implied that the unholy character of worldly power and glory would become apparent *as we began to act on our faith*, and that our faith would galvanize *as worldly power and glory sought to stifle and undo it.*

In predicting a millennial resistance by the world to the attitude he was calling for, Jesus was like someone who points at a pane of glass and who tells us that it is brittle. We cannot see its disposition from looking, and even when we touch it or tap it, it seems to be only hard and firm. But he assures us that it is brittle, and that it will shatter if we will simply strike it firmly with a hammer. Clearly, we can validate this prophecy only by doing what is asked. So long as we just look at it, study it, and accept it, we cannot know the real character of the glass. Similarly, the unholy nature of worldly power and glory becomes visible only when systems of command and status are hit with the hammer of faith.

This sort of coming-to-awareness is referred to as an "apocalypse." An apocalypse is not an Armageddon or world-ending conflagration; it is simply an awakening, when events unfold that reveal the reality of God. The word "apocalypse" comes from the Greek *apokalypsis*, which means "revelation" or "unveiling."[36] Jesus suggested that the coming of the kingdom of God would be a series of escalating apocalyptic cycles, because his coming and his prophecies would awaken people to the holy spirit within them, which would cause them to challenge authority and to ignore the social status of others.

An exchange between Jesus and Judas, recorded in *The Dialogue of the Savior*, describes the revealing (or apocalyptic) tension Jesus said existed between faith and power. Judas asked, "How is the spirit apparent?" Jesus answered with a rhetorical question, "How is the sword apparent?"[37] By the sword, Jesus meant the force and coercion underlying political authority and social rank. Generally it is invisible; those at both the top and the bottom of the social pyramid treat authority and inequality as if they were based not on the threat of punishment or death, but on totally reasonable grounds. The sword is exposed only when it is unsheathed, and it is unsheathed only when authority is defied or social rank is challenged or ignored. By the same token, the spirit becomes apparent when it motivates people to stand up to power and glory. Jesus expected the defiance he was inspiring to cause the sword to be drawn, and he predicted that, when it was, the spirit of holiness would grow stronger in response, thus initiating a chain reaction of spiritual conflict.

Jesus spoke of the kingdom of God both as something that is already here, and as something that is coming in the future, because of its character as a self-fulfilling prophecy, that is, a prophecy which itself causes a reaction that actually brings the prophecy to fruition. Other prophecies have had the same effect. One example is John the Baptist's decision to fulfill the prophecy of Isaiah by crying in the wilderness.[38] His lamentations stirred the spirit of God in Jesus. Another example of a self-fulfilling prophecy of this sort was the dream Jacob's son Joseph had about ruling over his brothers.[39] The latter became angry at Joseph *because of the dream*,[40] and sold him into to slavery. But *precisely because he was sold*, Joseph ended up in Egypt, became a powerful administrator for the Pharaoh, and was in charge of the food supplies when his brothers had to seek food in Egypt during the famine. Thus the dream caused its own fulfillment.

Theologians have puzzled for centuries over the fact that Jesus described the kingdom of God both as a prophecy and as an already-present reality. Some have suggested that the kingdom is just the body of believers, such as the church or the group the church represents. Others have said the kingdom is coming in the future through the power of God, who will resurrect the believers and have them rule the world with Jesus at their head. However, a political interpretation implies, instead, that the kingdom exists now in the spirit of holiness within us, but it will not be actualized until we realize our faith and the implications of our faith. As we do, those who have earthly power and glory will mock and persecute us, which in turn will expose their evil nature and strengthen our spirit, until eventually power and glory will be obliterated by our own growing refusal to acknowledge them.

5. The Spiritual Foundations of Society

The idea that politics is a spiritual phenomenon may strike modern ears as strange, but this is only because we have become accustomed to the conception of spirituality found in traditional Christianity and enshrined in the modern separation of church and state. When we think of religion, we imagine something private. We believe that each person's faith is a personal decision based on conscience, and that it has few implications, either for us or for them, outside a narrow realm of moral questions, such as what church to be married in or how to handle such private issues as birth control and sexual orientation. Even when people unite to worship together, they generally do so in a place separate from the sphere of politics—in a church or synagogue. Aside from a few charged issues like abortion, in our era virtually the only impact religion has on work and politics is in the designation of holidays.

We also hold a similarly distorted image of politics. Because we have isolated faith from other areas of our lives, we think of politics as spiritless, as something governed by self-interest, strategy, and manipulation. The belief that politics is an enterprise of calculation rather than conviction permeates our conception of the American political process; it is shared by politicians and citizens alike.

A thumbnail sketch of our vision of politics would go something like this: Our leaders compete for control of the central government by seeking support from certain blocs of voters. The wealthier elements of society form one coalition of voting blocs, and the poorer elements comprise another. In political campaigns, the leaders of each coalition focus on the middle class and try to tilt the electoral balance by pulling middle class voters into their camp. Most of the time, the government is almost paralyzed, because the difference in size and ideology between coalitions is so small that each side can veto, stall, or subvert the initiatives of the other. Nevertheless, middle class voters do occasionally shift rather dramatically to one side or another, and a big change is introduced. Almost invariably this is because of the economy. When times are bad, the middle class, which is always the swing vote, shifts to the coalition that is out of power.

Clearly, we believe self-interest dominates the process, and in a sense it does. People do vote their pocketbooks.

But this is *not* because politics is inherently a conflict over who gets what; the selfish character of electoral disputes in modern societies stems from the values of the citizens and the issues leaders put before them. Spiritual yearnings have been set aside. Because the whole social order is organized around a complex and fragile production process whose rewards are exclusively material, the only thing most people care about is having access to a good livelihood. They want economic security and growth, because their jobs are always at risk and the social order produces nothing else of value. At each presidential election, the candidates ask them whether they are better off now than they were four years earlier, and they answer with their votes. Truly, modern politics has no soul.

Nevertheless, despite our economy-centered political process and our jaded political attitudes, we know, at the same time, that much of politics and society is spiritual in nature. For example, we speak of the "spirit of capitalism," because we recognize that successful economic competition requires an ethos of risk-taking, hard work, and acquisitiveness. Similarly, we look back at the age of exploration, when the Americas were claimed by the Europeans, and say that it was fueled by a "spirit of discovery." By the same token, anyone who has worked in science knows there is a "scientific spirit," a professional culture of criticism, focus, and tough-mindedness. The idea that society is spiritual is widely accepted.

We also know that real shifts in politics—fundamental changes with enduring effects, not the little adjustments in American government that occur when the middle class votes out the incumbents—result almost always from changes in people's spirit; that is, they occur when the spirit of one group or another in a political struggle finally fails. The spiritual basis of politics explains why governments, as we say, "collapse," rather than wane or decline. The communist government of the Soviet Union did not wither away; it fell apart when the communists lost faith in their system. Every political order that fails does so in the same way: it trembles, reacts, tries to maintain itself, but finally disintegrates suddenly, as if a dam has broken—and indeed it has: the dam is the spirit of the coalition that had been in power.

Wars, which are political struggles between nations rather than within them, follow the same pattern. The victor is the side that keeps its fighting spirit longest. A war can drag on for years, even decades, with one side predominating entirely, and so long as the other side keeps its spirit, the war is not over. However, once the spirit is lost, the war is lost too. Recall the United States in Vietnam: The U.S. pummeled the North Vietnamese through the 1960s and was surely the dominant party in the conflict. However, once the U.S. lost its spirit, its effort fell apart, and it had to withdraw from Vietnam like an army routed. The same collapse occurred for Napoleon's forces in Russia when they encountered the Russian winter, and for Hitler's troops in France after the Battle of the Bulge. Once the spirit is broken, the will to fight is lost.

Political campaigns are also spiritual in this sense. After the major parties have selected their presidential candidates in the summer of election year and the campaigns, as we say, "heat up," they have all the characteristics of a military struggle. Each side maneuvers, trying to present itself in a positive light while raising doubts about the opposition. When a candidate is really "tagged," by, say, a self-inflicted gaffe or by a disclosure that exposes weaknesses in the candidate's character, the candidacy can quickly become a futile exercise as the campaign's spirit at the grassroots is lost.

The same thing often happens on a small scale in business meetings and social gatherings. A group can be functioning well—solving problems, flowing with a positive give-and-take. But if just one person becomes sour or negative, his or her attitude can throw a pall over the whole event. The spirit of the group is lost. This is where we get such phrases as, "he took the wind out of my sails," and "he was a wet blanket."

Sporting competitions frequently follow this pattern. A team can be doing well, but if it experiences a few bad breaks and loses its spirit, it will be overwhelmed by the opposition. Think of how many football games. "break open" in the last quarter. Teams have cheerleaders precisely because they know how important it is to try to maintain a competitive spirit among players and fans alike.

Even advertising, which is driven entirely by the aim of making money, pays homage to the spiritual foundations of society. When companies market their products on television, they do not focus exclusively or even primarily on the economic features of their commodities. To the contrary, they display an image of social life and of how their products fit within it. People are shown playing at the beach or having fun in spirited games, and, only then, do they drink a Coca Cola. Coke is the "real thing," not because it has certain ingredients, but because it is part of *real life*, which is an activity of the heart more than of the stomach. Advertising for almost everything—cars, beer, cereal, clothes—takes this form. Human beings do not live by bread alone, and they do not select one brand of bread over another for narrowly economic reasons.

Jesus understood politics and society very well, certainly better than most social scientists do today. He saw millions of people spread across the face of the earth, with spirits moving through them like winds. Families, groups—even nations and peoples—are held together fundamentally by their spiritual bonds. Nations may rise to global power, but when they lose faith in their purpose, they dissolve, like so many others, into a sea of forgotten peoples.

Political ideologies, as Jesus said of Satan, are like lightning falling from the sky.[41] They do not provide lasting illumination, but instead pull people together only for moments—flashes in the long, dark night of history. The beliefs that have united people in the quests we call nations and empires are almost countless. The Romans wanted law, order, and justice. The Crusaders pursued the Holy Grail. The European monarchies aimed to colonize the world. The Nazis sought purity for the Aryan race. The Soviets hoped for an industrial society without classes. The Americans call for democracy and freedom. The goals change, but it is still the same phenomenon, the politics of the spirit.

Into this swirling mixture of inspirations, Jesus sought to inject a new and radical motivation, the spirit of holiness. He wanted to pull us up from our petty preoccupations and give us a spirit that would conquer all others.

6. From Jesus to Mass Christianity

The shift within Christianity from a political, action-causing conception of spirituality, to a doctrine calling for guilt and humility, can be traced in the Acts of the Apostles. Organized, mass Christianity is the legacy not of Jesus, but of Peter. I apologize to Christians for these strong words, but they must be said: Peter was the rock that crushed the true spirit of Jesus during the first generation after the crucifixion. Jesus had spoken subtly of a spirit in humanity that would eventually dismantle all worldly systems of power and glory, but Peter preached about a "holy ghost" that would merely help people cope until Jesus returned to resurrect them and to establish a heavenly order.

I know that this assessment of Peter will be deeply offensive to many Christians, and especially Catholics, but I ask you to hear me out. We can see that Peter retreated from the teachings of Jesus even before Jesus was crucified. Recall that Jesus had told his disciples how to invoke the spirit of holiness: They were to be brought before kings and governors, and they were to block out concerns about the future and just answer with their hearts. When Peter had his first opportunity to do this—the night Jesus was arrested by the high priest—he did exactly the opposite, fearing the consequences and denying his faith, even though that very evening Jesus had warned him that his spirit might not be strong enough to stand up to the authorities.[42] As Peter lingered outside the hall where Jesus was being tried, a woman who worked for the high priest approached him and accused him of being one of Jesus' disciples, "but he denied, saying, I know not, neither understand I what thou sayest."[43] Before dawn, he did the same thing two more times.[44] How could Peter build the Church on Jesus' teachings about the spirit of holiness when Peter was too fearful to follow these teachings himself?[45]

In addition to being afraid, Peter was also ambitious. At one point, he asked Jesus directly what reward the disciples would receive for having become Jesus' students. "Behold, we have forsaken all, and followed thee; what shall we have therefore?"[46]

Peter's fear and ambition combined to make him want to establish a large church, even though his effort to recruit a huge flock was contrary both to the teachings of Jesus and to Jesus' actions. Jesus spoke on a number of occasions to very large crowds. His sermon on the mount was to a huge audience,[47] and at another time the crowd was so large that he had to address it from a boat at the shore where the people were gathered.[48] However, in no instance did Jesus try to organize a large congregation of adherents. He never performed mass baptisms, nor did he ask the crowds to follow him. Whenever Jesus sought disciples, he always addressed individuals, not groups. Indeed, as we have seen, Jesus spoke very carefully to the multitudes so that he would be understood by only a few of those who heard him, namely, by those who were predisposed to understand his political message. If Jesus had wanted a huge following, he would have recruited it while he was alive; he would not have expected Peter to gather it after the crucifixion.

Just as Jesus declined to assemble a mass following, he also rejected structured authority. When Jesus subtly advocated a revolution of passive disobedience against the Roman Empire and all other worldly powers, his purpose was not to establish another organized world-order. Assuming that this was his aim is one of the most serious mistakes made by both the Christian churches and the Islamic religion. We have already examined the contradiction between Jesus' teachings and organized Christianity, which is a hierarchical religious structure standing beside, and in many respects mirroring, the command-pyramids and status-ladders of government and business. No better is the Islamic strategy of establishing a society ruled by priests. It leaves power and glory intact, and merely makes the king or president a theologian. The Islamic kingdom is the spiritual kingdom that dies by the sword, or that loses its holiness because it lives by the sword, or relies on power.

In his teachings about heaven and earth, Jesus in no way suggested that we should put holy people in charge or on pedestals as the churches have done since Peter first laid claim to the leadership of the disciples after Jesus' execution. To the contrary, Jesus said that we must do away with power and glory *altogether*. He explained that there is a profound separation between heaven and earth. Heaven is ruled by God, who is loving and merciful, while the earth is ruled by Satan, who wants humanity to set up its own standards of ethics and power. The only link between these two realms is humanity, which was formed from earth but which has God's holy breath within it. The kingdom of God, which Jesus urged us to establish, involves expelling Satan from our lives and bringing the divine order of heaven down to earth. People are to become as perfect as angels; because of its perfection, humanity will no longer need the coercion of power and glory, and will be able to rule itself, as God rules heaven, with love and mercy.

The theological, as opposed to the political, claim Jesus made, was that God will help us do this if we will just take the first step. Bringing about the kingdom of God means turning our eyes and minds to heaven, and living as if we were truly citizens of God's domain. It is impossible for us to perfect ourselves in an instant, but as we begin to try, God will enter our minds and strengthen our resolve, which in turn will allow us to be better, and this will enhance God's presence still further, and on and on. Our political action of rejecting worldly power and glory is thus a religious action with supernatural consequences.

This action does not require, and indeed is negated by, the kind of organization Peter established after Jesus was gone. The spiritual revolution Jesus advocated was to take place through a change of heart and habit in every sphere of life. Putting this new wine in a new bottle, as Peter did when he established his new church, would keep it from bursting the old bottles it was intended to explode.

In effect, Jesus told us to overthrow power and glory by seeking God's help in making power and glory unnecessary. The philosophers of ancient Greece said, and the social scientists of modern society proclaim, that people are evil, and that coercion and social ranks are necessary to maintain order and keep workers working. But Jesus claimed exactly the opposite; he assured us that people have an angelic potential which has merely been imprisoned by the satanic force of social and political stratification.

And yet, while Jesus sought to subvert power and glory, Peter and his followers sought to claim power and glory for themselves. Jesus knew that this was Peter's inclination. Jesus conducted a ceremony, now largely forgotten by the Christian churches, of washing his disciples' feet. His intention was to show those who would follow him how to handle their spiritual status and authority: they were to serve rather than to be served. But when Peter's turn came in the ceremony, Peter said he did not want his feet to be washed, at which point Jesus threatened to send him away, permanently: "If I wash thee not, thou hast no part with me."[49] Peter relented so that he could remain a disciple, but his initial reluctance to participate shows that he either did not understand what Jesus was about, or he *did* understand but failed to agree with Jesus' political teachings.

There are reasons to believe that Peter differed with Jesus, and that Jesus knew this. In addition to Jesus' strong words to Peter when he was washing the disciples' feet, he also told Peter, on the night that he was arrested by the high priest, that "thou savourest not the things that be of God, but the things that be of men."[50] Moreover, Peter himself is reported to have made remarks and to have behaved in ways that were contrary to Jesus' teachings. It was Peter who carried a sword into the garden where Jesus was arrested, and who cut off the ear of Malchus, one of the servants who had accompanied the high priest when he came to seize the Messiah.[51] Jesus had to explain to Peter that his violence showed a complete lack of faith in God: "Put up thy sword into the sheath: the cup which my Father hath given me, shall I not drink it?"[52] One of the last things Jesus said to Peter was, "Simon, Simon, behold, Satan hath desired to have you, that he may sift you as wheat: But I have prayed for thee, that thy faith fail not: and when thou art converted, strengthen thy brethren."[53] Jesus thought Peter needed to be converted, but perhaps Peter never was.

In any event, the group of disciples who rallied around Peter after the crucifixion concerned themselves almost exclusively with recruiting a large membership for an international religious organization. We are told, for example, that Peter baptized over three thousand people at one gathering,[54] and five thousand at another.[55] Clearly,

Peter was intent on becoming the head of a huge movement.

Not all of the disciples took Peter's path toward mass Christianity. The Acts note that Philip went elsewhere and sought to instruct the learned.[56] The Acts also say that Philip preached "the things concerning the kingdom of God,"[57] which were the secret teachings of Jesus for subverting earthly power and glory. Philip, along with Mary Magdalene and Thomas, adhered to Jesus' instruction that "many be called but few chosen."[58] Their teachings became the gnostic tradition.

In contrast, the mass Christianity of Peter and his followers was based not on a political view of the kingdom of God, but on a mystical interpretation of Jesus' encoded messages. Peter preached "the remission of sins" and "the resurrection from the dead."[59] Rather than saying "few would be chosen," he exclaimed that the faith was open to "as many as the Lord our God shall call."[60] It is exactly at this point in history that Christianity became an organized mass religion preoccupied with sin, submissive to authority, and looking forward to some never-to-come day when God would descend to earth to resurrect the faithful.

7. Was Peter a False Prophet?

I apologize again for saying things that may hurt the feelings of Christians who are comfortable in their beliefs, but I cannot go further in my account of the teachings of Jesus without asking a troubling question: Was Peter one of the false prophets who Jesus said would come after him and against whom he had warned us?[61] At the last supper, Jesus predicted that Peter would deny him before the authorities,[62] and he even referred to Peter as Satan.[63] Jesus also said that we should evaluate every prophet according to his effects.[64]

Peter founded an organization that has many faults and a tragic history of oppression and corruption. It is especially preoccupied with the idea of sin. It says that human beings are inherently sinful; it asks for sins to be confessed or acknowledged; it presents itself as the only route by which divine forgiveness from sins can be obtained; and it claims to be able to affect people's status in the afterlife, both those

MELVIN LAND
JOHN 13: 34 - 35

who are alive now and those who are already dead.

In reality, Jesus preached the exact opposite of a sin-oriented faith. He was criticized for his willingness to associate with harlots. To the Pharisees, who were maniacs about law, ritual, and sin, Jesus said, "Ye judge after the flesh; I judge no man."[65] He specifically admonished us to "judge not, that ye be not judged."[66] He himself refused to judge, even though he was asked to cast judgement many times. To those who wanted him to judge an adulteress, he said, "Let he who is without sin cast the stone first."[67] To the young man who wanted him to speak to his brother about dividing the latter's inheritance, Jesus responded, "Man, who made me a judge or a divider over you?"[68]

This is not to claim that Jesus preached against all standards or commandments. Quite the opposite; he often told people to repent and to "sin no more."[69] But he taught that we should always keep in mind two things before we judge either ourselves or a fellow sinner.

One is that we should recognize and accept our weaknesses. In God's eyes, there are only small distinctions between human beings in terms of their moral goodness. We all fall terribly far short of God's perfection.[70] Jesus told the parable of a servant who, although having been forgiven of an enormous debt by his king, would not forgive the much smaller debts of another.[71] The implication of the parable was that we should be lenient with one another, or else God will judge us as critically as we actually deserve to be judged.

The second thing Jesus stressed when he taught us about enforcing commandments was to keep our priorities straight. The problem he had with the Pharisees was that they were always putting minor rules ahead of major ones. He said that they made much of giving expensive donations to the synagogue, donations of "mint and anise and cumin," but they "omitted the weightier matters of the law, judgement, mercy, and faith."[72] Jesus openly challenged the Pharisees' prohibition against work on the sabbath. He healed the sick on the day of rest, because he said it was more important to aid the suffering than to celebrate the creation:

What man shall there be among you, that shall have one sheep, and if it fall into a pit on the sabbath day, will he not lay hold on it, and lift it out? How much then is a man better than a sheep? Wherefore it is lawful to do well on the sabbath days.[73]

Jesus preached against legalism and sin-mongering because his whole aim was to replace worldly authority and status with a society of love through allegiance to God. He declared that the commandments of Moses and all the laws could be reduced to two principles: to love God and neighbor. The *Gospel of Thomas* tells us that his disciples asked him whether they should fast, pray, and give alms, and what diet they should observe. Jesus said merely, "Do not tell lies, and do not do what you hate."[74] Jesus wanted law and power to be dissolved by spirituality, and he knew that if people simply were honest and assertive, worldly power and glory would collapse. The *Gospel of Mary* relates an incident where Peter wanted Jesus to explain "what is the sin of the world." Given Peter's subsequent role in turning the Jesus movement into a religion of guilt, it is not coincidental that he asked this question. Jesus answered, "There is no sin, but it is you who make sin when you do the things that are like the nature of adultery, which is called 'sin.'" He went on to say, "Go then and preach the gospel of the kingdom. Do not lay down rules beyond what I appointed to you, and do not give a law like the lawgiver [Moses] lest you be constrained by it."[75]

When Peter established mass Christianity by preaching about sin and repentance, he was not elaborating the teachings of Jesus; he was rejecting them.

8. The Holy Spirit According to the First Christian Martyr

Peter and his followers' lack of the true ethos of Jesus is also reflected in how they responded to their congregation's call for assistance for impoverished widows. As told in the Acts, the congregation wanted Peter and the others to minister to the poor, but the disciples said it would not be reasonable for them to "leave the word of God, and serve tables."[76] Instead, they asked the multitude to select, from among themselves, seven men to be appointed "over this business," while they, the disciples, would devote all of their own time "continually to prayer, and to the ministry of the word."[77] Service, which Jesus had said should be each person's highest calling—especially the calling of those who would be spiritual leaders—was beneath the founders of the Christian church.

To minister to the needs of the poor, the multitude selected, along with six others, Stephen, "a man full of faith, and of the Holy Ghost."[78] Stephen—not Peter or any of the original disciples—would be the first Christian martyr after Jesus was crucified.

Stephen was accused of blasphemy by the members of various synagogues in Jerusalem. They brought him before the Sanhedrin, the same body which had tried Jesus. Stephen was charged with saying that "Jesus of Nazareth shall destroy this place and shall change the customs which Moses delivered us."[79] In his defense, Stephen did not deny the accusations. Instead, he made a long and wonderful speech about the conflict between power and glory on the one hand, and the holy spirit on the other.

He gave three examples of this conflict in the history of the Jews. The first was when the brothers of Joseph sold Joseph into slavery because his dream, which had been inspired by the holy spirit, offended them. They were the older brothers, and they therefore expected Joseph to serve them and to give to them all the glory in the family, but Joseph said that in his dream he, instead of them, was the master and they bowed down before him. Stephen reminded the Sanhedrin that the men who betrayed their blessed brother by selling him into slavery—the men who were offended that their social status was challenged in a dream—were the Patriarchs of Israel, the founders of eleven of the twelve tribes.

Stephen's second example was Moses, who was guided by the holy spirit when he led the Jews out of Egypt. Just as the Patriarchs had become angry when the spirit of holiness took hold of their little brother Joseph, the Jews turned away from the holy spirit when it came to them through Moses. When Moses initially sought to help the Jews—killing one of their Egyptian oppressors and urging them to unite as brothers—one of the Israelites who was exploiting the others rebuffed him, saying, "Who made thee a ruler and a judge over us? Wilt thou kill me, as thou diddest the Egyptian yesterday?"[80] Even when the Jews had left Egypt and had been shown repeated examples of God's powers—the miraculous plagues, the parting of the Red Sea, the drowning of the Pharaoh's troops—they continued to falter in their faith, turning to the worship of idols and planets.[81]

Stephen's third example applied directly to his own day, and to the judgement that he knew the Sanhedrin would render. He said the holy spirit had repeatedly inspired the prophets to tell the Israelites that "the most High dwelleth not in temples made with hands."[82] He paraphrased Isaiah: "Heaven is my throne, and earth is my footstool: what house will ye build me, saith the Lord."[83] However, Stephen pointed out, the Israelites had demanded to be led not by prophets but by kings, and the kings had built them a temple whose priests had laid upon the people all manner of law and ritual. The latest voice of the holy spirit, which had always spoken against the power of the state and the temple (and, in Joseph's case, the family), had been Jesus, who the priests had slain. Stephen laid the Sanhedrin's spiritual betrayal right at its own feet: "Ye stiffnecked and uncircumcised in heart and ears, ye do always resist the Holy Ghost: as your fathers did, so do ye."[84]

Stephen must have known he was going to be killed because, without giving his accusers time to ask it, he answered the question that is always put to the those who are about to die for claiming to speak for the holy spirit, that is, why God does not deliver them from their fate. Everyone had asked this of Jesus when he was crucified. Passers-by said, "Thou that destroyest the temple, and buildest it in three days, save thyself. If thou be the son of God, come down from the cross."[85] The chief priests, scribes, and elders mocked Jesus: "He saved others; himself he cannot save."[86] Even the thieves who were crucified alongside the Messiah "cast the same in his teeth."[87]

Stephen implied in his speech to the Sanhedrin that those who persecuted the prophets and the Messiah were carrying out the holy spirit's intentions unawares. The *Gospel of Philip*, which presents an image of the holy spirit similar to the conception voiced by Stephen, says it bluntly: "The rulers thought that it was by their own power and will that they were doing what they did, but the holy spirit in secret was accomplishing everything through them as it wished. Truth, which existed since the beginning, is sown everywhere. And many see it being sown, but few are they who see it being reaped."[88] For those who understood the spirit in this way, the Sanhedrin was like the brothers of Joseph; by attacking an inspired person such as Stephen, the council revealed its own corruption and thereby strengthened the very spirit it sought to suppress.

Stephen was treated even worse by the Sanhedrin than was Jesus. The council became so angry that it rushed Stephen out of the city and stoned him to death, then and there. In so doing, the Sanhedrin not only acted precipitously and unjustly, it violated Roman law, which stipulated that the Roman governor must approve all capital punishment. The latter requirement is why the Sanhedrin had taken Jesus to Pontius Pilate.

Stephen was treated more angrily than Jesus because Stephen spoke more directly. He made it clear that the spirit of holiness called for authority, even the authority of the temple, to be torn down, because God does not recognize the commandments of men and women or the rankings they establish among themselves.

Where were the apostles, and why did they not challenge the Sanhedrin on the illegality of its actions? The explanation offered in the Acts is weak: "At that time there was a great persecution against the church which was at Jerusalem; and they were all scattered abroad throughout the regions of Judea and Samaria, except the apostles."[89] Apparently, the persecution was not severe enough to drive out Stephen, or even to silence or subdue him. However, it appears to have silenced Peter. In the same way that he denied Jesus three times during Jesus' trial and crucifixion, he was nowhere to be seen at the martyrdom of Stephen. It is clear that Stephen indeed had the spirit of holiness, while Peter did not.

9. How Mass Christianity Lost the Holy Spirit

After the martyrdom of Stephen, or perhaps because of it, the apostles led by Peter developed an even more personal, non-political account of the holy spirit. Whereas Jesus had revealed that the spirit of holiness would provide strength and inspiration in the face of political oppression and persecution, Peter and those with him began to describe the spirit as something like a ghost. Indeed, many translators of the Bible substitute the phrase "Holy Ghost" for "holy spirit" in the Acts, despite the fact that the same Greek words, *pneuma hagion*, are used throughout the New Testament. The translators recognize that the words may not change from the gospels to the Acts, but the meaning does.

Peter and the others took their ghostly account of the spirit so far they began to claim that they could transmit the spirit by "the laying on of hands."[90] There is nothing in any of the gospels to suggest that this tactile process of ghost-transmission was taught by Jesus. To the contrary, when Jesus had offered the disciples a ceremony for kindling the spirit of holiness in others, it involved him breathing on them, not laying on his hands. John reports that Jesus gave his disciples the holy spirit when he appeared to them after his resurrection. "Jesus said to them again, Peace be unto you: as my Father hath sent me, even so I send you. And when he had said this, he breathed on them, and saith unto them, Receive ye the Holy Ghost."[91]

When Jesus referred to "laying his hands" on people, it was with respect to healing them, not transmitting a spirit.[92] The idea of healing by touching is unsurprising; we know how important it is to touch people, particularly the young and the sick. But Jesus intended more than just this. First, he wanted to expose the perversity of the Pharisees' laws regarding cleanliness. They would not touch the lepers or others who were sick, nor would they allow them into the synagogue. Their disdain for the sick was another one of their inventions, their "commandments of men." In the parable about the good Samaritan, Jesus says that the first person to pass by and step around the wounded man without helping him was a priest.[93] Jesus shocked the crowds by defying the practice of the Pharisees and touching the sick, and then he chided the Pharisees for their lack of compassion, implying that, with their rigid rules, they violated one of the highest commandments, which is to love your neighbor.[94] When the apostles used the "laying on of hands" not for healing but for delivering the "Holy Ghost," they lost this implicit critique Jesus had made against the social division between the healthy and the sick. Jesus was always tearing down social rankings, and here was one he destroyed even though most people would never have dreamed of challenging it.

The other point Jesus had made by "laying his hands" on the sick was to show how political power could be transformed from something oppressive into something uplifting. Before Jesus, the phrase "lay hands on" was used in Israel to mean "to officially arrest or capture." For example, when the priests and other officials sought to capture Jesus and take him to trial, they were said to want to "lay their hands on Jesus."[95] So, as Jesus used this same phrase in his healing, he was contrasting his vision of political power with an image that was more common, that is, of "laying hands on" to harm or control.

When the apostles began to claim that they could transmit the spirit of holiness by "laying on hands," it appears that they were met with opposition, at least by the emerging gnostic wing of the Jesus movement. The person who confronted them was Simon, the so-called "magician." The Acts give an account of this confrontation, but they must be read with the recognition that they are a document, not of the gnostics, but of the organizers of mass Christianity. Simon had been brought to Christianity by Philip, who, as mentioned earlier, had departed from the other apostles when they decided to focus on wholesale recruitment rather than on personalized instruction. Simon was a revered teacher, probably better known and more widely acclaimed than Jesus. The Acts say that Simon was acknowledged by all classes of people, "from the least to the greatest, saying, This man is the great power of God."[96] When he was converted by Philip to believe in the kingdom of God and the other teachings of Jesus, it was a wonderful day for the faith. Indeed, when the apostles in Jerusalem heard about the conversion, they immediately sent Peter and John to Samaria, where Simon and Philip were teaching.

Perhaps Peter and John felt threatened by Philip's success. Certainly, this would have been natural, for Philip had taken a different tack, the tack advised by Jesus of teaching rather than preaching, and the contrast between Philip's results and those achieved by Peter and the others could not have been more stark. Philip had demonstrated the effectiveness of a targeted recruitment by bringing into the fold a person who was widely acclaimed to be a god. In contrast, Peter, John, and the others had become so preoccupied with their mass recruitment that they had refused to minister to the poor, and then they had seen their followers scattered and Stephen stoned to death by the Sanhedrin. In any event, whether or not they felt threatened, they definitely tried to make an impression on the multitudes; when Peter and John arrived in Samaria and began to preach, they unveiled the so-called "laying on of hands."

What the Acts report next must be viewed critically. Simon is said to have "offered them money, saying, Give me also this power, that on whomsoever I lay hands, he may receive the Holy Ghost." Simon has gone down in history for this remark; the word "simony," which means to buy religious office or favors, comes from his name. But given his astuteness and the instruction he received from Philip, Simon was very probably speaking sarcastically. He was saying to Peter and John that, if the spirit of holiness could be transmitted by the "laying on of hands," then the spirit itself, which is the Spirit of God, could be controlled—even bought and sold. And yet obviously such a notion is contradicted by our most basic understanding of God.

Simon was probably also being sarcastic when he responded to Peter after Peter chastised him for offering to buy the supernatural power. Peter said, "thy money perish with thee," and Simon replied, presumably with mock fright, "Pray ye to the Lord that none of these things which ye have spoken come upon me." It seems doubtful that Simon would have actually been frightened. Rather, it would have been reasonable for Simon to ridicule someone who claimed to follow Jesus but who called on God to kill people for their words. Simon could not have missed this irony, given that he knew that Jesus himself had been executed for what he said, and that he had said only that the Pharisees claimed wrongly to have access to God and to God's spirit.

No doubt, we shall never know exactly what happened between Peter and Simon. But in Chapter 8 of the Acts, we see the three main strands of the Jesus movement go their separate ways. After the confrontation with Simon, Peter and John returned to Jerusalem to continue building mass Christianity, based on the remission of sins and on a belief in a future resurrection and second coming. Philip left to teach others, and from this root grew Christian gnosticism. For his part, Simon stayed in Samaria and either initiated or was incorporated into the Plato-influenced religion of the Manicheans and similar sects.[97]

10. Why Peter Prevailed Over Philip

The Christianity that we have today—the Christianity of fearful and ambitious Peter, the Christianity of the man who hid when Jesus was crucified and when Stephen was stoned—is nothing like the message Jesus revealed in his preaching. Peter's Christianity focuses almost exclusively on personal sin while ignoring the sacrilege of political power and social status. The shift to a personalized religion is obvious by the time Christianity gets to Paul. His letter to the Romans defines the holy spirit not as an inspiration giving people strength to stand up to authority, but as a support for withstanding carnal desires.[98] To be sure, Jesus did preach about the conflict between the flesh and the spirit, but he was not an ascetic. He came "eating and drinking."[99] Rather than hating the flesh, he counseled understanding it. According to the *Gospel of Thomas*, Jesus said, "Woe to the flesh that depends on the soul; woe to the soul that depends on the flesh."[100] Jesus did not want to neglect or crush the body; rather, he wanted to uplift the soul by establishing a social and political order oriented toward God. He saw the anti-flesh teachings of the Pharisees and others as just another trap that divides people and places some above, and in charge of, others.

It is easy to understand how the anti-political teachings of Jesus were transmogrified into the mystical religion of mass Christianity. The idea being proposed by Jesus esoterically to his disciples and in parables to the multitude was one of bringing down the entire social order, wiping away the rule not just of Rome but of the state and the temple generally, and establishing a kingdom governed by love, mercy, and a complete absence of distinctions between people in terms of power and status or glory. Clearly, Jesus could not preach openly the destruction of political power and glory, for this would have been a direct challenge to both Rome and Jerusalem and would have resulted in his immediate execution. Instead, he spoke of the kingdom of God and said that this kingdom, as he put it to Pontius Pilate, was "not of this world."[101] Of course, Jesus' kingdom was indeed not from this world, it was from heaven above; but it was being brought into this world, and it would cause earth-shaking changes.

CHAPTER THREE

Satan is Worldly Law and Order

LET US turn now to the other spirit, the evil spirit, about which Jesus preached. The founders of organized Christianity distorted Jesus' revelations about Satan in exactly the same way that they perverted his ideas about the holy spirit. In both cases, Peter and his followers thought of spirits as *phantoms* rather than as *motivations* arising from the political struggles of humankind. Just as Peter described the spirit of holiness as a ghost who helps the faithful fend off carnal desires, he depicted Satan as an evil angel who tempts people to satisfy greedy and lustful impulses.

But this view completely missed the point. Actually, Jesus taught that the conflict with Satan is a battle not with fleshly desires, but with the whole earthly system of power and glory.

1. Satan's Sole Possession: Worldly Power and Glory

What Jesus meant by Satan—the force or spirit in all worldly kingdoms—is obvious from what he said about the temptations he experienced during his period of fasting in the desert. He explained that Satan appeared to him and tempted him, initially, with powers Jesus already possessed. When this failed, Satan came forth with the things only Satan himself could provide.[1]

The first temptation was technology. It is important to recognize that Satan did not extend riches to Jesus, presumably because they are not Satan's to give.[2] Satan could tempt Jesus only to pursue riches himself, that is, to forget God and to focus exclusively on production, on transforming nature into commodities. He dared Jesus to "command this stone that it be made bread."[3] Although modern society would later take this route, Jesus rejected it because he knew it would be unfulfilling. In his words, "Man shall not live by bread alone."[4]

Satan then tempted Jesus with the powers of mysticism and other forms of worship that seek to control God for personal gratification or security.[5] Again, Satan himself did not offer Jesus protection from the world's dangers. He merely goaded Jesus to stand atop the highest temple and cast himself to the ground so that God would save him; that is, Satan urged Jesus to establish a creed aimed at manipulating God for worldly safety. This is in part what Christianity would eventually become, as we can see from all the Saint Christopher medallions, the benedictions at ceremonies to dedicate buildings, the prayers of soldiers before battles and of football players before games, and so on. But Jesus repudiated a religion of superstition because it reduces God to a servant and leaves people enmeshed in their world-centered fears.

When these snares failed, Satan finally turned to the only prizes that were his and his alone to offer. In the last, and presumably most enticing temptation, the devil displayed "all the kingdoms of the world in a moment of time," and he said to Jesus, "All this power will I give thee, and the glory of them: *for that is delivered unto me; and to whomsoever I will I give it.*"[6] What Satan possessed himself were power and glory. No doubt, Jesus could have easily inspired the creation of an earthly kingdom. In fact, his teachings were perverted, first, by Peter and Paul to support the "Holy" Roman Empire and, a few centuries later, by Mohammed to establish the empire of Islam.[7] But Jesus himself rejected earthly kingdoms, because he understood them to be forms of idolatry. He said that to join them is to worship and serve someone other than God.

Clearly, the Satan about which Jesus spoke was not the instigator of little misdeeds of the flesh. He was, and is, the spirit that creates human pyramids of command and status.

2. The Tyrannies of Everyday Life

When, in recounting his temptations, Jesus said that all earthly kingdoms and their glory are possessed (or owned) by Satan, he meant that they have no connection whatsoever to God; they are totally evil. This idea fell on rocky soil and never grew up within organized Christianity not only because it challenged the legitimacy of the Roman Empire, with which Christianity eventually made peace, but also because it was, and still is, totally contrary to widely shared beliefs about government. People have always been accustomed to evaluating legal systems against higher principles, and they have known that all systems have weaknesses. But they have believed that almost every government contains at least some goodness and justice. The only exceptions are evil tyrannies like Stalin's Soviet Union or Hitler's Germany. How, then, can *every* social order be satanic?

The answer lies in the essential characteristics of human society. Jesus explained to us in his subtle way that all human life is organized as a kingdom, a system of power and glory. People come together as a collective—a group or nation—and the collective has a life or spirit that operates over and above the will of any of its members acting individually. This is a basic fact of human life as we know it; we are all subjects in a kingdom. We may not recognize the masters in our lives because there are so many of them, but they rule us nonetheless. They control us in our families, police us in our cities, mold us in our schools, command us in our jobs, and tell us what is right and wrong in sex, fashion, and speech.

To see the controls permeating our lives, you must merely look for them during the course of an average day. When the morning alarm goes off, the hand of the kingdom has already taken hold of you, for the time of day is itself set by the laws that determine the time zones. As you lie in bed with your wife, husband, or lover, your relations with each other are defined by law, including the sexual acts that are permitted and the financial obligations of each of you if the relationship is terminated. As you flip on the morning news, you should realize that the television station is federally licensed and restricted. As you drive to work, note that your automobile's seat belts, emission standards, and lead-free fuel systems are all federal requirements; that the station playing on the radio is licensed; and that the road system is built and policed by government. At work, your wages and conditions of employment are governed by law. The food you eat at lunch is government-inspected and in some instances graded. After work, your ability to consume various drugs, such as nicotine and alcohol, is regulated.

The list could go on and on, and these are only the formal controls.

The informal rules of our worldly kingdom are even more extensive and detailed. All you must do to see them is to violate them. Wear strange clothes; cut your hair in a peculiar way; show more affection, anger, or faith than is normal; and you will learn quickly about the invisible fences of conformity that permeate human existence.

To be sure, many people would argue that most of society's laws and customs are, if not essential, at least helpful in maintaining order. How could we travel in cars without traffic laws? How could society survive without rules governing family relations? How could mass communications function without central regulation?

But these questions take the social order as it is and then merely point to the obvious need for rules to manage it. Forget the way the world is, and consider the aspirations of the soul!

What if we began from the premise not that we want to maintain a social formation based on industrialism and competition, but that our aim is a society of humility and love? Rather than establishing complicated social systems and promoting aggressive behavior that must then be regulated by extensive legal systems and social norms, we could just as well seek to avoid social patterns and habits that necessitate a counterbalancing web of restrictions.

When Jesus spoke of the kingdom of God, he was drawing our attention to the pervasive tyrannies in the kingdoms of men and women. Almost every moment of every day, we bow to a multitude of laws, rules, regulations, pressures, fashions, and unstated social expectations. Some of them are for our own good, but most are just conventions. Why must men wear neckties? Why do we work forty-hour weeks? Why is speech protected, while dignity is not? Why are managers paid more than the people who do the hardest labor? Why are soldiers glorified, while housewives are belittled? And, most importantly, where is God in all of this? Do these rules, judgements, and social habits save our souls, or strangle them?

3. Power and Glory Are Idols of the Heart

Jesus said that the kingdoms holding us exist through power and glory. *Power is the right granted by a group or nation, either explicitly or tacitly, to particular individuals to make and enforce decisions governing the whole.* Democracy is a myth, like the belief in the Middle Ages that kings receive their authority directly from God; no democracy has ever existed, but the idea of democracy is cited to justify the power-laden systems in which we actually find ourselves. All societies are run by relatively small numbers of leaders, and the leaders themselves always grant power over themselves to one of their members. In other words, or in the words of Jesus, all societies are kingdoms, and all kingdoms have a king, no matter how much they may want to deny it. They may call the king a president or a prime minister; they may hold periodic elections; they may even put some issues directly before the electorate for a vote. But they all have a top official and a set of top leaders who have the power to tell everyone else what to do.

Further, all earthly kingdoms are built on coercion or the threat of coercion. Governments may claim to operate primarily or even exclusively through reason, but in actuality no earthly power rules without force. Indeed, the word "power" in Greek is *dunamis*, which means "force." In systems of power, one or a few people are given the right to speak for the whole group and to direct the force of the whole group onto individuals, as when the police make an arrest or the courts order an execution. When a person or a group of leaders is accepted as speaking for the collective, its pronouncements are called "laws."

The force used to enforce laws varies, depending on whether the unit through which the power of the system is implemented is a family, a school, a business, the police, the military, or some other agent of social control. Sometimes the force is limited to restrictions on movement, reduced access to necessities or commodities, invasions of privacy, or actions that humiliate. In other cases, it can also include violence against the body, and even death.

All of these sanctions are an integral part of society as we know it. Up to now, there has been no social order among human beings that has not rested on force.

Glory, like power, is also something that the collective grants to only a few of its members. Glory is the status, esteem, and recognition that the collective bestows on the people it selects to be valued. Power and glory are often connected, but not always; powerful rulers can be hated, and lowly servants can be exalted. Attributes that gain people glory independent of power include beauty, wit, strength, intelligence, size, bravery, and other personal characteristics, plus rare things purchasable with wealth, such as special jewelry, clothing, or vehicles.

Just as laws are merely the commands of rulers backed by collective force, glory is simply the judgement of individuals backed by mass opinion. In Greek, the word *glory* is *doxa*, which also means "opinion." *Glory is a widely shared bias that certain individuals are more valuable than everyone else.*

All earthly kingdoms are contrary to the spirit of God because they involve granting power and glory to people rather than to the Creator. Power and glory are human fabrications that substitute human judgement for God's. The Creator scoffs at these presumptuous rankings. In Isaiah's words, "All nations before him are as nothing; and they are counted to him less than nothing, and vanity."[8]

Every person recognizes intuitively that a conflict exists between his or her spirit and the social order's requirements. The divine spirit within human beings leads them to expect to be treated as reasonable and willful, that is, to be treated as creatures who deserve to be respected and reasoned with. And yet, belonging to a system of power inevitably means giving up freedom for servitude and dignity for status, for it places the individual under the rule of others and puts judgements about his or her value not in the hands of a merciful Creator, but of a fickle crowd.

4. The Possibility of Orderly Anarchy

To further understand what Jesus meant when he implied that power and glory have satanic origins, we must remind ourselves that the core of Jesus' teaching is that power and glory are completely unnecessary for, and are actually inimical to, social order. We have been indoctrinated to believe otherwise—to think that, without sanctions and incentives to control them, people would degenerate into gluttons and thieves, and society would dissolve into chaos. But, for Jesus, our tendency toward evil comes not from within us, but from outside.

It is an unfortunate characteristic of human beings that they try to rationalize the demonic systems of power and glory in which they all live. They assume that social and political organization is necessary for individual and collective security. When they evaluate one kingdom against another, it is merely in terms of how much control the mass public exerts over its masters, and the extent to which the public is open to different ideas about who should be given glory. If the handful of leaders who run the social order must face election every few years; if the few people who are given glory are selected more or less fairly from among different genders and races; and if law is codified and applied somewhat uniformly across social, economic, and political classes; then the system is considered to be laudable. It does not matter that the vast majority of people have almost no real freedom and must scramble for crumbs of esteem. Jesus, who had faith in God and the afterlife, saw such thinking as the equivalent of making a bargain with the devil.

The proposition that a force or spirit exists independent of human beings which makes them behave inhumanly, is simply to say, conversely, that human beings will be compassionate and merciful so long as this force or creature does not subdue or beguile them. If human beings deal with one another face to face, recognizing their deep alikeness, the problems of the world disappear. When people identify with others, they inevitably love them and treat them as they would want to be treated themselves. The golden rule is built into the soul of every human being. Only the powers of darkness and the prince of the world can deactivate this inherent lovingness.

The prophets and the messiah have told us that the source of humanity's drive toward dehumanization is an inclination to turn away from God, away from responsibility, and away from one's fellow men and women. When Jesus spoke of Satan, he was not talking about some malicious ghost; he was pointing out to us that people are faced with a spirit that tempts them away from their humanity, away from their soul-given connection with God and with one another. The Hebrew word *Satan* comes from the same root as *seteh*, which means "to turn away."[9] Satan is a spirit of *worldliness*, a spirit that turns our thoughts from God and the afterlife and toward matters of this life and this world. When the connection between our souls and God is broken, we lose our humanity, the spirit of God within us, and we behave as if other people were soulless also.

5. The Evil Spirit of the State

The idea that political systems are moved by a spirit, over and above the human beings who comprise them, is entirely consistent with our experience. Systems of command and status are inhuman and demonic because, in essence, they are decision-making processes that disperse responsibility and make accountability impossible. By spreading the ownership of actions, social organization creates a thing, a machine, a *beast*, that is bigger than any one of its members individually or even all of them if they were each acting independently. When Nazi soldiers were asked how they could murder millions of innocent Jews, they referred to the collective; they said they were "just following orders," as if they themselves did not have minds of their own. By the same token, today as in the days of Jesus, food and shelter are denied to the poor, not by other human beings, but by "the bank," or "the city," or "the bureaucracy," or just "the system." Such inhumanity is a crime against our Creator, not only because it debases and destroys his creation, but also because it is seen, by both those who commit it and those who experience it, as an accident or an unfortunate circumstance.

The satanic tendencies or temptations of social and political organization are difficult to combat because they are totally bound up with what seems to be good, useful, and necessary. Just as the serpent lived among the other creatures in the Garden of Eden and was perhaps the most interesting of these creatures, so the dark force in the world dwells beside the light. The soldiers who implemented the holocaust were surely evil, but they were also patriotic and law-abiding, and were the most willing of their countrymen to die for what they saw as high ideals. The modern industrial system, which leaves many people impoverished and dehumanized, is the very same system that flew men to the moon, cured polio and tuberculosis, and achieved almost universal literacy. Good and evil are mixed together like marble's white and grey.

Certainly the world in which Jesus lived was an amalgamation of good and evil as terrifyingly convoluted as that found in the modern era. The Roman Empire had brought order to the Mediterranean world, and it offered rights to everyone, including slaves and occupied nations. Israel, like other subject states, could continue to practice its religion and be governed by its own laws so long as it paid tribute to the Empire and respected the Roman version of international order. But the system thus established was still pitiless and inhuman. Although viewed then and today as one of the greatest political orders ever formed, it was a mechanistic decision-making process that ground up everything human in its path. It coopted the Jewish priesthood, authorized the sale and transport of slaves, placed puppets at the head of Israel's government, and divided authority between powers so that it was possible at once both to order a crucifixion and to wash one's hands of responsibility.

Today these same satanic tendencies continue to operate even if civil authority is clothed in democratic rather than in imperial garb. Why do we feel that civilization is running amok? That we must watch helplessly as our cities, our families, and our children crumble? That wars and riots erupt like volcanoes beyond human control? Because our society truly functions in this fashion! As Paul noted in his letter to the Ephesians, "we wrestle not against flesh and blood, but against principalities, against powers, against rulers of the darkness of this world, against spiritual wickedness in high places."[10] What Paul failed to see was that as long as we have "high places," we will have wickedness, for the two come together. Jesus said that all worldly power is satanic precisely because it is abstract, collective, dispersed, and therefore inhuman or mechanistic. The teachings of Jesus were a direct response to the evil inherent in the world, the evil that causes people to create a beast to rule them.

6. Human Law is the Orginal Sin

I believe, when Jesus said human law and status are satanic, he was being entirely consistent with the revelations of the Old Testament.

We in the modern era are inclined, like the Pharisees of Jesus' day, to think of the religious law of the Old Testament as very detailed, rigorous, and extensive. And, in a sense, it is. Deuteronomy, in particular, contains numerous injunctions and laws about worship, cleanliness, eating, and other routines of daily life. But Jesus was telling us to read the Bible more carefully. When he disputed the Pharisees, it was never by rejecting earlier prophecies, but rather by explaining their deeper meaning.

Two of the earliest and most important stories in the Bible, if read carefully, can be seen to confirm the teaching of Jesus that earthly kingdoms are inherently evil. One is the account of how Adam and Eve came to be expelled from the Garden of Eden. The other is the record of the conflict between Cain and Abel.

The Christian churches have completely misunderstood the story about Adam and Eve in the Garden of Eden. They have interpreted it to mean that human beings are inherently sinful. On this view, laws and governments are necessary to keep human sinfulness in bounds.

But the report in Genesis of the so called "fall" of Adam and Eve is primarily about the origin of power, and only secondarily about the birth of sin. Adam and Eve had been situated initially in a place where they could do generally as they wished. There were no man-made laws or rules to constrain them, and the two of them were completely equal in power and glory—all power and glory were God's—so they did not command one another. They were governed only by the commandments of God, which apparently were very broad. God imposed no sexual prohibitions, no requirements about clothes, no rules about worship, no regulations about when to rise or when to sleep, no rules about cleanliness. The only commandment was to accept God's definitions of right and wrong; that is, Adam and Eve were prohibited from eating from the tree of knowledge of good and evil.

When the Bible says Adam and Eve ate from the tree of knowledge, it means they invented human laws. This is explained in the gnostic *Gospel of Philip*. The tree of knowledge of good and evil is man-made law: "The law was the tree. It has power to give the knowledge of good and evil. . . . For when he said, 'Eat this, and do not eat that,' it became the beginning of death."[11] The original sin of mankind was indeed turning away from the commandments of God, but the sin was not becoming law-*less*, but law-*full*.

Adam and Eve were exiled from the Garden of Eden, from a life of peace and love, because they put their own laws ahead of God's. We can see this from what happened after they ate from the tree. Eve ate first, but her mind did not suddenly change. Only after she and Adam had both eaten did they cover their nakedness. God had issued no commandment about wearing clothes. Adam and Eve invented this rule themselves, and when God saw that they had done so, he sent them away.

A similar message can be discerned in the story of Cain and Abel. This story has been interpreted by organized Christianity to be about the first murder, but it is really about the origin of government and is intended to explain that government is rooted in the greatest possible sin. To comprehend the meaning of the story, we must understand Cain. His problem was not that he was lawless or rebellious. He worshipped God righteously, and he obeyed all of God's commandments. When God had ejected Adam and Eve from the Garden of Eden, he had told Adam that mankind must "eat the herb of the field,"[12] and Cain obeyed this commandment. When he sacrificed to God, he offered to him "the fruit of the ground."[13] Even when Cain killed Abel, he was not breaking God's laws; at that time, God had given no commandment prohibiting murder.

Cain's problem was that he wanted glory, and he wanted glory to be awarded according to his own standards of value. He became jealous of Abel and angry at God because God had liked Abel's sacrifice more than his, even though Abel had broken God's commandment by not sticking to a vegetarian regimen; Abel's sacrifice was "the firstlings of his flock,"[14] not the "fruit of the ground." Cain's anger toward God is visible in how he spoke to God after the murder. When God asked him where Abel was, Cain answered him with an insolent question: "Am I my brother's keeper?" Cain's retort was not intended to be evasive; after all, he could have lied and said he had seen Abel elsewhere, or that Abel had been attacked by wild animals. Cain's response was angry and petulant because Cain was judging God. Cain killed Abel because God gave Abel what, in Cain's view, was undeserved glory. As with the original sin of Adam and Eve, this, the second sin of humanity, grew from putting human judgements ahead of God's. Hate and bigotry, and the crimes they inspire, come from the law, or from the belief that people have the ability to judge one another's goodness and badness.

Significantly, the Bible says that Cain went on to found what we call civilization.[15] After God sent him away, Cain established the first political organization, the city that he named after his son, Enoch. And Cain's descendants invented both music and metallurgy, which eventually would evolve into what we call entertainment and technology. Worldly civilization, or the line of civilization that flows from Cain rather than from Adam and Eve's other son, Seth, is rooted in a turning-away-from-God and a desire for human standards of justice rather than God's.

The prophets who foretold the coming of Jesus said that he would "utter things which have been kept secret from the foundation of the world."[16] This is the secret Jesus told: that human law is an invention, a groundless constraint, and, moreover, a sin against God. This is the secret that the high and mighty have kept since the beginning of civilization.

7. The Ways of Satan

The New Testament contains two lengthy examples of the way Satan operates as a spirit behind or below the power of the law. Both examples involve executions. The first is John the Baptist, and the second is Jesus. In each case, people dispersed responsibility so that they could conceal the evilness of their actions even from themselves and be swept along unawares by their shared decision-making.

Herod arrested John the Baptist because apparently he feared John's growing influence, but at least initially he did not execute him because the people viewed John as a prophet and Herod probably feared that an execution might spark unrest. However, at some point John criticized Herod for incest and adultery—Herod had married his own niece, Herodias, who previously had been married to Herod's brother— and this criticism sparked an evil scenario of dispersed responsibility that culminated in John's murder.

The event took place on Herod's birthday.[17] Herod's daughter or stepdaughter danced for him, and he was so delighted, he said he would give her anything she wanted, up to half his kingdom. She consulted with her mother, who John had insulted, and on her mother's instructions, she asked for John's head to be delivered to her on a platter. Herod protested but nevertheless said he was bound by his oath, so he had John executed as requested.

In this case, Satan, or the spirit of evil tempting humanity, operated through a process in which everyone participated partially so that no one was fully to blame. The daughter could be somewhat absolved because she acted hastily, she was a child, and in a bizarre sense she was being a good daughter in trying to please her mother. Herod could claim to be guiltless because he had never intended for John to be executed but had been tricked into doing so. In fact, Herod, too, could be said to be acting at least somewhat righteously because he held to his oath. For her part, even though she benefitted from the execution, Herodias avoided responsibility because she acted through her daughter, who was acting through Herod. John's execution thus had the appearance of an accident, a mistake which no one intended.

The same satanic path of unreality that characterized the execution of John, where everyone participated and yet no one was to blame, was even more apparent in the trial of Jesus. In Jesus' case, the blame was spread between the Jewish religious court or Sanhedrin, the Roman governor Pontius Pilate, and the multitude. The Sanhedrin accused Jesus of blasphemy and asked Pontius Pilate to have him killed.[18] Pilate told them to do it themselves, but they refused and said it was Pilate's responsibility as governor.[19] Pilate interrogated Jesus, as did Herod, and neither found anything to warrant the death penalty.[20] Pilate proposed releasing Jesus in the annual program to pardon one criminal at Passover. However, when the multitude was consulted, it chose Barabas rather than Jesus.[21] At this point, Pilate ordered the crucifixion but washed his hands of responsibility.[22]

Who was to blame for the crucifixion of Jesus? Not the Sanhedrin, because it did not carry out the execution. Not Pontius Pilate, because he was merely capitulating to the demands of his host country and the wishes of the crowd. And not the multitude, because they were allowed to free only one prisoner, and they chose Barabas out of ignorance. Clearly, some force or spirit was at work to keep Jesus from being dealt with humanely, that is, responsibly, by one human being to another. As with the execution of John, Jesus was crucified, not by a person, but by an evil spirit that emerged like a monster from the buck-passing actions of several groups and individuals trying to avoid responsibility.

Jesus said ahead of time that this is how his execution would happen. It would be carried out almost unconsciously, as if by a collective mind, but those involved would still be responsible. This is why he told his disciples at the last supper that "the Son of man goeth as it is written of him: but woe unto that man by whom the Son of man is betrayed! It had been good for that man if he had not been born."[23] Jesus knew that his execution was inevitable, that the forces swirling around him were leading irreversibly to his crucifixion, but he pointed out that these forces emerged from human will, or more precisely from a lack of will, from particular people allowing these political currents to possess or sweep them along.

8. The Faith of Satan

Just as there is a set of beliefs, a faith, that gives people a spirit of holiness, there is also a creed that induces the spirit of Satan, the willingness to turn away from one's humanity and join into malicious systems of power and status. This evil creed is simply the opposite of the teachings of Jesus. It is a belief that there is no God, no afterlife, and therefore no ultimate justice.

Even though atheism is always present in every social order and indeed makes political power possible, it is never widely acknowledged, and it is never total. It stands in the shadows of the social order because it is always confronted by at least a glimmer of faith. It is for this reason that a doctrine of religious doubt has at no time in history been fully accepted by any society or people. The closest that an atheistic set of ideas has come to being incorporated into the life practices of a population is in the Roman Empire and, of course, in our own era. But even in these cases, the bulk of the populace has continued to believe, at least marginally, in a supernatural justice; then and now, atheism has been concentrated among the classes that possess the bulk of the social order's power and glory. Significantly, this is exactly what Jesus said: Satan will give power and glory to those who will turn away from God.

Rather than being stated baldly as a lack of faith in God, atheism emerges subtly as an alternative confidence in the world or in some aspect of the world. Those who are without faith seldom say, "I do not believe in God." In fact, they may not even be aware of their creed of doubt. They talk instead about in what they *do* believe, which is always the world or some feature of the world.

One expression of this confidence in workaday reality is the belief that the cosmos is orderly and stable, and that it always will be. The opinion that there is no God, implies that the world is eternal, for, if there was no creator, then the cosmos must have existed forever. The world may change forms; it may move through stages of birth, decay, death, and rebirth; it may, over billions of years, go from an expanding universe to a glob of matter that collapses in upon itself, only to explode once more in a big bang, to start expanding again; but in theory it has been here forever, and nothing stands outside it to end its existence. Regardless of whether those who are unsure about the existence of God want to avoid placing their trust in another being, they are led by the logic of their doubt to put their faith in the world.

We see the premise of the world's eternal life in both Greek philosophy and modern science. The ancient Greeks claimed that the world is held together by abstract Ideas or "Forms." Plato said that oaks, poplars, and pines all have a similar structure because they are governed by the Form we call "tree." While particular trees may grow, wither, and eventually die, the Forms, Plato asserted, are eternal. Similarly, modern science assumes that law-like principles underlie the dynamics of all events. Circumstances may change, but the laws of physics do not.

The overarching concept that emerged in Greek philosophy and that continues to be used to this day in science to capture the idea of an orderly, eternal universe is the word "nature." This concept, which has had as much influence as monotheism on the course of Western civilization, was coined by Plato's teacher Socrates.[24] The notion is that all things, human and nonhuman alike, have no deeper origin than themselves and are governed solely by internal principles. Whereas the Judeo-Christian tradition contrasts "the world" with "heaven," the atheistic tradition of Greek philosophy and modern science speaks of "nature" and looks for wisdom not above it, but within it.

The hidden faith or counter-faith of atheism is also expressed in the thesis that humanity's highest aims are to understand the world and to conform to its principles. If the cosmos is eternal, then there are no higher principles than cosmic principles. It is pointless to ask who created the world, or for what purpose. The ultimate question is, How does the cosmos operate? And the ultimate value is to use such knowledge for ends chosen by humanity.

This explains why today as well as in the Roman Empire of Pontius Pilate, the word "nature" is not simply a descriptive term like "sky" or "earth," but instead a concept that suggests worth. To say that something is "natural" implies that it is good and wholesome, and that it will occur in a desirable way if not impeded. To this very day, people want to behave "naturally," and to follow nature's example. Although atheists and others with similar doubts may claim to be without theological convictions, their creed of uncertainty inevitably spawns a religion of nature. In contrast, the tradition of Judaism and Christianity rejects the glorification of nature because the Bible points to a higher dimension and says that the world is just brute creation, not to be worshipped in its own right but rather to be seen as evidence of the great power of the Creator above and outside it.

Still a third cryptic expression of atheism, in addition to the opinions that the world is eternal and that nature presents a model for emulation, is the belief that the most important thing in life is life itself. The creed of Satan that there is no God and no heaven leads to an overwhelming preoccupation with the self. For, if there is no afterlife, then the only experiences that matter are those that affect a person in the here-and-now. By extension, self-sacrifice is irrational, unless it will be rewarded here on earth.

This is why the culture of both the Roman Empire and the modern era have been characterized by such hedonism. To the extent that people do not believe in an afterlife, they want to pack as much into their present lives as possible. They are terrified of pain and death and are generally unwilling to die for a higher cause, because they see no ultimate reward. They are also calculating and self-centered, because they anticipate no punishment for unexposed wrongs. Similarly, appearance comes to matter more to them than truth, for they doubt that truth has an advocate or an avenger.

If atheism ever penetrated society thoroughly, we would see what we catch only glimpses of today. People would be totally vicious and calculating. They would organize into gangs, cities, or nations for the sole purpose of dominating others and extracting as much as possible from the bounty of nature—working to turn stones into bread, desperately fearing old age and death, seeking solace not in God but in talismans and positive thinking. To be sure, they would be quite natural people: They would act on their impulses, take what they want, crush the weak, and bow to the strong, just like all other animals. Indeed, they would see themselves as animals, and as nothing more than products of the earth, children not of humanity but of nature. Necessarily, their society would be built entirely around promises of rewards and punishments, because this is all they would value.

We can see, in fact, that political power is based on these very premises, but it is held in check because a certain amount of faith persists even in the most godless societies. People grant power to rulers, obey their masters' commands, and follow the public's prejudices in assigning worth to one another, because they value their earthly lives and are afraid of pain, humiliation, and death. But there are limits to their faithlessness and to the inhumanity it engenders. The social order remains humane because it is still held together by a weak but nevertheless essential faith. Most people want to be good, even if it costs them some benefits. They may not have enough faith to ignore political power and social status altogether, but they do have enough to be decent and moral, at least if does not mean risking their lives or incomes. Civilization continues to survive, because the spirit of Satan is counterbalanced by the spirit of holiness.

Of course, the danger exists that atheism will spread unchecked in the modern era. Many people know they have doubts about the existence of God, but they do not see how far their lack of faith

influences their treatment of others and their own goals for themselves. They think of their religious beliefs as a private matter, not as
the main factor that determines the spirit of both the individual and
the social order. They do not know how different they would be if they
truly believed in God and his judgement, because they have never dealt
with their lack of faith aggressively and have therefore never seen the
transformation that faith brings.

9. The World is Tempting Because God is in Heaven

The revelation by Jesus that the world contains a satanic spirit, or
that the world inspires a satanic spirit in the unwary, amplified the
teachings of earlier prophets and highlighted the political implications of a nature-oriented philosophy, a philosophy Jesus recognized
in the Roman Empire and anticipated for the modern era. One of the
central if not overriding points of the Old Testament is that God and
nature are two very separate things. The religion against which the
ancient Israelites had rebelled was essentially one of nature-worship.
The idolatry of the Canaanites and Egyptians involved creating
images that depicted forces of nature, while the religion in Babylon,
where the Jews were held in captivity, was astrology, which saw human
life as governed by the movement of the stars and planets.

The Old Testament prophets preached forcefully against this subjugation of humanity to nature. Although they did not have the
revelations that Jesus would bring about Satan, they understood the
world's allure. The prophets said that people are predisposed to
worship the things on earth and in the cosmos, because the world is so
awesome in its beauty, complexity, and scale. This is one meaning of
the symbolism of saying that Adam and Eve ate from a forbidden tree
when they really just invented human laws. The temptation human
beings face is from the earth and how the earth strikes the human eye;
Eve ate from the tree of knowledge of good and evil only after she
looked at the tree and "saw that the tree was good for food, and that
it was pleasant to the eyes."[25] Likewise, Deuteronomy, the last testament of Moses, warns against the enticement of worshiping the
likenesses of men and women, beasts, birds, and fish, and especially

against the appeal of developing a cosmic religion, "lest thou lift up thine eyes unto heaven, and when thou seest the sun, and the moon, and the stars, even all the host of heaven, shouldest be driven to worship them, and serve them."[26] The Bible warns that the world is seductive.

The Old Testament says over and over in different ways that God is not nature, that he is not any part of the world except for the divine spark in each human being. No doubt, this is why many biblical stories say that God must "come down" to the earth to deal with human beings. When Adam and Eve ate from the tree of the knowledge of good and evil, we are told that God was not on the scene and that he was not aware of the sin committed by his creations until he came and saw that they hid their nakedness.[27] The same was true with respect to Cain and Abel; God learned of Cain's crime when he heard Abel's blood cry out to him from the soil.[28] Similarly, when the descendants of Noah built the tower of Babel, God is said to have decided to "go down" to see what they had built.[29] The Old Testament prophets understood thoroughly that the world is devoid of God except for the spirit of God within humanity. If God appears on earth, it is because he has chosen to descend from his higher abode, which completely transcends the world.

The Old Testament also makes it clear with this same reasoning why sin and worldliness are connected. The explanation is given in the story of Adam and Eve. The world tempts the human mind to a great arrogance, not just to worshiping the animals and forces of nature, but to a belief that human judgement is the highest judgement. The world enticed Eve through its promise of wisdom, of ultimate knowledge. The serpent is the ancient symbol for wisdom. Jesus acknowledged this when he told his disciples to be "wise as serpents."[30] Eve was beguiled by the serpent, by the promise of wisdom, to seek her own knowledge of good and evil in the center of nature, in "the midst of the garden."[31] When the story says that Adam and Eve ate from the tree of knowledge of good and evil, it means that nature tempted them, and when they turned to nature for wisdom, they began to invent their own standards of good and evil. God had created them in nakedness and had left them naked, but after seeking wisdom in nature rather than from God, they had decided together that nakedness is bad. The world tempts human beings not merely to worship it, but to become embedded in it, and to think that nothing is higher than the world and therefore that no judgement is higher than their own.

Jesus tried to explain to us that the search for wisdom in nature is a terrible mistake. It is a temptation that ends not in humanity's liberation and exaltation, but in slavery and degradation. God is in heaven. If we worship the world, then we will become the subjects of the world and will be less than the world; we will be ruled by the lord of flies.

10. The Lesson of Job: The World is Chance and Causality

We can see now that Jesus was trying to tell us that human society contains a conflict between spirits. On the one hand, all of us have a spirit of holiness, even if it is very weak, because we are all born with an innate awareness of being observed, judged, and affected by a supernatural intelligence. This spirit lifts us above the world like a wind, and allows us to place truth, love, and mercy ahead of our personal interests. On the other hand, we are also prone to a spirit of worldliness, because we find the world to be astounding, pleasurable, and never completely satiating. This spirit leads us to value our lives above all else, to glorify nature and human reason, and to trade our freedom for the security of government and human law. Whether the holy spirit or the spirit of worldliness dominates a person or a social order depends on faith. Most people and all societies waver in the balance, accepting the kingdoms of men and women but never relinquishing entirely their desire for a kingdom of God.

The spiritual conflict described by Jesus is the subject of the Book of Job. Indeed, when Jesus used "Satan" as the name for the devil, he was referring us to this book, for it is the only one in the Old Testament that speaks at any length about Satan and his ways.[32] The Book of Job is surely based on a revelation, but it is not written in the usual manner of the Bible. It does not recount historically significant events or relate specific spiritual experiences. Instead, it is a story.

In this account, Satan comes before God and accuses humanity of loving God only for the riches, safety, health, and other benefits God is believed to provide. Recall that this was the second temptation Satan presented to Jesus; Satan urged Jesus to create a faith based on asking God for protection from physical harm. In the Book of Job, God seems to agree with Satan that in many cases people worship him only in hope of gaining earthly advantages, but God says this is not true of Job, and he allows Satan to tempt and torment Job in order to determine the basis for Job's righteousness. Job then experiences what today we would call a terrible run of "bad luck." His livelihood is destroyed, members of his family die, and he develops horrible boils.

The heart of the story is a dialogue between Job and his friends, who try to understand why Job has encountered so many calamities. His friends say it is either because Job has sinned, or because God is uncaring and unfair. Job protests that he has not sinned, but he refuses to believe that God is tormenting him gratuitously. Toward the end of the dialogue, a young boy appears from nowhere and explains to Job that he must hold firm, that it is easy to love God when things are going well but that the true test of faith is loving God during periods of adversity. Job understands this message and is saved, and he goes on to live a happy and prosperous life.

The Book of Job uses a story and a dialogue to explain to us how faith and doubt interact in the competition for our convictions. First, it tells us why doubt is always a temptation. We are inevitably prone to atheism precisely because God and the world are separate. Human beings are not protected by God on a constant basis but instead are embedded in an order of luck or probability into which God occasionally intervenes. Everyone is at the mercy of the world's forces, which are governed by chance, struggle, and death. God is in heaven, and he comes to earth, or reaches out to a person, only a few times in his or her life. An angel, or a spirit of holiness, will intervene at decisive points to show each individual the way to God, or the means to protect the soul, when he or she is most in danger of losing faith. In the Book of Job, this angel appears as a boy who bolsters Job's wavering conviction that God is good. One can accept the assistance, as Job did, and survive the spiritual test, or one can capitulate and prostrate oneself to the world's forces, trying, like ancient pagans or modern scientists, to predict and manipulate the powers of chance.

The usual absence of God explains why atheistic and scientific accounts of the world seem plausible. Most of the time, nature does indeed behave according to laws of causality and probability. God suspends the laws of nature only rarely. This is why we call such events "miracles"; they do not occur every day. Further, science and other atheistic belief-systems are blind to God's occasional actions in the world because science and atheism look only for invariable connections and patterns. When nature behaves unnaturally, either the phenomenon goes unnoticed or it is discounted as an event which has natural causes that have yet to be discovered.

Second, the Book of Job tells us about the way Satan, or the spirit of worldliness, surfaces in our lives. Repeatedly in the story, Satan is said to be "going to and fro in the earth, and . . . walking up and down in it."[33] The spirit is not stable and enduring like the spirit of holiness, which is always in the background, if only weakly, and which repeatedly produces defiant offspring. Instead, it swirls about, popping up in one place one day and somewhere else the next.

Truly, this revelation is confirmed by experience. Is this not the way temptation operates? It comes and goes. And the same is true of evil leaders and evil nations: The world is not equally evil everywhere at once, but it always contains a brutal tyrant somewhere.

The satanic spirit moves in this way because it is rooted in doubt, which is a transitory state of mind. A fundamental fact of human experience is that we generally feel our lives to be connected to a higher power. Even with the constant propagandizing of science in the modern era, which disparages faith as wishful thinking, most people remain convinced that a basic fairness permeates the cosmos. Only during times of terrible misfortune do human beings lose this belief that they are under the eye of a caring observer. Doubt creeps in when we see good people suffer wrongs and bad people prosper. This is as true of nations as of individuals. Tyranny is the child of despair, not of prosperity.

A third and related point is that the power of evil in human life is always limited. The author of Job implies that God gives Satan the power to test each person's faith, but God limits what Satan can do.

When God tells Satan he can work on Job, God says, "Behold, he is in thine hand; but save his life."[34] Satan can tempt by harming a person's holdings, health, or loved ones, but Satan cannot simply reach in and take a soul.

The same notion that there are limits to Satan's powers is expressed in John's Book of Revelation; in several instances, Satan or his minions are said to be given power on earth, but the power is always limited in extent and time.[35] Satan is in the world, but nonetheless each person remains capable of choosing God.

This revelation, too, is borne out by experience. All people can see that the world is full of evil. They recognize cruelty and deception in every aspect of life—in government, business, entertainment; even in the churches—as well as in themselves. But no matter how much people may try to hide from their obligations to one another and from their accountability to God; no matter how often they may seek to blame others for the evil they themselves carry out; no matter how widely responsibility is dispersed and concealed, the spirit of holiness remains visible and exerts an influence. The most merciless people and the most dastardly nations always try to account for their actions in terms that appeal to the goodness in humankind, not to the demon. Herod executed John, but he pleaded that he was bound by an oath. Pontius Pilate ordered the crucifixion of Jesus, but he sought to wash his hands of blame. Hitler and Stalin murdered millions, but they did so in the name of helping the brave and the poor. The spirit of worldliness emerges and exists only within the confines of an ever-present faith, a faith which may be undermined by doubt but which can never be entirely extinguished, in either a people or a single individual.

Fourth, Job is the first book in the Bible to suggest that there are intertwined dramas occurring on earth and in heaven, and that not only do actions in heaven affect those on earth, but those on earth affect God in heaven. Whereas the Greek philosophers had depicted the heavens as governed by unvarying principles, and the Babylonian, Persian, Greek and Egyptian pagans had seen the heavens as filled with scheming gods who intervene in the affairs of the earth only for sport or for their own vanity, the author of the Book of Job revealed to humankind that heaven and earth are intertwined reciprocally. An accuser stands in heaven and seeks to divide the Creator from the created by telling God that he is loved only for his earthly benefits and by tempting humanity with the belief that God is indifferent. Humanity's relationship with God depends on whether people confirm or disconfirm this accusation. The relationship can be either extensive or nonexistent, depending on our own actions and beliefs.

This is what makes a kingdom of God possible. If God merely stood aloof in heaven and left the world always to operate by cause and chance, or if he intervened in our lives only whimsically, it would be impossible for us to expand our connection with him. But the Book of Job explains that God's presence depends on people's faith. When they hold firm to their faith even in times of adversity—even when, as now, they are told that God is dead—God will send a spirit to strengthen them in their times of need. For individuals, it may be a meaningful encounter with someone else who gives them fortitude, as the boy did in the discussion with Job. For a nation or a people, it will be a Moses or an Elijah or a Jesus. To the extent that people maintain their belief in God, they will have experiences that will reveal God's presence, and they will have leaders who will bring God's word. The faithful can see God and are led by prophets. In contrast, because they set up nature as their idol and science as their creed, atheists live in a kingdom of hell and are governed by heartless rulers—by Caesars, Pilates, Hitlers, and Stalins.

11. Jesus Wanted to Free Us from Sin by Putting an End to Human Laws

Jesus sought to remake human society by overthrowing human laws and replacing them with the most basic of God's commandments. When Jesus said that earthly kingdoms are possessed by Satan, he meant it. He did not want to make our governments marginally better. His aim was not to achieve equal opportunity for power and glory, but to dethrone human law altogether. His teachings were totally contrary to the philosophical traditions of the Roman Empire in which he lived and from which the political and social structures of the modern era are derived. Scolding us for our belief that we possess knowledge of good and evil—for our presumption that we are capable of deciding who among us is best and who is worst—he called for an end to all judging, all commanding, and all ranking.

Although Jesus was often circumspect when he explained his revelations, we can see very clearly his radical political agenda in the way he treated his own crucifixion. He responded very differently from Socrates, the founder of Greek and Roman philosophy, who was similarly executed for his beliefs. Jesus used his own death to call for an end to law, while Socrates used his as an example to show that human laws should be obeyed at all costs.

Socrates was tried and convicted by an Athenian jury and sentenced to death by poisoning. Like Jesus, he should never have been charged and certainly never executed, for he had done nothing more than to challenge the legal and religious conventions of his day. But political turmoil in Athens had made the public afraid of new ideas, and Socrates was a well known philosopher. Twenty-five years earlier, his name had become a household word because of a play by Aristophanes, *The Clouds*, which had depicted him as hostile to the traditional religious beliefs of the Greeks.[36] At his trial, Socrates was accused of "not recognizing the gods recognized by the State, but introducing new deities, and corrupting the young."[37] The new gods that Socrates had introduced were the forces of nature, which he did indeed deify.

Socrates could have easily avoided execution. After his conviction, he most certainly would have received leniency from the jury in sentencing if he had simply asked for mercy, but instead he chose to be hostile and defiant.[38] Further, after the sentence of death was imposed, he could have easily escaped the execution, because his friends offered to bribe his guards and transport him secretly out of the city. But Socrates not only chose to stay, he stressed that the laws of the city had to be obeyed, for he said, without law, even imperfect law, civilization would crumble.[39] Believing not in God but in nature, Socrates saw no laws higher than human laws, and hence he concluded that there was no option but to accept them. From the point of view of Socrates and the Greek and Roman philosophers who followed him, law was an end in itself. It could be criticized in particular instances for being against nature or for being based on something other than prudence or reason, but ultimately it was essential to the social order and had to be obeyed.

Pontius Pilate was merely conforming to the traditions of Greece and Rome when he washed his hands at the decision to crucify Jesus. He implied by this act that the laws of Israel were wrong in leading a blameless man to be condemned to death. And yet, at the same time, his act, which was to deny responsibility for the execution, also said that the laws of Israel had to be carried out even if he might personally object. It was, from Pilate's perspective, beyond his reach.

Jesus, though, drew on the Judaic tradition to make a totally different point. He implied that his execution showed that the law, far from being too important to challenge, is just a superstition; it is an opinion to which people cling to make themselves feel safe and in control.

Aware that he was the target of plots and that eventually he would be arrested and executed, Jesus compared himself to a sacrificial lamb, which is killed on the altar as an atonement for the congregation's sins. Early on, John the Baptist referred to Jesus as "the Lamb of God, which taketh away the sin of the world,"[40] and at the last supper, Jesus himself said that his blood would be "shed for many for the remission of sins."[41] In comparing himself to a sacrificial lamb, Jesus was suggesting that the sins for which he was being persecuted had actually been committed, not by him, but by those who were doing the sacrificing. Their sin, "the sin of the world," was the sin of replacing God's commandments with human laws, as Adam and Eve had done in the Garden of Eden; this is "the sin of the world" in the sense that it is common to people everywhere and at all times. Jesus obeyed the commandments of God to love God and to love all people. He was sacrificed on the altar of human vanity, the belief that human law is higher than God's law, because he challenged the laws of men and women and all of their self-exalting power and glory.

When Jesus prophesied that his crucifixion would bring "the remission of sins," he meant that it would lead to the overthrow of human law. In the New Testament, the original word for *remission* is *aphesis*, which means freedom. Jesus expected his execution to bring many people freedom from sins because he knew that his death would strengthen the growing cry of humankind for a divine order, which, once established, would put an end to humanity's petty little laws and would release everyone from being constantly judged, condemned, and punished. To be sure, not all laws would be lifted, and not all sins would be forgiven; the commandments of God would still be in force, and sins against God, such as ridiculing the holy spirit, would still be condemned. But the legal and moral inventions of humankind, from dress codes and sexual mores to laws parceling out power and glory, would be thrown out, along with the guilt and blame they previously imposed. People would be given freedom from many sins because many actions would no longer be defined as sinful.

In short, Jesus saw his death, and urged others to see his death, not like Socrates, as a statement affirming the ultimate validity of earthly law and order, but as an event that revealed the vacuous foundation of all kingdoms of humankind.

12. Jesus Did Not Turn the Other Cheek

At his trial, Jesus also presented a model for confronting worldly authority. He did not seek to provoke his accusers, as Socrates did, because Jesus recognized that the problem is not people but rather the whole system of power and glory. The challenge in dealing effectively with the satanic forces of society and government is to make the individuals involved in collective decisions recognize and accept personal responsibility for their decrees. Tweaking the nose of one's masters or accusers, as Socrates did, is not the right strategy. The agent of power, who is possessed by a spirit of worldliness and by the fear and the conformity it engenders, must somehow be brought to see the humanity of those he or she commands and judges.

When he was being interrogated by the high priest and later by Pontius Pilate, Jesus made two statements that attempted to require the people interrogating him to take responsibility for their actions even though a satanic spirit was causing them to place a veil of irresponsibility between them and him. At one point, Jesus was asked by the high priest to explain his doctrine, and Jesus refused, telling the priest that he had spoken "openly to the world" and that if the priest wanted to know his views he should "ask them which heard me."[42] Jesus knew that he had spoken obliquely, and that only those with "ears to hear" could have understood his teachings about the kingdom of God, so he demanded that the priest take responsibility for showing that Jesus had been blasphemous, which would have required the priest to interpret Jesus' teachings and thereby render a personal judgement as to their meaning and acceptability. But as soon as Jesus had spoken, he was slapped by one of the officers of the court, who said, "Answerest thou the high priest so?"[43] The officer was demanding that Jesus acknowledge the power and glory of the high priest by being less assertive in his answers. Significantly, at this point Jesus did not turn the other cheek. Instead, he argued back, telling the guard, "If I have spoken evil, bear witness of the evil: but if well, why smitest thou me?"[44] Again, Jesus insisted that those who persecuted him should show why they believed he was guilty, not just mindlessly join the collective condemnation; and he refused to bow to their status and authority.

The idea that Jesus advocated passive obedience to authority because he said that people should turn the other cheek when they are struck is a complete misinterpretation of his teachings. His remark about turning the other cheek was simply an example given in his Sermon on the Mount to stress the importance of becoming as perfect as possible so that law and power will not be needed to maintain order; he pointed out that the law said we should not strike or get angry with one another, and he said that his view was that even if you were struck you should turn the other cheek.[45] This remark was a call for love, not for mindless obedience to the law or to abuse. Jesus' real attitude toward authority was revealed in his reaction to the guard and to the high priest; he stood up to them and demanded that they be accountable for their actions.

Jesus did the same thing directly to Pontius Pilate when Pilate asked him whether he claimed to be the king of the Jews. Jesus responded, "Sayest thou this thing of thyself, or did others tell thee of it?"[46] Jesus was not seeking to understand the basis of Pilate's accusation; he knew that he was being accused of attempting to organize the Jews in rebellion. Rather, he was trying to force Pilate to take, or at least to assign, responsibility for the charges. Once again, Jesus was pushing the issue of accountability. He wanted Pilate to be specific as to who was making the charges because he knew well that the Sanhedrin and the Roman authorities, like all worldly power, operated in exactly the opposite fashion, that is, to detach actions from individuals and thereby create larger "forces" that move along as if they were beyond any single individual's control.

Jesus understood his crucifixion correctly to be potentially an explosive event in the evil system of power surrounding him. He wanted those responsible to be identified with their actions. By not physically fighting back or verbally mocking his accusers, he denied his captors the opportunity of blaming him for their decision. Through his life and death, Jesus showed the world the human face of those who were then, and are still now, allowing themselves to be swept along by the dark forces of power and glory.

This effort by Jesus to shine a light on the people who stood in the shadows of the system of power explains one of the remarkable features of the gospels: they are filled with names. Those who knew Jesus understood the importance of confronting power with humanity. They did not report to history that John had been executed by the puppet ruler of Israel; they explained that John was a prophet and a just man, and that he was executed through the demonic collaboration of Herod, Herodias, and their daughter. The authors of the gospels did not write that Jesus was executed by "the Romans," but rather by the high priest Caiaphas and the governor Pontius Pilate. They listed the names of the disciples, of Jesus' parents and brothers, of many of the people he healed, of the towns that he visited, of the criminal who was released when Jesus was condemned, of the Cyrenian who carried his cross, of the man in whose crypt Jesus was buried. The gospels are an account of real people, inspired by the spirit of holiness, pulling the mask of anonymity from the face of power.

With his death, Jesus hoped to show us the strength of the holy spirit in confrontations with the satanic spirit of earthly power and glory. No matter how complex the system of power becomes, and regardless of how wide the gap is between the glory of the highest official and the meekness of the lowest citizen, decisions are always made and implemented, ultimately, by individuals. Evil is a retreat from God and from accountability. Jesus demonstrated everyone's power to confront evil with its own actions and thereby break the veil of secrecy.

Satan, he said, is the "father of the lie,"[47] and he can be defeated by the spirit of truth. The lie is that human beings have ultimate knowledge of good and evil. The truth is that the only commandments we are required to obey are to love God and neighbor. Jesus called for each of us to personally confront the countless Satans who seek to judge and control us with "the commandments of men."

CHAPTER FOUR

Hell is the Destiny
of All Worldly Kingdoms

IN the past three chapters, we focused on uncovering the political meaning in Jesus' teachings about the kingdom of God, the holy spirit, and Satan. I want to turn now to some of the implications of these teachings for the modern era. Specifically, we need to consider Jesus' prophecy that a cataclysm will occur before the kingdom of God is established.

The key to understanding this prophecy is knowing the meaning that Jesus attached to what we have come to call "hell." The idea of hell as a realm where evil souls are punished is a Christian distortion. Actually, when Jesus spoke of hell, damnation, eternal judgement, and the like, he was not describing some region beneath the earth where a fallen angel punishes sinners; he was talking about the inevitable destination of all worldly kingdoms. Jesus prophesied that humanity's faith in its own opinions about good and evil would eventually entangle humankind almost without limit, and would produce the most horrible social order imaginable. He warned that society's constant judging and ranking would become like a "fire that can never be quenched."[1] Although ultimately the holy spirit would reemerge and triumph, it would not be before humanity creates a hellish society consumed by criticism, insecurity, and the slavish pursuit of status.

I believe that this prophecy is about our own times, or at least about the future the modern era is embracing. In the creed we refer to as "science," we face the world-exalting religion Jesus told us was germinating in the Roman Empire. This prideful faith now extends around the globe and causes people everywhere to believe that humankind will eventually solve all the mysteries of the universe, even the question of our own origins and purpose. In the gnostic *Book of Thomas the Contender*, Jesus seems to have spoken directly to our scientific presuppositions when he said, "Your hope is set upon the world, and your god is this life!"[2]

Also increasingly apparent in the modern era is the constant criticism—the eternal judgement—from which Jesus came to save us. Because most people think that they, rather than God, are the ultimate assayers of one another's value, they constantly maneuver to gain recognition and rank—dressing, speaking, and acting with the aim of impressing or of showing dominance. In the words of Jesus, "Their mind is directed to their own selves, for their thought is occupied with their deeds. But it is the fire that will burn them!"[3] The flames of hell are being kindled today in the ever more exacting judgements people are imposing on one another in every area of life.

1. The Fires of Desire for Power and Glory

The teachings of organized Christianity about hell and more generally about the endtimes, the judgement, and the establishment of the kingdom of God, are based on an unfortunate misunderstanding. Again, I know that many Christians may find this assertion objectionable, and I apologize for challenging widely accepted doctrines, but I believe that Christian dogma is refuted by the gospels themselves. I am also concerned that we learn the truth about Jesus' teachings, even if the truth conflicts with our traditional ideas.

The mistaken conclusion drawn by Christianity that hell is a place of punishment in the afterlife arose from an understandable tendency of the apostles and Church founders to fuse two of Jesus' teachings that were actually quite separate. One concerned God's judgement in the afterlife. The other had to do with the cataclysm that Jesus said would occur later in history, shortly before the kingdom of God is established. In trying to understand these revelations, Christian priests and writers concocted the notion of a burning pit in the afterlife, ruled over by Satan, where evil souls would spend eternity while good souls lived forever in the kingdom of God.

I am not going to trace the development of this idea, because it is unnecessary. To see that it is an invention, you need only to look at the gospels. Although Jesus often spoke of the afterlife, he did not say that some people go to heaven and some to hell. Indeed, Jesus never used any word at all that meant "hell" in the sense that we apply to the term today.

Jesus is reported to have spoken on three occasions about "Hades,"[4] but Hades referred to the land or state of the dead—*all* of the dead— not to a place or condition experienced by evil souls alone. That Hades was simply the phrase Jesus used for the afterlife in general can be seen in his parable about the wealthy man and the poor beggar Lazarus. Jesus said they both died and were buried, and then they opened their eyes "in Hades"[5] and saw each other in very different conditions. Lazarus was in the bosom of Abraham, but the wealthy man was being tormented by a flame. The implication was that the afterlife is the same basic condition for everyone—everyone is conscious—but some people experience happiness while others suffer, depending on how they behaved in their pre-death existence.

When Jesus spoke of what we have come to call "hell," he used the word *Geena* or *Ge-Hinnom*, which was short for the "Valley of Hinnom."[6] This is a gorge outside the city of Jerusalem. It was notorious in the Old Testament as the place where the idols of Baal and Molek were worshiped during the reign of King Manasseh. The temple at Hinnom was called "Tophet." The idolatrous Israelites expressed reverence to Baal and Molek by burning alive *their own children* at Tophet's altar. In the case of Molek, the idol was made of brass and was hollow. A fire was built inside it, and after the statue became very hot, the priest took a baby from its father and placed it in the idol's arms, where it was slowly cooked as drums played to drown out its screams.[7] The valley of Hinnom was not a realm of the afterlife; it was an actual abyss of terror into which the Jews had stumbled earlier in their history.

Where the Bible says that Jesus warned people about "hell," translators have substituted the word "hell" for "Ge-Hinnom." To understand what Jesus meant, we must go back to his original words. Jesus told his followers not to fear those who can kill their body, but rather those who "hath power to cast into Ge-Hinnom."[8] He pointed out that it is better to pluck out an offensive eye than to have two eyes and "be cast into Hinnom Valley."[9] He chastised the Pharisees for making their proselytes "twofold more the child of Ge-Hinnom" than they were themselves.[10] He cautioned those who ridiculed others that they were "in danger of the fire of Hinnom Valley."[11] Repeatedly, Jesus pointed to certain beliefs and actions as leading, not to punishment in the afterlife, but to the chasm where human life is sacrificed, as he himself would be, on the altar of human opinion about good and evil.

As usual, for those who were steeped in biblical traditions the reference to Ge-Hinnom had subtle but very significant political overtones because of the connection to Molek. When it is written in Hebrew, Molek's name is identical to the word for "king," which is "Melek." The identity occurs because Hebrew writing omits vowels; hence they both appear as MLK. In fact, the god was probably referred to originally as Melek or king, just as Beelzebub had first been called "Baal" or "lord." The Old Testament authors had subverted "Molek's" name by replacing the two es in Melek with the vowels from the Hebrew word for "shame," which is "boshet."[12] Through this artful contraction, they depicted the god *Melek* as *Molek*, a "king of shame," and implied that those who worshiped him bowed to the ultimate false god rather than to the true king Jehovah.

In the context of his teachings about the kingdom of God, Jesus' repeated references to the Valley of Hinnom sent a clear signal to those with ears to hear his political message. Jesus was warning us that worldly power and glory are a shameful kingship that culminates, eventually, in humanity's self-destruction. Whenever we exalt ourselves above God; whenever we assume that one person has the power to command and judge another; whenever we put human laws and values ahead of God's, we build a fire that we cannot extinguish.

Experience shows that, in socially and politically stratified settings, our desire for control and esteem has no end. No matter how powerful or socially elevated we become, we always want to surpass someone higher. Even the mightiest kings look back in history to rulers they feel the need to outdo. Authority can be divided with checks and balances, and access to status can be equalized across races and genders, but the thirst for power and glory eventually leads to destruction so long as power and glory exist at all. For in any system of ranks and command, the values of social advancement eventually come to permeate the social order, and the spirit of Satan is unleashed.

This is why Jesus prophesied that the future would bring a great "dryness." By this he meant that the "living water" of faith would evaporate, and human society would become a spiritual desert.[13] The prophet Isaiah had made a similar prediction seven centuries earlier, when he had foretold the coming of Jesus. Isaiah claimed a time would arrive when people would thirst for faith as if they were "a garden that hath no water."[14] A little over a century after Isaiah, the Prophet Jeremiah screamed the same warning. He predicted that the name of Tophet and Ge-Hinnom would be changed to the "valley of slaughter" because "they shall bury in Tophet, till there be no place."[15] Jesus did not believe that the dry times had yet arrived; as we saw earlier in Chapter 1, he said at his crucifixion that the world was still in a "green tree," and he wondered aloud at "what shall be done in the dry."[16] But Jesus anticipated a hellish future because he saw that power and glory had been unleashed by humanity's original sin, that is, its belief that it has access to ultimate knowledge of good and evil.

Jesus announced that the new fire of Hinnom would eventually produce a spiritual and political cataclysm. This is what he intended when he spoke of "damnation." The original Greek word for "damnation" was *krisis*, which meant "judgement," not the act of sending souls to a tortuous abode. Thus, when Jesus warned against blasphemy directed at the spirit of holiness, he said it could lead to a state of eternal damnation or "endless judgement."[17] If we avoid the mistake of Christianity and keep this teaching separate from what Jesus said about "Hades" or the afterlife, it becomes apparent that by "endless judgement" Jesus had in mind, not disembodied minds baking in a fiery afterlife, but the incessant judging and jealousy that take over a social order to the extent that it loses the holy spirit. Jesus was saying that a social order built, like ours, on power and glory, will eventually become consumed by its own envy, bitterness, and cruel ranking. Without faith in God and the detachment from society it inspires, everyone descends into Hinnom Valley. Some stand higher than others on the steep slope of the gorge, but all kneel to Tophet and burn in the arms of Molek. In the words of the psalmist, "The wicked shall be turned into hell, and all nations that forget God."[18]

2. The Three "Days," or Stages, Preceding the Kingdom

At this point we can begin to decode Jesus' most famous words—or at least the words that were best known during the era when he lived and was crucified. After he drove the money changers from the temple, some of the people in the temple challenged him, saying, "What sign showest thou unto us, seeing that thou doest these things." Jesus responded, "I will destroy this temple that is made with hands, and within three days I will build another made without hands."[19] Out of the numerous parables and aphorism that Jesus offered during his brief ministry, this was the only statement brought forward at his trial before the Sanhedrin.[20] By then, the comment had become so notorious that, not only did witnesses report it to the high priests, but those who watched him be crucified quoted it as well and mocked Jesus for having said it.[21]

The meaning of this statement was, and still is, the central question surrounding the mission, nature, and destiny of the movement Jesus initiated. However much modern Christians may wish to assume that the meaning is obvious—that Jesus was referring to his resurrection after the crucifixion—the people who lived during the beginning of the Christian era were deeply divided over the message Jesus intended.

Several interpretations are obvious in the Bible. The people to whom Jesus made the remark took him literally; they thought he was saying that he could *physically* replace the temple in three days. They asked in astonishment, "Forty and six years was this temple in building, and wilt thou rear it up in three days?"[22] In contrast, at the trial when the remark was reported by witnesses, the high priest did not understand it, and he asked Jesus to explain it.[23] Later, the people who wrote the canon gospels interpreted the statement to refer to Jesus' bodily resurrection; in John's words, Jesus "spake of the temple of his body."[24] However, Stephen, the first martyr after Jesus, preached something else entirely; Stephen taught that when Jesus said "he shall destroy this place," Jesus meant that he would "change the customs which Moses delivered us."[25] As we have seen, at his own trial before the Sanhedrin, Stephen tried to defend this account of Jesus' teachings by quoting Isaiah to the effect that "the most High dwelleth not in temples made with hands."[26] In short, some of Jesus' listeners thought he was speaking of the temple literally as a building, others concluded that he was speaking figuratively about his own body, and still others decided that he intended the temple as a symbol for the laws of humankind.

The traditional account of Christianity that Jesus was referring to his own resurrection makes sense if one considers only the reference to the "three days," for Jesus showed himself to some of his followers three days after the crucifixion. But this interpretation is less satisfying when trying to understand Jesus' point about tearing down a temple "that is made with hands," and building another that is "made without hands." Was the body of Jesus "made with hands"?

Conversely, Stephen's view makes sense when it comes to understanding the meaning of a temple "made without hands," but Stephen's analysis is weaker when trying to explicate the symbolism of the reference to "three days." Stephen points out that Jesus' reference to a temple "made without hands" was drawn from Isaiah, and that it implied that the made-up laws of kings and priests, who built temples of stone, would be replaced by the true laws of God, who dwells above the whole of creation. This is clear enough, but why would the new laws take "three days" to create? If Stephen's account is complete, why did Jesus not say that the new temple, the temple "made without hands," would be built "eventually," or "when the wickedness of this generation has passed," or some other phrase to indicate a lengthy or even not-so-lengthy passage of time? Were the new laws really to come "within three days"?

My own view is that both Stephen and the founders of organized Christianity captured part of Jesus' meaning, but each missed the totality. Stephen was correct that Jesus was talking about replacing human laws with God's commandments, but Stephen failed to grasp how this shift in values was to take place, because he ignored Jesus' point about the temple's reconstruction taking "three days." Conversely, the founders of organized Christianity were right that the notion of "three days" *does* have a special meaning, but the meaning they gave to it was inaccurate, because they were focusing on building churches "made *with* hands," and hence they glossed over Jesus' point that the spiritual transformation he was initiating would yield a temple "made *without* hands."

I believe that when Jesus said the kingdom of God will come in three *days*, he meant that it will come in three *stages*. Jesus depicted history as a conflict between faith in the world and faith in God, or between Satan and the holy spirit. The stages leading up to the kingdom of God will occur as the intentions of humanity vacillate back and forth between worldliness and holiness. At one period in time, humanity will be preoccupied with the world, while at the next period it will react in holiness, and so on down the line until eventually faith in God triumphs once and for all. The arrival of the kingdom of God will thus be preceded by "days," that is, by clearly demarcated periods of darkness and light.

We can understand why Jesus would say that history will take this form when we recall Jesus' teachings about Satan and the holy spirit. Jesus revealed that each of these spirits exists in the world side by side. He warned that "he who is near me is near the fire."[27] Satan, or the spirit of Satan, is embodied in worldly systems of power and status. The spirit of holiness is rooted in every person's innate sense of being watched over by a higher intelligence who judges the heart. Those who are inspired by the spirit of holiness see the atheism inherent in power and glory, and their detachment from the world causes a hostile reaction from those who stand at the top of the social pyramid. In turn, to the extent that the latter reveal the force and oppression by which they maintain their positions of rank, the spirit of holiness will grow stronger among the multitudes. Civilization swings back and forth between the spirit of God and the spirit of Satan, with the conflict becoming clearer at each step.

Jesus described all of history leading up to the kingdom of God as a single "generation" to help us see that our spiritual vacillation is all part of single movement. The movement is similar to the spiritual awakening of a single individual. People hear God or see God in their lives, but they always approach God in fits and starts because God is not the only power pulling on their souls; the temptation of the world attracts them as well.

This is why Jesus made another prediction at the very same time that he declared his ability to replace the temple in three "days." In a parable that could not be comprehended until the modern era, he foretold that an initial period of faith inspired by his teachings would be followed by an era of even greater atheism than he had found in the Roman Empire:

> When the unclean spirit is gone out of a man, he walketh through dry places, seeking rest, and findeth none. Then he saith, I will return into my house from whence I came out; and when he is come, he findeth it empty, swept, and garnished. Then goeth he, and taketh with himself seven other spirits more wicked than himself, and they enter in and dwell there: and the last state of that man is worse than the first. Even so shall it be also unto this wicked generation.[28]

We are still part of the "wicked generation" to which Jesus was referring because we are still part of a civilization built on worldly power and glory. The modern era is "the state of man" that is "worse than the first"; the modern era has ushered in the spirits of science, capitalism, competition, and other systems of worldliness. These spirits came to humanity after the age of Peter's Christianity, because Christianity swept our house clean of paganism and idolatry, a cleaning which made modern science possible. But "seven other spirits" left the state of humanity in a worse state than before, because they caused humanity to deny God and to embrace the world even more thoroughly than had pre-Christian polytheism.

The three "days" leading up the kingdom of God, the temple that is "made without hands," can thus be seen to be (1) the age of organized Christianity, (2) the modern era of science, and, at some future point, (3) the day or age of judgement. At each stage, both the spirit of holiness and the spirit of worldliness have become, or will become, stronger, because each spirit is reacting to the other and is propelling it forward. Science was definitely launched in reaction to Christian dogmatism and still defines itself in distinction to belief systems based on faith. Presumably, the modern day, the day preceding the day of judgment, the day we are now in, will become a Ge-Hinnom, because the spirit of worldliness will grow to enormous proportions.

3. Jesus' Vision of History Contrasted with Our Own

It may be useful to compare Jesus' vision of history with the self-image of the modern era. Most people in the current epoch are blind to the spiritual dangers of our times because our civilization—the conglomerate of "Western" nations that grew from the Judeo-Christian tradition—has succumbed to a terribly distorted account of its development. We have been taught to believe that the West has emerged as the dominant culture on the planet, not because of the religious beliefs at its core, but because the West has replaced faith with reason. Rather than seeing a series of "days" leading eventually to humanity's complete emancipation from itself, modern scholars envision nothing better than what we have now, and hence they divide all of history merely into the darkness of antiquity and the supposed enlightenment of today.

This is the premise underlying our idea that the modern era is "modern," or fundamentally more advanced than its predecessors. In theory, all ages before ours were mired in superstition and wishful thinking. The current epoch began, we are told, when courageous freethinkers demanded realism. They tested ideas against facts and observations, and rejected all suppositions—including belief in a Creator—that could not be subjected to experimentation and analysis. Modern civilization is supposedly the result not of a spiritual struggle in history between faith in God and faith in the world, but of reason's victory over illusion.

In contrast, from his vantage point two thousand years ago, Jesus offers us a very different analysis of both our development and our current situation. His account of history as a spiritual struggle implies that the West has risen to world dominance not by rejecting its faith but by holding to it.

To see the value of this lesson, we must recognize that the lengthy survival and great success of Western civilization are unparalleled phenomena. The greatest historians of the twentieth century, Oswald Spengler and Arnold Toynbee, concluded that the invariable pattern in history is just the reverse; after an initial burst of success, all civilizations have declined and eventually collapsed. In fact, Spengler and Toynbee predicted that the West would disintegrate soon because it had already outlived its life expectancy.

Spengler presented his views in *The Decline of the West,* an enormously influential analysis written shortly before World War I. Pointing to cultures that had died in earlier centuries—ancient Egypt, Babylon, Persia, China, and others—he argued that the end of Western civilization is inevitable: "Each culture has its own new possibilities of self-expression which arise, ripen, decay, and never return."[29] Failing to question or even to perceive his unstated premise that the West is exactly like all other cultures, Spengler inferred from the decadence and political instability of the twentieth century that the decline of Western civilization had already begun.

Toynbee conducted a similar study and reached an identical conclusion in his ten-volume work, *A Study of History,* which was published not long after World War II. After reviewing the histories of all twenty-one of the world's known civilizations, he theorized that the West was following the same life-cycle evidenced by others.[30] He also inferred that Western civilization was near the end of its existence because it had recently become radically secular, a trait that Toynbee found had always marked a civilization's final stage.[31]

Spengler and Toynbee may have been right about *other* civilizations, but they were wrong about the West. Although all other civilizations have eventually collapsed because they have succumbed to a secular ideology, Western culture is different because it has contained within it, from the very beginning, the compelling idea of a social order governed solely by God. This vision and the spirit of holiness it inspires have repeatedly reemerged whenever Western civilization has fallen under the influence of worldly faiths.[32] While other cultures have been burned to nothingness in the arms of Molek, ours has repeatedly renewed itself through a resurrection of faith. Western civilization has emerged as the preeminent civilization on the planet,[33] outlasting all others and taking charge of intellectual life on all continents, because it has been energized by the holy spirit.

The essence of the Judeo-Christian tradition is a warning against abandoning our saving faith. The account of Adam and Eve in the Garden of Eden is in part about what happens when people turn away from God and put human laws ahead of divine commandments; they lose God's protection and nurturing. The lesson presented in the events surrounding the Tower of Babel is that God will scatter any people who seek to become gods themselves by constructing a stairway to heaven. The report of what happened to the Israelites in the wilderness when they began to worship a golden calf is a caution against idolatry. So are the Old Testament's frequent assertions that the oppression of Israel under various peoples was traceable to the idolatrous ways of some of its kings, notably Jereboam, Manasseh, and Ahab. By the same token, in the days of Jesus the fire of Molek and the Valley of Hinnom were synonyms for the terrible consequences of turning away from God. Clearly, the Bible is filled with frightening examples of what happens whenever faith is replaced by idolatry or atheism.

When Jesus announced that it would take him three "days" to establish a social order governed totally by spirituality, he was reminding us that our history of spiritual growth has not occurred in one uninterrupted stream, but rather has been characterized by many missteps and regressions. The historical sequence that will eventually result in the resurrection of the true spirit of Jesus began with the Roman Empire. The Empire threatened to destroy monotheistic faith because it offered a tempting trade; it allowed religious freedom in return for adherence to secular law. Jesus came to save the world from this bargain with Satan and lead it back to its aspiration for a divine order. Even though his teachings were distorted by Peter, Paul, and the other founders of the Church, organized Christianity still inspired the multitudes to transfer their allegiance from Rome to God, and clearly this transformed the Roman Empire and humanized our civilization. Thus, the first "day" in the process of establishing the "temple made without hands" involved at least a partial subjugation of power to faith.

The arrival of the second day, the modern era, which occurred in reaction to the corruption of the Church in the fourteenth and fifteenth centuries, did not represent a victory of reason over superstition, it marked a return to the relationship between power and faith under Caesar's Rome, although this time both the spirit of worldliness and the spirit of holiness were much stronger. On the one hand, the holy spirit regained some of the vigor it had lost since the Church had accommodated itself to the Empire. In reaction to the Church's decadence, a broad-based spiritual movement emerged which came to be called the "Reformation."

The Protestants took back the holy spirit from the Church, which had claimed to control it since the days when Peter first invented the "laying on of hands," and returned it to the people. The Reformation's leaders devoted themselves to translating the Bible from Latin into the common languages of Europe and England, giving the citizenry an opportunity, for the first time, to inhale the biblical spirit into its own lungs. Suddenly, prophecy returned. Preachers and martyrs such as Thomas Muntzer, Andreas Karlstadt, Ulrich Zwingli, Martin Luther, John Huss, Jacob Boehme, John Calvin—the list could go on indefinitely—demanded the right to a personal relationship with God through their own souls, unmediated by a religious hierarchy. This movement, which is still in its early phase of development, restructured the Church into numerous sects of conscience, brought down the monarchies of eighteenth-century Europe, and gave us the few freedoms we have today by spawning the modern era's idea of liberty.

On the other hand, the coming of the modern era also witnessed a counterrevolution by the world's systems of power and glory. Through a lengthy historical process, leaders in the political sphere succeeded in institutionalizing a boundary between church and state—a boundary similar to what had been practiced under the Roman Empire. Although many people were misled into believing that the new border separating power and faith created a realm of religious freedom, the actual effect was to cordon off the holy spirit so that it could not challenge authority or status. This depoliticization of the Judeo-

Christian tradition was possible only because organized Christianity had misunderstood the teachings of Jesus to be exclusively about the afterlife and the judgement, and not also about dismantling power and glory in the here-and-now. But once the church-state boundary was in place, the social order suddenly had enormous freedom to expand its system of ranks, command, and esteem, just as the Roman Empire did before Jesus.

4. The Scientization of the Bible

I wish I could be optimistic about the modern era and believe that somehow the spirit of holiness will solidify rapidly to dismantle our expanding systems of command and status before they go much further in placing us under our own severe judgments, but I can understand why Jesus said that we would first descend into the Valley of Hinnom. The basic problem, as I see it, is that the scientific ethos is systematically deconstructing our belief in the Creator. If the bulk of humankind loses faith in God and the afterlife, the spirit of holiness will be reduced almost to nothing, and the result will be a kingdom of hell, at least until the holy spirit reawakens.

Most Christians have reacted to the scientific invasion of Western culture in the same way that the Pharisees responded to the arrival of Roman legions in ancient Israel: They have tried to defend themselves by withdrawing into their religion just as the Pharisees withdrew into their homes and temples. Arguing to themselves and to others that the Bible reveals the world's purpose, whereas science focuses on the world's composition and dynamics, modern Christians hope to protect their faith by declaring it to be outside science's jurisdiction.

Unfortunately, though, this strategy of privatism is ineffective, not only because it leaves the rest of the cultural city open to looting by the occupation forces, but also because science, like the Roman legions, recognizes no restrictions on its own actions. Just as the Pharisees found that obeying the laws of Rome meant that they had to give up all doctrines that conflicted with Roman edicts—including their faith that earthly kings are subordinate to God—modern Christians who have accepted the principles of science have learned that science will not leave their religious beliefs alone. Science does not see itself as just another system of belief; it declares itself to be the only legitimate framework of thought, and it actively seeks out opposing viewpoints.

Make no mistake; the great minds of science have not been, and are not now, people merely interested in learning about nature. They have targeted the Bible and have sought to replace its central principles with their own. Galileo was not attacked by the Church when he just taught about the Copernican theory that the earth goes around the sun; he was brought before the Church authorities only after he made a point of ridiculing biblical statements about miracles involving the planets. Darwin, Marx, and Freud were no less frontal; each wrote works directed specifically at overturning belief in a divine Creator. To be sure, the assault by science on faith would have been unsuccessful if organized Christianity had not established a rigid creed that was actually inconsistent with the Bible, a book which is much more subtle and complex than most Christian exegetes and scientists recognize. But this does not mean that science undermined faith by accident or simply because religious people were foolish; science *as an enterprise* has earned its place in the modern world by going after religious doctrines.

This is why the body of knowledge generated by science addresses, almost one-for-one, the revelations provided by faith. The disciplines that comprise science are not just a reflection of reality; some parts of the world receive intense study, while others go completely unexamined. We know a tremendous amount about the stars and planets, but nothing about the economic systems of fan clubs or the average size of the nose hairs of horses. The subject matters of science have been selected—from among an infinite number of potential topics—to deal with the very same questions answered by the Prophets. Scientists do not examine just *any* patch of reality; they study things that may help them develop nature-based accounts of the creation of the universe, the origins of human beings and other creatures, the sources of human happiness, the means to social and economic prosperity, the roots of political stability and freedom, and so on. Science is a threat to faith precisely because it seeks to show that the essential features of the world, the features that concern human beings, can be accounted for *without God.*

The technique used by scientists in their assault on the Judeo-Christian tradition is to supplant biblical teachings about God's role in the world with ideas that rely solely on the automatic workings of nature. The account of creation in Genesis is replaced by theories of cosmic explosions, chemical reactions, and natural selection. Biblical revelations about the rules that should govern human life are rejected in favor of theories that yield similar moral codes, but that do so by citing human nature rather than God. Natural explanations are offered for such supernatural events as the parting of the Red Sea and the resurrection of Jesus, without considering the possibility that biblical accounts of these events contain elements of symbolism. Moses is redefined as a defector from the Egyptian upper classes who wanted to found his own nation, and Jesus is reconstructed as a great psychologist who could heal by suggestion and mass hypnosis. As the scientific legions march through the streets and search the homes of Western civilization, no revelation or doctrine is excluded from their effort to rework Western culture.

The scientific subjugation of the Judeo-Christian tradition has already reached beyond the centers of power into the private lives of ordinary people. While the core beliefs of the Judeo-Christian tradition are being deconstructed and rebuilt along scientific lines in the universities and academic journals, popular culture is being manufactured in the same image. In many science fiction movies and television shows, the biblical cosmology of God versus Satan has been reconfigured into the more scientifically acceptable format of conflicting "forces": the "light side" against the "dark side." God is sometimes depicted as a higher "level of being" or an extraordinary "form of consciousness," while the traditional idea of heaven is reformulated in the terms of modern physics, as an alternate dimension populated by ghosts and spirits. For those who have eyes to see it, the scientific crucifixion of faith is occurring everywhere in modern society; biblical revelations hang on scientific crosses all around us.

5. The Modern Form of the Holy Spirit

The scientific assault on faith and the rapid expansion of our worldly systems of power and glory already appear to be sparking a faint but nevertheless important stirring of the holy spirit. The growth of worldliness in the modern era does not mean that the holy spirit has been, or will be, obliterated without remainder. The Bible assures us that this is impossible; every human being—even those raised in depravity and subjected to an atheistic culture—always has a measure of connection to God, and every social order contains at least a residue of faith. If the holy spirit were not an innate and indestructible element of human nature, scientists would not feel it necessary to direct their intellectual lasers at religious beliefs, and tyrants of all sorts would not constantly find themselves confronted by opponents willing to die for their convictions. The teachings of Jesus suggest that it is the new form of the holy spirit—the spirit being born in reaction to the Ge-Hinnom of the modern era—that will eventually overtake our worldliness and usher in the kingdom of God.

The modern face of the holy spirit is not to be found in our anger, even in the anger being generated by the scientific ethos. To be sure, we see disaffection everywhere: in the anarchy of the inner cities, where lives are traded for cars, gold, and other symbols of status; in the rock-and-roll subcultures of our children, who mock authority by exalting those who deride it; in movements that seek to exit modernity by returning to nature; even in the middle class, which hides from the surrounding values-vacuum by burying its head in work, family, and television. Antipathy toward modern life is so common that scientists have coined a term to describe it; they call it "alienation."

But such disaffection for modern life is not the holy spirit returning, for it has little impact. Scattered and misdirected, it quickly evaporates under the hot sun of this era's great power and glory. The inner-city poor self-destruct in their introjected rage. Young rebels either join the system or become permanently mired in their subculture of opposition. Social dropouts just disappear. Workaholics die young. Suburban families reproduce and then scatter. Each enclave of disaffection is a miniature Hinnom Valley, burning in its own flames.

No, the spirit of holiness, which Jesus said would stir in reaction to

Satan's temporary victory, is not to be found in the smoldering crevices of our culture. Quite the reverse. It is blowing like a faint breeze, a wind gathering from many directions, as if the distant air were awakening from a long sleep.

The spirit of holiness Jesus foresaw is emerging as a world mind. For the first time in human history, a global public opinion is beginning to form, a gentle collective-will that can influence world events simply through its judgements. Although it is not easily seen, it becomes visible whenever it ruffles the leaves of the trees. It condemns human bondage. It sings. It opens its arms to children. It heals the sick. It cares for the disabled. It sends food to the victims of droughts and floods. Occasionally, it even blows down great empires and ruthless rulers.

The holiness of this spirit—its sense of separateness from the world—can be felt in the tension between our aspirations and the reality of our society. We know that our growing awareness of global unity—our growing knowledge that each of us is a child of human-kind—is dwarfed by the world's towers of command and obedience. In control of enormous resources, global corporations destroy entire communities solely for the purpose of enriching a few stockholders and managers. All sorts of "systems"—financial, defense, communica-tions—surround the globe like a net of steel; everyone is at once both connected and tied down. Nuclear armaments are pointed like dooms-day spears at virtually every population center on the planet. We may be beginning to think with one mind, but we are embedded in a social order that is fragmented, ruthless, and out of control. The conflict that Jesus said would occur between Satan and the holy spirit is material-izing right in front of us, at the point of contact between our global humanity and our ever-expanding systems of power and status.

Significantly, Jesus told us that this is precisely where we should look for his spirit to return. Perhaps predicting the false Christianity of Peter, he said there would "arise false Christs and false prophets," and that they would fool almost everyone, telling them that the spirit of Jesus was to be seen or found in insular subcultures or monastic sects.[34] But Jesus said he would actually be wherever the nations of the world are assembled, "for wheresoever the carcass is, there will the eagles be gathered together."[35] Today, the major powers of the world, the

American eagle and its allies, indeed stand over the body of Christ, the church that has become a carcass. But the spirit within the carcass is stirring, and the body may yet rise again.

6. Signs of the Apocalypse

Jesus said the dry times would bring terrible consequences, and he was right. As Satan materializes in his new form, the portents of impending horrors abound. The omens are not obvious; those who want a warning from heaven will not receive it. But Jesus pointed out that, just as an approaching storm can be discerned in a red morning sky, the coming conflagration can be seen in "the signs of the times."[36] One must merely "know how to read this moment."[37] Three signs stand out.

One is the emergent kingship of scientists. When modern science was first launched, it was envisioned as an open group of freethinkers who simply sought the truth, but today science is an enterprise of experts who stand above the public and direct the activities of the entire society. Scientists tell businesses how to increase efficiency, how to hook consumers with their products, and how to deal with bad press. They tell politicians how to get elected, bureaucrats how to manage the economy, and soldiers how to build weapons and destroy armies. They tell the public what to eat, how to raise children, and how the universe was created. They predict the future and explain the meaning of the past. Scientists are no longer merely seekers of truth; they are becoming the rulers of modern society.

What will the world be like when the values of science finally frame all decisions? Where will we find mercy, love, hope, and faith?

The complete scientization of modern society is not an idle potential; it is happening at this very moment! Marital relations, child-rearing, recreation, and many other areas of modern life that should be left open to spontaneity are being brought under the direction of scientific principles. The realm of technical control and efficiency is growing ever larger, while the sphere of real life gets pushed into a smaller and smaller corner.

Consider, too, the astonishing disparity between our ability to solve technological problems on the one hand, and moral or political problems on the other hand. Despite our tremendous ability to grow food, to manufacture commodities, to heal the sick, and to travel beneath the seas and into the distant heavens, our way of life and indeed the continued existence of our species is threatened by our own inability to govern ourselves. With science we have subdued nature, but our technology is running wild because science offers no guidance for technology's development and application.

At this very moment, technical processes and mechanisms are being formed that could steal the very essence of our humanity. What will be done with our new powers of computing, electronic surveillance, and genetic engineering? If scientific values of efficiency and mastery govern their usage, these technical abilities will simply be absorbed into our expanding systems of command and status, increasing the power of the mighty and reducing the influence of the emergent global congregation.

Still a third sign of the hell into which science is taking us is the deterioration of social relations. The advance of science has been accompanied by a loss of faith and charity. As scientific values have gained ascendancy, the ethical bonds made possible historically by the spirit of holiness have been dissolving. Crime, suicide, and divorce have been rising right along with the gross national product. Steadily, the spiritual framework of civility has been disintegrating around us, only to be replaced by the fabricated structures of schools, courts, jails, and bureaucratic rules and regulations.

Overall, the modern era appears to be a living contradiction because it has elevated human opinion about good and evil above the commandments of our Creator. Professing a belief in reason, the social order refuses to reason about God. Supposedly committed to free thought, it subjects its citizens to the most sophisticated techniques of mass indoctrination ever imagined. Claiming to exist for security and protection, it routinely exposes its population to nuclear annihilation as it jockeys with other nations for control over territory and resources. A democracy in name, it uses modern communication technologies not to enhance popular control of government but to manipulate public opinion and tighten the state's grip on the electorate.

The modern era is at once the age of a new, worldwide hope, and the era of mankind's greatest danger and uncertainty. Satan rises tall before us as the spirit of holiness, stirring faintly in the background, is assaulted at a thousand points by the insidious anti-faith of science.

7. The Psychology of Evil

Of course, Jesus never really expected us to be moved from our worldly preoccupations by such distant portents of political and cultural tyranny. He foresaw that the only truly convincing sign of our spiritual holocaust would be the mental anguish we would experience immediately in the here-and-now. Jesus said that the expansion of worldly systems of power and glory—the coming of the dry times—would exact a spiritual toll. We would literally begin to lose ourselves in the growing web of commands and external judgements entangling us. Jesus could see already in the Roman Empire, when raw power was merely in its infancy, that this spiritual death is terribly painful, even if those who are experiencing it do not understand what is happening or recognize that it comes from being possessed by the world. When Jesus warned us to beware of the dangers of Hinnom Valley, one message he was delivering is that worldly power and glory can incinerate our very souls. He spent much of his ministry not only agitating groups to spiritually reject civil authority and social status, but also extricating individual sufferers from Satan's grip.

Sadly, the prophecy is fulfilled. It has become commonplace in the modern era for people to lose control of their own volition and judgement. Many of us have become the slaves of our desires, fears, or wishful thinking. In some instances, this mechanization of the soul has taken the form of an unyielding compulsion, such as an addiction to drugs, food, or sex. In other cases, it has been characterized by a terrible mood which cannot be shaken. In still other instances, our intentions have become jumbled and fragmented to the point that the self seems to dissolve. Virtually everyone in modern society has experienced some of these tendencies. If they had not, there would no need for the plethora of diet books, drug counselors, psychotherapists, and Alcoholics Anonymous groups to help people regain their willpower.

Unable to ignore our widespread suffering, scientists have offered an explanation for it and have tried to develop a cure. They have argued that the apparent destruction of self-control stems not from a satanic spirit that is taking possession of modern men and women, but from unfortunate circumstances during our upbringing. Their theory is that emotions flow from a deep reservoir of primal instincts which must be properly shaped during childhood. Personality disorders, such as addictive tendencies and fragmentation of the self, are supposedly caused by frightening or exciting childhood events which create permanent emotional reactions. According to this hypothesis, the split-off personality, unconscious impulse, or neurotic symptom arises from a fear, lust, or hurt that occurred in a tragic childhood event. The remedy prescribed by psychoanalytic theory is to talk these feelings out, draining their psychic energy by expressing the emotions through words.

Ironically, modern psychoanalytic theory, which is one of the main ideologies of the modern era people use to avoid moral responsibility, has depicted Christianity as a faith that itself blames human actions on external forces. The idea of people being possessed by demonic spirits is characterized by science as a strategy for escaping blame by saying "the devil made me do it."

But Jesus' teachings about Satan's influence on the mind is exactly the opposite of this caricature. In attacking the devils that were bedeviling his countrymen, Jesus was demanding the same kind of personal responsibility he insisted on from the political and religious authorities.

Jesus explained that the world is a satanic web of power and glory. Participation in this kingdom will inevitably cause a deformity in the soul. The center of the self, the individual's freedom of will, is gradually abdicated to the multitude of pressures and interpersonal distinctions into which the will is enmeshed. Intentions are replaced by reactions, and real relations between people are replaced by proprieties. Having given others the power to command us and to assess our worth, we begin to lose not only our freedom and dignity, but control of our own volition and judgement.

In short, to the extent that we acknowledge power and glory, we behave in a mindless fashion identical to the systems in which we are embedded. It is the same phenomenon that the psalmist observed with idols: "They that make them are like unto them; so is every one that trusteth in them."[38]

We are accustomed to thinking of the neurotic person or the split personality as sick, and in a sense he or she is, but such personalities are just an extreme version of the normal self, which is also fragmented by distractions and prone to preoccupations. We all know what it is like to be very worried, afraid, or hopeful. When we have been in a dangerous or exciting situation, we may, for a long time afterward, find fears or desires repeatedly intruding into our thoughts like unwelcome winds, disturbing our thinking despite our best efforts. Neurotic or split personalities are merely caught in such events inextricably. The world holds them in a place, and the mood evoked in this place takes possession of their will.

This is what Jesus meant when he spoke of people's souls being possessed. To be possessed by a devil or spirit is really just the opposite of being whole or integrated. The word *religion* comes from the Latin *religari*, to tie together. When someone has a religious or intact soul, he or she can behave consistently, or with integrity, from one situation to the next, exerting will over events rather than the reverse. In contrast, insofar as an individual becomes tied emotionally to the world, his or her will is broken into pieces by the world's demands, temptations, pressures, and threats. When Jesus asked the man who was not in his "right mind"[39] what his name was, the man replied, "My name is Legion: for we are many."[40] When Jesus healed this man and those like him, he was said to have "made them whole."[41] To become immersed in the world is to give the world possession of your soul and to lose your humanity.

We know how preoccupation with the world robs us of our compassion and empathy. In the ancient era, Jesus' parable of the good Samaritan pointed to the fact that most people just ignored the suffering around them. Surely this is true today. Each of us has driven by the homeless in our streets as they stood beside the road with their signs asking for food and work. Each of us has jockeyed for position within our families, schools, and workplaces, pursuing aggressively our own interests against the humanity of our fellows. It is almost a defining feature of modern life that all face-to-face relations are characterized by strategy, manipulation, and selfish goal-seeking, even in what are supposed to be our most intimate connections. Somehow, we simply convince ourselves that these self-serving relationships are inevitable, that we must look out for our own interest or we will be fleeced like sheep.

Indeed, we have become so accustomed to this satanic, selfish attitude that we have defined it as the norm. We have been taught by science to deny our moral responsibilities. We have been persuaded that our feelings are beyond our control and that they must be expressed or acted on if we are to avoid emotional problems. Is this not the essence of modern psychoanalytic theory? However much we may give lip service to the idea of free will, it is commonplace today to regularly attribute our actions to factors over which we have no control. Our selfishness is said to be assertiveness. Our anger is defended as honest outrage at frustration. Our lust is chalked up to childhood "repression." Rather than rising above our feelings, we prostrate ourselves before them, at most hoping to reduce their intensity by expressing them or talking them through.

The strategy Jesus proposed for dealing with the spirits that trouble our minds—the fears, anger, desires, anxieties, and other images that break in upon our thoughts and distort our intentions—was far different from the remedy proposed by psychoanalysis. Because he saw that these spirits originate from the demonic attraction of the world and from too much concern about the world, he instructed the suffering souls he encountered to turn their eyes upward toward heaven. The problem and the solution are not emotional but rather spiritual.

8. How Modern Men and Women Lose Their Souls to the World

From Jesus' perspective, we in the modern era have given ourselves over to Satan almost totally, for the approach we take toward the self or the soul is exactly the opposite of what Jesus counseled. Jesus said the highest commandment is that "the Lord our God is one God" and we are to love him with all our "heart, soul, mind, and strength."[42] But we have turned ourselves away from God and toward the world. I can cite at least three ways in which we have become totally consumed by the sensations the world generates within us.

Perhaps the best example of our self-absorption, of our tendency to set our feelings up as idols to be worshiped, is the influence of psychoanalysis on everyday life. Psychoanalytic theory may appear to be reasonable in suggesting that childhood events influence adult character, but the theory actually has satanic implications. In personal relations it leads to a complete break in the transcendence achieved by love, forgiveness, empathy, and compassion. Those who are unloving or inconsiderate can blame their untoward actions on problems they experienced as children, thus allowing them to avoid the difficult task of working cooperatively in marriage, parenting, and other relationships where partnership is a necessity. At the same time, psychoanalytic theory leads one to reject the arguments of the other; any complaints he or she might have can be attributed to other concerns or "deeper" issues. How many times do husbands and wives in modern society say, "Now, what are you *really* angry about?" Rather than dealing with each other face-to-face as free moral creatures expecting to be reasoned with, we treat our minds and intentions as if they were caused from outside, and we wrestle with each other's illusions or speculations about what the other needs or wants. As one modern poet put it, "I pretend to touch you, and you pretend to feel."[43]

A second way in which individuals subjugate their souls to the world is by trying to transform their own bodies into idols. Increasingly, in the modern era the human body is considered as a slab of flesh to be sculpted and perfected. Excluding work and sleep, the vast majority of time and effort for many Americans is devoted to dieting and exercise. On top of the molded physique is added a layer of style in the cut of hair, the fashion of clothes, and, for women, cosmetics. In the end, each individual's soul becomes buried behind a veneer of flesh and illusion.

But of course, this is the objective. We who are slavishly devoted to our appearance are not seeking beauty for ourselves; rather we are trying to gain the adoration of others. We want glory. We want all eyes to gaze at us with envy. We desire not merely to be appreciated or loved, but to be lusted after and worshiped.

And yet the price we pay is precisely what Jesus said; it is the loss of our souls. As we define ourselves in terms of the attention we receive from others, the core of our self disappears altogether, for how we feel is dependent on the reactions of those we encounter. If people are impressed, we become confident and puffed up. If we are ignored or ridiculed, our self-esteem bursts like a bubble.

This is true even for those among us who construct their appearance in opposition to prevailing fashion. An irony often noted is that people who seem to themselves to be expressing individuality through their body-sculpting and facade of style are often those who have lost themselves to complete conformity. The punk rock-and-roll addicts who rip their jeans, put nails through their earlobes, and tattoo their arms are not free spirits; they are freakish clones of nonconformity.

A third technique where we have subordinated ourselves to the world is in the widespread effort to manipulate moods and feelings through the use of external stimuli. An obvious example is the rampant use of drugs in modern society, from tobacco, alcohol, and caffeine to illegal substances such as marijuana, cocaine, and lysergic acid. But mood-manipulation is much more pervasive than the ingestion of foreign substances. In essence, to create select states of mind and feelings is the goal of the entire entertainment industry. People watch action movies to become excited. Comedies to be light. Romance and drama to experience grief and the weight of difficult choices. Sporting events to feel the tingling sensation of competition and the adrenaline rush of fear and anger. And for those who need help in becoming sexually excited there are always X-rated movies and pornographic magazines. Entertainment in the modern era is simply a mind-drug that is ingested not through the skin or mouth, but through the eyes and ears.

All of these self-manipulating and world-enmeshing processes are occurring virtually all the time. We arise in the morning and have a cup of coffee to wake up. We speak to our spouses or children about our feelings, always with the assumption that there is or could be something behind them, some displaced anger or some residue of hurt from long ago. We drive to work in our automobiles with the radios playing, provoking memories of our teenage days or stimulating our hearts to pound with a frantic rhythm. At the office, we become a part of the big machine and experience the death that it is. We process or construct or serve or carry out. After work, many of us scurry off to the exercise room to keep our bodies sculpted. Then we don our mask of style and fashion and go out into the world of superficiality, or we head home to barrage ourselves with entertainment, three hours or so of mirth or thin action, the substance of which we will never recall—only how it made us feel, whether, that is, we thought it was funny or exciting or just boring. The body becomes like a machine in which we live, and our free will is reduced to a pinpoint inside of it. We are swept along by the situations we establish around us, the pressures of work, the commitments of families or friends. And we sell our free will for the pleasure of drink or food or a week's wages. As a modern poet put it, "time pulls on my finger, and I light another cigarette."[44]

Exactly as Jesus explained, the hell we enter after turning away from God is the loss of our souls, our free wills. We are not responsible for our actions; we can chalk them up to sad childhoods, and we can ignore the protests of our loved ones by dismissing their pleas as misunderstood feelings. But we recognize at some level of our minds that our essence has been reduced to a minimum, and that in a sense we are dead.

9. The Democratic Illusion

Still, Jesus never wanted us to forget that our suffering, no matter how personal, has political roots. His ministry of healing was not conducted in a vacuum; it was carried out as part of his teaching about the kingdom of God. If we are finding ourselves possessed by the world and unable to control our wills, with our souls burning in the flames of our own desires and judgements, it is because we reside in a kingdom of worldly power and glory.

The evil described in the Old Testament and highlighted by Jesus, the evil of decision-making processes that disperse responsibility and drain face-to-face humanity from the social order, is virtually the hallmark of modern political, economic, and cultural systems. As faith has declined in the modern era and been replaced by atheism, science, and other forms of religious doubt, modern society has become no more than a far-flung, complicated network of power that throws a veil over decision-making and shields everyone from accountability. Personal problems which affect real flesh-and-blood human beings are increasingly depersonalized and collectivized. The hunger of a million people, each with his or her own history, goals, and needs just like our own, are lumped together as "poverty" or "homelessness." And those who are ultimately responsible for the suffering of these many people are hidden behind the complexity of their unconscious collaboration. Everyone laments the problems, but no one accepts blame for causing them, and in fact responsibility is difficult to assign.

Is it any wonder that we treat our own bodies and minds like machines, manipulating them with entertainment and drugs, sculpting our physiques, thinking of our feelings as currents that change of their own accord? Is this not the way the social order itself functions? Although it is run by people, it operates like a mechanism, because the people in it have turned over their freedom to incentives, sanctions, fashions, and trends. Financial markets rise and recede like the tides. The mood of the public shifts from confidence to fear, and back. Elections operate as a thermostat, throwing out the incumbents and causing the government to act whenever the economy "cools off." We are becoming machines because we live in a mechanistic society.

To be sure, citizens in modern systems do not see their social formations as inhuman, oppressive, or morally evasive. Quite the reverse. The modern social order is thought by leaders and citizens alike to be a system of self-government. Previous political and economic orders are said to have been based on slavery justified by religion and backed by force. Modern society is depicted as an entirely new social formation, emerging from aspirations for freedom rather than from the human tragedy of domination.

But in reality, despite all its pretensions to being liberal, free, and governed in the public interest, modern industrial society is exactly like every other worldly kingdom. It is a social order founded on power and glory, on distinctions of rank and status between persons, where respect and obedience are given to people rather than to God. Just as the power of Babylon and Rome grew like a vine in the atheistic soil of Greek philosophy to entangle the soul of the ancient world, so today the undergrowth of authority and rank in modern society has been nurtured by science and now ensnarls the whole social formation.

The only divergence between modern society and the social order of antiquity is that, today, the power of command is somewhat more widely distributed and access to status is based more on competition than on parentage. But this is a minor difference; it means merely that each person has many masters, not that lordship has been eliminated. Power and dominion are exercised at virtually every moment and at every point in the society. The prophet Isaiah foresaw the loveless social order we now inhabit: "The people shall be oppressed, every one by another, and every one by his neighbor."[45]

If anything, the oppression of modern society is greater than earlier social formations because it is concealed behind an illusion of democracy. People naively believe that the iron cage of laws and regulations covering almost every aspect of their lives is somehow constructed by their own wills. The bureaucratization of life is seen as an expression of self-government.

In reality, however, the political process is as far from democratic as it is possible to be without becoming a blatant tyranny. The system is elitist to the extreme. Out of a population of over 250 million U.S. residents, effective control over the political command centers is wielded by fewer than ten thousand people. Elections are so unimportant that in even the most visible races—such as those for the U.S. President—only about a quarter of the people who are eligible to vote actually go to the polls. Further, political assassinations, manipulation of public opinion, and corruption of all sorts are commonplace. As Isaiah anticipated, "the princes," the politicians, are "companions of thieves," and all of them "loveth gifts, and followeth after rewards."[46]

Behind the curtain of democracy stands a military-industrial leviathan. Almost all the laws, regulations, social programs, education benefits, investment incentives, and other outputs of the command structure are driven by a commitment to economic growth and military power. There is no need for democracy, because no one in charge really cares what the people want. Leaders simply direct all activities toward expanding production and consumption, and everyone else takes up a position inside the beast. Women work and breed, and try to have it all. Men strive for dignity in a persona of strength while sacrificing their health for shiny cars. Little girls are readied for the next round of child-bearing. Little boys prepare for wars to come. All the while, the beast keeps grazing on human souls.

10. Power and Glory in Families, Schools, and Business

If power and glory were just features of the larger social formation—structures which could be evaded like bad television—the creeping mechanization of modern society might be tolerable, but thistles of authority and status are taking root in every field of modern life. The family, which God gave to us as love's home and incubator, is becoming an emotional wasteland. Increasingly, relations between husbands and wives are based not on mutual respect and affection, but on resources. When the husband is the sole breadwinner, or when, because of his education, experience, or other factors, he has more extensive opportunities for work than his mate, the marriage is patriarchal, and the wife is a second class citizen in the family, having the status of something between an adult male and a child. Even though the woman may be employed forty hours a week or more, she often has a servant role in the household and does most of the cooking, cleaning, and child rearing. Further, if for some reason the economic advantage of the union is lost, or if one or both parties believe they can find a better mate elsewhere, the couple often just divorces.

Ironically, women have responded to this absence of love by becoming as calculating and manipulative as men are stingy and demanding. Women speak of liberation, but what they mean by this is equal opportunity to oppress. The idea of motherhood, which is a social role rooted in love rather than acquisition, has been almost lost. Ultimately, the duties of both husband and wife may become economic positions rather than social commitments; if the logic of power and money continues to replace the spirit of love, men and women will pay one another for their services, and families will cease to exist.

Already, much of the parenting function in families has been shunted off into schools, which exercise their responsibilities with power rather than with affection. Children are no longer loved so much as they are "socialized." Schools are organized not on the model of a family, but of a factory in which each child is molded to a predetermined slot. The poorer children are shunted off into trade schools; middle class youngsters are channeled into community colleges and state universities; and the wealthy, who can afford exorbitant tuition, enter private universities and pick up the credentials and connections to join the elite class of rulers.

Just as power has subverted the social function of families, it has also come to define our relations at work. The economic system may be described by scholars as a process based entirely on exchange rather than power, but in reality it is just a thousand or a million self-contained dictatorships, each vying for dominion over the others. Owners and managers have the power to make and enforce decisions, while the employees can do little but obey. Although workers can leave to find other jobs and are free to band together and bargain collectively, the right to quit is no more than the right to choose another master.

The contemporary view of modern government, business, families, and schools—the almost universal belief that modern life is free of power, at least in its "democratic" institutions and in the private sphere—qualifies as a profound collective delusion, for it ignores the exercise of dominion and power in virtually every sphere of life. Whether or not the origin of this mass madness is Satan, the reality is clear. Modern society is a web of power, control, status, domination, deprivation, and subjugation, all glorified as somehow fair and appropriate. Each person is at one moment a victim, at another moment a victimizer. Women and men, blacks and whites, young and old, all compete with more or less equal opportunity to exercise dominion over one another. Everyone serves someone else. The modern social order is a circular chain gang of masters and slaves, in which everyone worships someone and is glorified in turn, but where no one has real dignity or more than momentary love.

11. The End of Modern Life

Of course, it could be argued that modern society has not yet completed its development, that its perfection is unfolding. Is this not the idea of progress and modernization? Those who believe in the world as a thing-becoming, those who accept all of these criticisms of the modern social order but who nevertheless maintain a businesslike and scientific faith that things are improving, would undoubtedly argue that vestiges of raw power in modern life are not expanding with spreading atheism, but instead are withering away because of heightened awareness. In just the past century, they would point out, labor has organized to counterbalance the controls of management; racism has been unmasked and condemned; women have fought for their rights and have already won many of them; child abuse has been brought into the light of day and appropriately outlawed; and environmentalists have rallied and have begun to stop the unbridled destruction of the global ecosystem. Defenders of modern society could easily make a case that the social order should be appreciated for its emerging perfection, rather than denounced for its current problems.

Where, though, is the world headed? If the aim of Western civilization is no longer spiritual salvation, then what is it? To know this, one must merely ask what goals are articulated today, and what Western civilization would be like if they were achieved. Our era espouses at least four great aspirations.

One is world peace. The hope is that the world will become a planet of self-governing, autonomous nation-states. The latter are to be defined largely around peoples with common backgrounds and histories, and each nation is to be represented in some sort of world congress like the United Nations. If one of the nation-states steps out of line by intruding upon the land of its neighbors or by violating basic human standards of law and order on its own peoples, then the planetary congress will intervene like a police officer among nations.

Note, however, that there is no aim to establish true self-government, whether for the world as a whole or for individual nations. The growing power and dominion in families, corporations, and the modern government of bureaucrats and elected officials will not be dismantled, although they may be constrained by new international laws. Instead, yet another layer of power and glory will be constructed at a higher level. The world-kingdom will be a system of interacting nations, supported by the tribute or taxes of the various citizenries, and defended by a common army or militia.

How is this different from the Roman Empire? It does not establish a global congregation of equal souls but merely creates a larger framework of rank and command. If anything, the coercive power in businesses, schools, and families, which is replacing the bonds of love, will be reinforced and supported. As with the Roman Empire, each nation will be allowed to have its own religion and customs, and the laws of all nations will be made more uniform by being subjected to a higher authority. But law, power, status, rank, privilege, inequality, domination, and control will persist, and will be stronger and more extensive than ever.

A second goal of the modern era is to eliminate the arbitrary exercise of force, a goal which defenders of our social order might argue is making all power more humane and therefore more acceptable. Employers can no longer hire, fire, and promote whomever they please; they must be unbiased with respect to race, religion, gender, and national origin. The power of parents and teachers to inflict corporal punishment on children is being taken away. The subtle oppression perpetuated in language, as when women are called "girls" and black men are referred to as "boys," is being rooted out and prohibited. Oppression and exploitation may yet be visible, but they are being steadily and systematically dismantled.

Again, though, what sort of society is being constructed? People are to be respectful out of fear, not love. Everyone is to have equal access to the pinnacle of control, but rank and power prevail. The social order is becoming a giant bureaucracy, governed by countless rules and regulations, where everyone is on the lookout for racist or sexist comments or actions, but where no one works to build relations of trust and mercy.

A similar situation prevails with the third goal of the modern social order, which is economic prosperity. The aim is not merely to assure that everyone has a basic minimum, or even a little excess. The overriding objective is to produce luxuries without limit. When the measure of production, the gross national product, fails to grow, or when the rate of growth levels off or declines, it is called a "recession" and the social order goes into a panic. Presidents of the United States are reluctant even to mention the word. The whole economic, political, and cultural system is predicated on ceaseless expansion. The same is true for individuals and families; each person expects to be better off each year, and each generation wants a higher "standard of living" than the generation that preceded it. Dancing in everyone's heads are visions of new cars, tools, furniture, clothes, jewelry. If the civilization is successful, people will be receiving service from robots, traveling to distant planets, preparing food with the touch of button, and always receiving more.

But what will this bring us, if not disaster? If we are learning anything from modern prosperity, it is that *things* are never satisfying. As soon as a new product is purchased, an even newer or better one is desired. Further, people use their acquisitions to reinforce the system of rank and privilege by signaling one another about their status. Everyone learns that Cross pens are better than Bics, Polo shirts are better than Izods, Cadillacs are better than Fords. And those who display the better products are given the glory. Far from freeing humanity from want, technology and the splendid things it produces are enslaving us more than ever. We are becoming dominated by our own wants, which have been unleashed by the dazzling choices presented to us, and we now value one another not according to our essential worth as human beings, but on the basis of our possessions.

Finally, a fourth objective of the modern era is environmental protection, which entails a new relationship between humanity and nature. The aim is to adjust human society to the "ecosystem." Nature is thought to function as an interrelated, self-stabilizing organism of which human beings are simply a part, no more important than any other element. To eliminate one component, whether it is a species or a type of habitat, is to jeopardize the operation of the whole system.

Although the goal of bringing humanity into harmony with nature may seem absolutely essential, this is only because another precondition of modern society is endless economic expansion. Unwilling to reexamine the latter, we are forced into an environmental ethos. If we are to keep growing, we must make all the adjustments necessary to avoid environmental limits; we, as a social collective, must identify the practices that are environmentally hazardous, and we must, as a collective, prohibit such actions by limiting individual discretion. If this entails limits on cherished rights, then so be it, for the survival of the collective is at stake, or at least the survival of the social order as we know it, with its boundless plenty.

The kind of society entailed by this way of thinking is the same sort of monolithic, nature-centered society of pagan antiquity, in which life was an eternally recurring series of activities organized around the seasons. The Nile floods, then planting season, then harvesting, then the flooding again, all overseen by Isis and Ra, and everyone paying homage to the nature-gods' awesome stability and inevitability.[47] In an age that has seen Hitler, Stalin, and Mao, it should not take much imagination to recognize that a society regulated according to nature could be incredibly tyrannical. Plants and animals will be valued more highly than human beings, and the social order will be restructured accordingly to assure that the normal pattern of nature is maintained intact even if it means a drastic increase in human suffering and abandonment of Western civilization's ambitions for a social order ruled totally by love. Modern fears of tyranny will be realized not in political oppression by a clique or ruling elite, but in a self-imposed tyranny of nature.

In short, when we carefully consider where the modern social order is headed, we can see the nightmarish future or Ge-Hinnom that Satan, or the spirit that has lead us to turn away from our biblical heritage, is preparing for us. It will be a global bureaucracy subsuming a million principalities and petty tyrannies, where glory is literally worn on one's sleeve, and human life is governed according to the needs of Nature, the great but fragile ecosystem that supports us as we gorge our limitless appetites. It is a kingdom only an antichrist could imagine, and it has become our highest aspiration.

CHAPTER FIVE

The Lord's Prayer
is a Political Manifesto

THE nature of the divine kingdom Jesus called on us to create is described most directly albeit compactly in what has come to be called "the Lord's Prayer." Of all the writings of the New Testament, this prayer is most likely to be the exact words of Jesus, for one would have expected him to have had such a prayer and for the disciples to have carefully memorized it and to have passed it down to their followers. Several other prayers by Jesus are recorded in the canon gospels: Jesus thanked God for bringing Lazarus back to life;[1] he glorified God for revealing his mysteries "unto babes" while hiding them from "the wise and prudent";[2] he appealed to God to let him avoid crucifixion;[3] and during the crucifixion he asked God to forgive his executioners and to accept his spirit.[4] But, with the possible exception of the communion ceremony, the Lord's Prayer comprises the only words of worship Jesus actually taught others to recite.

Many people have tried to discern the characteristics of the kingdom of God by looking at what Jesus said about it in various contexts, but this is a misleading approach, because Jesus often spoke with the aim of concealing his political messages from the authorities. He might say one thing before a crowd; something else entirely to the priests, Herodians, or Romans; and still another thing to his disciples. We have seen this in Jesus' teachings about serving earthly power and glory: to the crowds, he described authority and status subtly as the kingdom of Satan; to the authorities, he said his view was to "render unto Caesar what is Caesar's"; and to the disciples, he declared that no one can serve two masters. Looking in various places for Jesus' description of the kingdom yields an image dotted with elements Jesus did not intend.

The Lord's Prayer is unique because Jesus taught virtually the same words to the crowds in public and to his disciples in private.[5] He did not suggest an exoteric prayer to the former and a secret prayer to the latter. The Lord's Prayer is thus a bridge between the public teaching and the private. It is a special declaration that could be relayed to both worlds and be understood by both worlds, although perhaps not in the same terms.

1. What Can Be Demanded of God

Two of the most important aspects of the Lord's Prayer are its structure and tone. Unlike many psalms, which extol God or plead to God for assistance, the Lord's Prayer speaks of a relationship with the Almighty very different from what organized Christianity eventually came to prescribe. The latter was transformed into a religion of atonement, where the priesthood mediates between the faithful and God for the purpose of delivering sinners from hell. But the only prayer Jesus taught his followers to recite strikes a very different stance.

In particular, the Lord's Prayer does not contain a single plea, a single word of request or supplication. Every line of the prayer is either a statement of will on the part of the ones who pray, or a demand imposed upon God. The prayer does not say "please forgive us for our trespasses," or "please give us our daily bread." It simply tells God to do these things.

This tone, like everything else in the prayer, has both a spiritual and a political implication. Spiritually, it requires us to adopt a particular attitude toward our Creator. We are to make our appeal to God with an unmitigated belief that it will be granted. We are not to ask with a timid heart, thinking that God might grant part of our request but deny the rest. We are to make our prayer virtually as a demand.

Recently, it has been noted by several authors that the new spirituality preached by Jesus can be seen in how he addressed God. Jesus often called God by the Hebrew word *Abba*, which is a familiar term for father similar to *papa* or *daddy*.[6] Certainly, there is some truth in the fact that this usage indicates a new stance toward the Creator, for the Israelites seldom described God as a father at all, much less as a papa. In all of the Old Testament, God is referred to as our "Father" only eight times.[7]

But the Lord's Prayer is doing more than merely teaching us to see God as our father. It is telling us that God is a unique kind of father. He is a father whom we can depend on totally, without any doubt or fear whatsoever.

The key is for us to demand only what we can rightfully expect. Jesus specifically instructed the multitudes not to approach God for reasons other than those contained in the Lord's Prayer. We are not to pray publicly with an eye toward gaining glory from those who see us praying.[8] Nor are we to seek to influence God with supplications, "for your Father knoweth what things ye have need of, before you ask him."[9] Seek forgiveness, daily bread, and deliverance from evil, and there is no need to plead or beg, or even to worry about having the prayer answered.

This explains why Jesus told his disciples that "whatever ye shall ask the Father in my name, he will give you."[10] Jesus was not saying that the name "Jesus" was some sort of magical talisman that would force God to respond to all of his followers' requests. The word for "name" in both Greek and Hebrew also meant "character" or "essence."[11] This is why the Lord's Prayer says "hallowed be thy name;" it means that we glorify God's disposition or spirit. When Jesus implied that his disciples should make their requests to God in the "name" of Jesus, he was saying that their prayers should conform to Jesus' teachings and manner. If they asked in the way that Jesus taught, they would seek only what God would give to them as a matter of course.

Spiritually, then, the Lord's Prayer is not intended to influence *God*, but rather *those who are praying*. They are to recognize what they can command from God, or what God will give them even without their asking. And in their manner of speaking, they are to assume that their requests will be granted. God may be their Papa and they may be like children, but they are assertive children indeed. Their prayer is stated like a child who says to his or her parent, "be sure to feed me today and clothe me today and help me be a good person." Good parents do not expect their children to beg for such things; they provide them without asking. God, Jesus constantly reminded us, is much better than any earthly parent, and he will behave accordingly.

2. The Lord's Prayer is Not a Prayer

Politically, the Lord's Prayer is akin to a pledge of allegiance. It not only states several expectations for God, it announces the intentions of those who are praying. They say, in effect, "We declare that God's kingdom has come, and we choose, here and now, to give all power and glory neither to the popular nor to the exalted, but to God alone." In this sense, the Lord's Prayer is not a prayer, but a vow.

This is why Jesus taught people to pray as a group, rather than individually. If it were not for its political intentions, the Lord's Prayer could just as well have begun, simply, "Father who art in heaven," or just "Father." But Jesus instructed us always to say *"Our* Father." Those reciting the prayer join together and, in effect, create the kingdom of God by the very words they say. The Lord's Prayer is a group or collective statement because it is designed to establish a group bond, a new kingdom independent of the power and glory of the world.

Those who pledge their allegiance to the new kingdom recognize that God is not near. They say, right up front, that God is "in heaven." They also recognize that God's will has not been done on earth as it has been in heaven; people are rewarded, according to their true worth, in the afterlife, but in their earthly existence people are given power and glory wrongfully on the basis of human judgement. Those who recite the Lord's Prayer praise God's name, that is, his character, because they recognize its infinite superiority to the justice achieved by humanity in the kingdoms of men and women.

The Lord's Prayer is a dramatic announcement of intent. The members of the congregation are going to make the will of God active in the world through their own wills. They themselves are going to implement God's love and mercy on earth and thereby establish a divine kingdom.

The context in which the Lord's Prayer is delivered in the Sermon on the Mount shows in detail how Jesus envisioned that we should bring God's will to earth. Those who reside in the world but belong to the kingdom of God, that is, those who declare themselves to be subject to God's rule, live in complete faith that there is an afterlife, a kingdom of heaven in which their actions will determine their positions and the rewards or punishments they receive. This is what Jesus meant when he said those who have riches on earth will not be rewarded in heaven; they have already been rewarded. And those who pray should do so quietly and in seclusion, rather than making a display of it like the Pharisees, because they will obtain their reward in heaven while the Pharisees have their reward already. The faith Jesus called on people to have is a faith that they are connected already and eternally with the kingdom of heaven. If they act on this faith, then they will behave precisely as the Lord's Prayer declares they will behave, and a spirit of holiness will emerge in their midst.

Indeed, if one examines the Lord's Prayer carefully and with a recognition that Jesus was offering messages with double meanings—a surface meaning for those without faith, and a deeper, revolutionary meaning for those who were prepared to join him in uniting under God's rulership as opposed to Caesar's and Herod's—it becomes clear that God need not even be listening. The prayer does not ask God to bring about the kingdom. It does not call for a supernatural blow against earthly rulers. Unlike many Psalms, it does not request of God that the mighty be brought down, or that the prideful be rebuked, or even that the good be rewarded. It is a prayer unlike any prayer ever before or after; it is a prayer that itself brings the spirit of holiness into being.

3. Jesus Saw Prayer as a Political Action

The peculiar character of the Lord's Prayer explains two puzzling features of the gospels. One is the apparent contradiction between, on the one hand, Jesus' admonition that we should not pray in public, and on the other hand the fact that Jesus taught a prayer and also prayed publicly himself. How could Jesus say, in one breath, "when thou prayest, enter into thy closet,"[12] and in the next breath instruct us to recite, "Our Father who art in heaven . . ."?[13] If prayer should be in secret, why would he have prayed publicly when raising Lazarus, rejoicing at his new understanding of the prophets, and before and during his crucifixion?

The answer is that he saw prayer as a political act. He prayed himself, and he asked others to pray, not to try to change God's mind or to point out some need to God—God does not require our help with such things—but to inspire ourselves and others. Jesus said as much when he resuscitated Lazarus:

> Jesus lifted up his eyes, and said, Father, I thank thee that thou hast heard me. And I knew that thou hearest me always: but because of the people which stand by I said it, that they may believe that thou hast sent me.[14]

Jesus prayed publicly to activate the spirit of holiness, and he urged others to pray for the same reason. Private prayer was for personal strength: Keep your heart soft by praying for those who use you;[15] pray for strength against the flesh, which is weak;[16] pray for release from a troubled spirit;[17] pray to avoid temptation.[18] Prayer in public, such as the Lord's Prayer, is, or should be, different; it is not prayer so much as it is spiritual activism.

The other puzzle explained by the political character of the Lord's Prayer is a strange feature of the gnostic gospels: They say that Jesus told his disciples not to pray at all. In the *Gospel of Thomas*, Jesus warns that, "if you pray, you will be condemned."[19] Jesus is quoted similarly in the *Gospel of Philip*.[20]

Presumably, Jesus instructed his followers not to pray in the traditional sense of the term. He did not believe that the kingdom of God, or any other form of earthly righteousness, could be brought about by repeating words to the sky. Jesus taught a new kind of prayer, because he brought a new revelation. If we want mercy and love, then we should not make a request of God, but rather a vow between people.

Jesus' belief that prayer is a political act may strike modern ears as cynical, but it actually has deep roots. Jesus was not trying to use religious ceremonies to dupe the multitudes into adopting a hostile attitude toward the authorities, he was reuniting spirituality and politics, which all earthly kingdoms strain to keep separate because of the anti-establishment implications of faith. Historically, government always emerges from religious convictions. All ancient kingdoms traced their origins to gods because they grew from the spiritual bonds of their subjects. Even the words "to vote" have a spiritual origin; they come from the Latin, *votum*, "to vow." In a kingdom of God, which is what Jesus wanted to establish, prayer is naturally a political act, because politics and faith are united.

4. The Economics of a Divine Kingdom

In addition to its political subtlety, the Lord's Prayer is also remarkable for the principles it lays out to govern the divine kingdom it establishes. After hallowing the nature of God, it expresses the intention that the divine kingdom should come into being, and that, through it, God's will should be done on earth. The prayer then states three precepts for the kingdom's governance. Those who recite the pledge ask for daily bread, forgiveness, and protection from temptation. As with the prayer in general, the political implications of these principles are not obvious; the prayer's elements seem on the surface to be merely requests of God. But a careful look shows that they are much more.

Consider, to start, the demand that God "give us this day our daily bread."[21] This expectation of God has three aspects. One is that it focuses only on a single period of twenty-four hours. Clearly, the prayer is to be said each morning, and, as far as material matters are concerned, its reciters are not to think beyond the rest of the day. Second, the food being requested is very basic. It does not ask for "nourishing meals" or "bread and meat," but instead only for bread. Third, even the bread is to be very limited in quantity. The Greek phrase which has been translated "daily bread" is *epiousios artos*. A more precise translation would be "necessary bread,"[22] that is, only the bread required for health. Thus, the overall effect of this sentence in the Lord's Prayer is to focus our intentions much more narrowly than normal: on the day and on the barest essentials.

As is typical for the aphorisms of Jesus, the spiritual effects of this principle are easier to see than the political. Spiritually, the impact is to minimize worries about the future. We tell God or ourselves that

God will give us our daily bread. This emphasis on not being concerned about tomorrow is consistent with many of Jesus' other sayings and his general teaching that we should turn away from our worldly preoccupations and obtain pleasure and meaning in the small things in life. The idea of expecting daily bread is a statement of how we who say this declaration are going to approach the world.

Politically, the principle is an incredibly insightful strategy of economics. It implies that we will stop seeking to accumulate wealth. We will go after only those things we require for sustenance and health. Poverty will not be eliminated with government programs or private charity, but through a worldwide spiritual transformation.

Certainly, nature is now and always has been capable of providing sufficient food and other goods to support humanity. The economic difficulty faced by mankind has not been that the world lacks resources adequate to carry us. The Old Testament, which Jesus read so carefully, is clear on this point: Although when God sent Adam and Eve from the Garden of Eden he initially placed them under a curse of scarcity (declaring that Adam would have to wrench food from the ground),[23] God lifted this curse after the great flood, and abundance was granted to all of humanity from Noah forward.[24] If we are not greedy, the world will give us what we need.

The economic problem has been that some people accumulate an enormous amount while others go hungry. Today, the poverty and deprivation in our inner cities is not due to our inability to produce enough food, clothes, and shelter to go around; it stems from the fact that a small segment of the population consumes gluttonously and without limit. Further, this same phenomenon is recapitulated globally. The hunger of undeveloped countries is not due to worldwide scarcity; it is a consequence of the Third World not having commodities to offer to those in the First World in return for food. The Third World goes hungry while the First World lives wastefully and with vast storehouses of food. Poverty, whether in a city, a nation, or a hemisphere, is merely the other side of wealth. This was the case two thousand years ago, and it remains so today.

Jesus sought to restrict our economic concerns to our daily bread because he recognized that poverty and deprivation are political or spiritual problems, not economic. Poverty is an inseparable aspect of all earthly kingdoms because these kingdoms are built on power and glory. Some people are assumed to be more important than others, and by various means they are given access to the lion's share of the social order's outputs. Others simply do without, because, in one way or another, they are judged less worthy. Poverty is not a problem that can be corrected by social programs or redistributive tax systems, or with everyone's favorite solution: education. Wealth and poverty flow from the spirit of the system, or from the values on which the social order is based and which it reproduces in each new generation.

Just look at the earthly kingdoms of today. Modern society is organized for the sole purpose of producing commodities, which are distributed according to a merciless system of judgement. Everything is driven by competition. Businesses that cannot constantly improve their productivity go under. People who are emotionally or educationally incapable of competing are left by the wayside like so much garbage, to be cleaned up by public or private charity. Science focuses almost exclusively on developing new technologies for the economy, and scientists who do not publish perish. Leaders are judged at the polls against their success at guiding the production process and protecting the nation's access to natural resources. As a whole, the social formation is just a giant mechanism for turning stones into bread, and it gives the most bread to those who work best within it.

The system continues to operate as it does, spewing out waste and crushed human beings, only because the people who comprise it have turned their souls over to the pursuit of property. Virtually everyone is preoccupied with the scramble for goods. Each day is approached, not as a blessing or an experience to be enjoyed, but merely as a stepping stone to some hoped-for acquisition. Some chase after a better apartment, a newer automobile, or a particular item of clothing, while others scheme ambitiously for great power and wealth. But the scale alone is all that varies; the motivational complex is always the same: every soul is little more than a bundle of wants.

5. The Glory of Poverty

The economic program contained in the Lord's Prayer strikes at the heart of the system of power and glory. In teaching us to seek and expect only our daily bread, Jesus was reconstructing the social order from the inside out. He did not call for economic redistribution. There is nothing in the Lord's Prayer that asks for God to give support to the poor or to distribute wealth more evenly. Jesus wanted to end inequality, not by taking from the rich and giving to the poor, but by convincing everyone—rich and poor alike—to stop trying to stockpile possessions. Much of the glorification of select individuals would end if the scramble for riches were called off. In the secret teachings of Jesus, poverty was not the problem, it was the solution.

This attitude toward indigence accounts for several strange features of Jesus' ministry that are often overlooked or misunderstood. For instance, it explains why Jesus never established a system of charity. On several occasions, he is reported to have told single individuals to sell all of their possessions and give them to the poor,[25] but, in all of his sermons to crowds, lectures in the synagogues, and instructions to his disciples, Jesus never asked his followers to take up collections for the poor. Instead, he praised the penniless and urged everyone to become like them.

The belief that poverty is an effective economic and political strategy against power and glory also puts the miracles of the loaves and fishes in a new light. Jesus performed two miraculous feedings of the multitude. First, he fed five thousand people with five loaves of bread and two fish,[26] and then four thousand with seven loaves and a few fish.[27] It is clear that these miracles puzzled the disciples. At first, the disciples did not even recognize them,[28] and even when they did, they seem to have thought that Jesus was just trying to be nice to the crowds while proving his divinity.

But Jesus was actually trying to make a point. He even said so afterwards: "Verily, verily, I say unto you, Ye seek me, not because ye saw the miracles, but because ye did eat of the loaves, and were filled. Labor not for the meat which perisheth, but for that meat which endureth unto everlasting life."[29] The loaves were a lesson: huge numbers of people could be nourished by very little if they would share equally and not expect to be stuffed. Further, by seeking only their "necessary bread," they would be released from their concerns about the world so that they could truly live. Christianity turned the breaking of bread into a mystical ceremony of absolution, but Jesus meant it to teach us about the freedom, equality, and holiness of spirit that can be ours if we collectively choose poverty rather than the pursuit of property.

A third peculiarity of Jesus' ministry that is explicable once we understand his economic strategy is his seeming lack of concern about the plight of the poor. The statement by Jesus that "the poor ye shall always have with you"[30] is frequently seen to imply that Jesus thought inequality is an unavoidable and intractable feature of human life. But in actuality, Jesus accepted the existence of poverty and saw no reason to try to end it because he wanted the whole world to adopt the same indigence. Similarly, when asked by John's disciples whether he was the messiah, Jesus cited as one sign of his divine mission that "the poor have the gospel preached to them."[31] As if it were the most important indication of all, this seemingly unconvincing evidence was listed last—after the testimony that "the blind receive their sight, and the lame walk, the lepers are cleansed, and the deaf hear, the dead are raised up"—because it was the most phenomenal: unlike virtually all do-gooders both then and now, Jesus did not try to help the poor become better off; he told them instead that they were fortunate for their lack of property. By the same token, Jesus said "Blessed be ye poor: for yours is the kingdom of God,"[32] because the new kingdom he was advocating would indeed be a kingdom of paupers.

It is easy to understand why organized Christianity misunderstood Jesus' economic program to be a call for charity and tithing rather than for the glorification of indigence. After all, helping the poor was a good mechanism for building the Church. Gifts to the Church could buy the wealthy an easier conscience and the respect of parishioners, while aid to the needy could win popularity with the multitudes. The problem is that this Robin Hood role for the Christian faith is totally contrary to Jesus' teachings. It means that, for the Church to have a function, it must accept the inequality of the social order rather than call people to poverty.

This unfortunate misunderstanding of Christianity has been a plague on our faith. It led to the selling of indulgences in the fifteenth century, when the Pope actually offered forgiveness of sins—even sins not yet committed—in return for money. It can also be seen today in various Christian theologies and political parties that call for income redistribution in the name of Jesus. However, a Church or political movement organized to provide welfare is anti-Christian! In the kingdom of God prophesied by Jesus and delineated in his prayer, we do not take from the rich to give to the poor; we teach by example and call through faith for people to stop accumulating and to start living. The answer to the world's economic problems is not collective but rather individual. Each person has the power to join the economic program of the kingdom of God through his or her own personal behavior by refusing to amass goods beyond his or her personal needs. If people did this on a large scale, the economies and distribution systems of the world would change automatically.

6. The Politics of Forgiveness

The second principle of the holy kingdom being created by the Lord's Prayer is forgiveness. Jesus makes it very clear in other statements that this is a radical form of mercy. It is not tit for tat. If you are struck by someone, turn the other cheek.[33] If someone takes you to court and sues you for one thing, give them even more.[34] Our forgiveness of others is not to be contingent upon their behavior in any way whatsoever. We are to love even our enemies.[35]

Again, this principle has both spiritual and political implications. Spiritually, it implies more than that an attitude of tolerance be adopted toward those who offend us. Jesus did not instruct us to say, "Forgive us our trespasses and help us forgive those who trespass against us." He taught us to declare a direct connection between our behavior toward one another on earth, and God's attitude toward us in heaven. We tell God in heaven to have mercy on us *in proportion to* our own mercifulness on earth. "For with what judgment ye judge, ye shall be judged: and with what measure ye mete, it shall be measured to you again."[36] Our forgiveness of others is to be rooted in our recognition that God forgives us of far more.

At first blush, this seems to be a rather straightforward idea, but it is actually a profound redefinition of the relationship between God and humanity. It is not insignificant that this is the only governance precept in the Lord's Prayer that establishes a contingency between our actions on earth and God's attitude toward us in heaven. The expectation that we will be given our daily bread and protected from temptation depends in no way on our own behavior; Jesus did not tell us to say, "Give us our daily bread if we work hard," or "Lead us not into temptation if we try to avoid sin." But when it came to forgiveness, Jesus instructed us to tie our union with God to our feelings toward one another: forgive us proportionate to our own judgement of others.

In this brief statement, the Old Testament covenant is being overlaid with a new agreement. The initial covenant was offered by God to man: God chose the Jews and demanded that they worship him alone, and in return they were made into a historic people, with their own land and with the ability to withstand efforts to absorb them culturally, politically, and militarily. This covenant between the Jews and God still stands, as we can see from the reestablishment of Israel in the Middle East. But a new and universal covenant now exists above it and extends to every human being who will join the kingdom of God. This covenant is a vow from humanity to the Creator: we will earn his forgiveness by being merciful to one another. The kingdom of Israel is subsumed within a kingdom of God through the unified will of humankind to join together in a holy union.

Spiritually, the principle of forgiveness frees us from the eternal hell of our incessant judging, which is the source of life's grief and bitterness. Jesus pointed out many times that most of us are completely consumed by our condemnation of one another. The anger that grows from each of the resentments we harbor is a flame that burns our souls, and so long as we bear our intolerant grudges, the fire can never be quenched. Hate feeds on hate. One person's resentment is repaid in kind, which in turn is itself revenged, and so on until the world is just a web of reciprocal animosity. All recognition of humanity is lost; our eyes are covered with scales of bitterness, so that we see in one another not the image of God, but only the weaknesses highlighted by our unwarranted self-righteousness.

By forgiving others, we free ourselves from this self-created hell and become capable, for the first time, of truly living. Our spirit rises above the resentments that clutch at our souls. Forgetting our hatreds, we naturally feel love. The tension between us and the world dissolves. We are reborn.

7. Law Without Judgement

As before, the social and political implications of this principle are far-reaching. With forgiveness as a guiding social precept, the whole character of law and justice would be transformed. The change would take place first in our hearts, and then in our institutions. Justice would be replaced by mercy.

The social and political change would be motivated by a new recognition that flows from faith in God and from the holy spirit this faith engenders. When we acknowledge our Creator, when we hallow his nature, we inevitably see our own sinfulness. The holy spirit is itself experienced as an elevation from our fleshly existence, and, as such, it causes us to understand just how strongly the world pulls at our minds, and how, even when deeply inspired, our hearts remain torn between the fear of the world and the hope of the afterlife. In the kingdom of God outlined by Jesus in the Lord's Prayer, this self-understanding is to be the foundation of our forgiveness of others. We know how much we need forgiveness from God, and we apply the mercy we desire from him to our evaluation of the trespasses of others.

Politically, this means that in the kingdom of God there can be no judges in the traditional sense of the term. Judges sit on high in their black robes and apply the social order's opinions about good and evil. All sorts of little rules about evidence, argument, and decorum are applied, and a verdict is rendered as to guilt or innocence. Judges aim to achieve justice, not mercy.

Jesus wanted to do away with "the commandments of men" and the eternal judgement they entail. In his own life, he repeatedly showed us how variable and trite are human laws. He said that we "judge after the flesh,"[37] but he came, "not to judge the world, but to save."[38] He was always being asked to apply the law: Should we pay taxes?[39] Should we divide our inheritances differently?[40] Should we be able to divorce our spouses?[41] Should we heal on the sabbath?[42] Yet he always either rebuked his interlocutors or gave them a parable or lesson intended to show them the misguided nature of their inquiry. Their laws always focused on actions rather than spirit;[43] they condemned those who would heal on the sabbath, while they glorified those who prayed insincerely just to gain the admiration of others. And just look how Jesus' own execution showed the whimsy of human laws from one people to another! The Jews had a law, which the Romans thought was ridiculous,[44] against healing on the sabbath, while the Romans would order executions and the Jews could not.[45] Human laws vary from one culture to another because they are merely inventions.

Jesus demonstrated his attitude toward "the commandments of men" when he was asked to judge the woman who was caught in the act of adultery. Those who brought her before him reminded him that Moses said, "Such should be stoned: but what sayest thou?"[46] They were trying to get Jesus to reject the law of Moses so that they could condemn him. Jesus did not answer them immediately, but instead, "stooped down, and with his finger wrote on the ground, as though he heard them not."[47] It is very significant that this is the only instance, *in his entire life*, where Jesus is reported to have written anything at all. The statement he was making by writing at this time, and in the sand, was that the law is just an arbitrary code, a rule book written in the sand, lacking spirit. Those who sought his judgement nevertheless pressed him for an answer, so Jesus stood and said, "He that is without sin among you, let him first cast a stone at her."[48] This wonderful challenge forced the woman's self-appointed judges to look at themselves and breathe spirit into their interpretation of Moses' law, and one by one they all turned and walked away. Jesus taught that we must wipe away the laws that have been written in sand, and resurrect the commandments that have been written in the spirit of humanity.

Jesus told us to begin undoing the worldly systems of judgement in our own lives by not taking our interpersonal grievances to the authorities for resolution. This does not necessarily mean ignoring trespasses against us. But it does mean limiting our laws to God's commandments—to love him and one another—and it does require us always to accept one another's apologies. "If thy brother trespass against thee, rebuke him; and if he repent, forgive him: And if he trespass against thee seven times in a day, and seven times a day turn again to thee, saying, I repent, thou shalt forgive him."[49]

Before judging others, we must judge ourselves. Jesus teaches in both the canon and gnostic gospels to strive for personal perfection rather than criticizing and condemning others. In the *Gospel of Thomas* he says:

> Love your brother like your soul, guard him like the pupil of your eye. . . . You see the mote in your brother's eye, but you do not see the beam in your own eye. When you cast out the beam out of your own eye, then you will see clearly to cast the mote from your brother's eye.[50]

The intent of this guideline is not for us to find a set of perfect judges to rule over us; it is for us to become as good as we can: "Be ye therefore perfect, even as your Father which is in heaven is perfect."[51] To the extent that we perfect ourselves according to the simple commandments to love God and neighbor, human law and judgement will become an edifice without inhabitants.

The effort of our earthly kingdoms of men and women to achieve justice is an aim rooted in atheism. Whenever we seek vengeance, or when, euphemistically, we demand that violators of our man-made laws pay "their debt to society," we are implicitly committing two sins as great as any crime that we may be condemning. We are presuming that we have ultimate knowledge of good and evil, that we know all the circumstances and the deepest secrets of the so-called offender, and that we are as capable as God of determining guilt and punishment. Jesus explained this with his parable of the tares, which is recounted in the *Gospel of Thomas*:

> The kingdom of the father is like a man who had good seed. His enemy came by night and sowed weeds among the good seed. The man did not allow them to pull up the weeds; he said to them, "I am afraid that you will go intending to pull up the weeds and pull up the wheat along with them." For on the day of the harvest the weeds will be plainly visible, and they will be pulled up and burned.[52]

If we go about condemning and punishing, we are quite likely to destroy the innocent. Was this not what happened to Jesus?

When we judge others, we are also demonstrating a complete lack of faith in God and the afterlife. For why would we seek an earthly verdict if we truly believed that a divine judgement awaited everyone at death? The system of law and judicial justice in modern as well as ancient society sets up human beings as gods. As we have seen, Jesus told Peter that this is the sin of the world.[53]

The Bible instructs us clearly that the power of judgement was never granted to humanity by God. The first judicial system in the Judeo-Christian tradition was established by Moses during the Exodus, but it was not prescribed to him by God, or even by a vision or a divine inspiration. It was proposed by his father-in-law, who said that Moses should judge only the larger matters, the "statutes of God," while appointing "rulers of thousands, and rulers of hundreds, and rulers of tens" to judge the people "at all seasons."[54] Those who in any way imply that the power to establish and enforce human laws was granted from God have read the Bible superficially. Jesus was consistent with the Old Testament when he said that earthly kingdoms of power originate from Satan.

Jesus offered us a simple system to resolve conflicts among ourselves, without a judge at all. If someone offends us, "go and tell him his fault between thee and him alone: if he shall hear thee, thou hast gained thy brother."[55] However, if there is no resolution to the dispute, take one or two other people with you, "that in the mouth of two or three witnesses every word may be established."[56] If that does not resolve the matter, then take it to the congregation that has pledged allegiance to the kingdom of God, and if the offender still refuses to listen, "let him be unto thee as a heathen and a publican."[57] This informal method of judgement calls on us to work things out among ourselves. The most severe penalty we can impose is not to take one another's freedom or life, but to place someone outside the kingdom, and, of course, when they apologize, we must forgive them and let them back in.

Does this sound naive? Only to the extent that you reject the overall kingdom of God. If you want a modern industrial society, with human pyramids of power and a demonic scramble for wealth and the glory that wealth buys, then a judgement-process rooted in forgiveness, which aims at love rather than justice, would sound preposterous. But the method for resolving conflicts that Jesus prescribed makes perfect sense if we accept his other teachings, particularly that we need to stop accumulating property, that we need to grant everyone dignity, and that we need to dismantle all relations of power and privilege. Most crimes center on these very issues, and once they have been removed the propensity to evil will be greatly reduced.

Further, as we begin to institute a divine system of judgement, we will transform the characters both of ourselves and of those to whom we show mercy, for when we forgive those who have wronged us, they will love us, and we ourselves will feel the spirit of God.

8. The Location of Temptation

The third spiritual and political principle prescribed in the Lord's Prayer is to avoid temptation. As with the precepts regarding daily bread and forgiveness, this is declared as an expectation of something God will do for us, but it also implies a certain state of mind and certain institutional arrangements.

Spiritually, the prayer's insistence that we not be led into temptation is very different from the attitude usually associated with organized Christianity. Because of the latter's emphasis on sin, most Christians believe that their main religious requirement from a personal point of view (as opposed to their social obligations to the Church, to the poor, etc.), is to fend off their carnal desires. But this is not the prescription in the Lord's Prayer; the prayer does not say "Give us the strength to master our cravings" or "Help us withstand our fleshly impulses." Rather than requesting aid in *overcoming* temptation, we demand to be delivered from temptation *altogether*.

What does this mean? How can human beings, who are always plagued by fears and urges, be totally removed from enticement?

To understand the intention of this principle of the Lord's Prayer, we must recognize the kind of temptation to which it is referring. The original Greek word for "temptation" is *peirasmos*, which is defined as "a putting to proof."[58] Thus, when the gospels mention "temptation," they are speaking, not of enticements or situations that provoke urges, but of exposing someone to a test. We can see this by looking at how the word "temptation" is used with respect to Christ. Jesus was said to have been "tempted" whenever the scribes and Pharisees posed questions that were designed to make him reveal his real intentions. He was "tempted" when he was asked whether the Jews should pay taxes to Rome;[59] if divorce was acceptable;[60] what is the greatest commandment;[61] whether an adulteress should be stoned;[62] and if he would provide a sign from heaven.[63] To be "tempted" meant being questioned or provoked in such a way that he was inclined to reveal his hostility to Rome, his departure from Judaic traditions, or his divine mission.

We can now understand that the point about temptation in the Lord's Prayer has to do not with our desires and impulses, but with our political posture toward authority. In establishing the kingdom of God, we are to avoid confrontations with the earthly system of power and glory. If we encounter a situation that would encourage us to reveal our disrespect for earthly rulers and social ranks, we will try to handle it just as Jesus did: we will speak obliquely, or answer a question with a question, or, if possible, simply avoid the situation entirely. Our aim is to circumvent the test and be delivered from the evil system that would crush us instantly if it knew our minds.

This is why the Lord's Prayer refers to being led *into* temptation rather than merely to *being tempted*. The thing to be avoided is not a state of mind—an inclination to do wrong—but a social or political situation. We create the kingdom of God by removing ourselves, as much as possible, from the kingdoms of men and women.

Spiritually, this implies a peculiar attitude toward authority and status. It means that we are not to be rebels, iconoclasts, or nonconformists; we are not, in other words, to define ourselves in opposition to worldly power and glory, for this just makes us mirror images of the power and glory we want to dissolve. Instead, we are to be indifferent. We render unto Caesar if we must, but we know that all Caesars stand on pedestals of atheism and are merely vanities in the eyes of God. We acknowledge the customs of our country, but we understand that all customs are simply inventions, and that the only true commandments are to love God and neighbor. We see that people want us to join with them in judging others, but rather than rebuking them for this, we simply suggest to them that they judge themselves first. We lead ourselves not into the worldly system of judgement, but away from it. We become, in Jesus' words, "passers-by."[64]

Politically, the principle in the Lord's Prayer against temptation (or testing) means that the kingdom of God is never to have any institutions that inquire into our faith or convictions. Such institutions comprise one of the defining characteristics of earthly kingdoms; the kingdoms of men and women demand loyalty, and they have means of assuring it. The words "census" and "censorship" are connected because, historically, being counted in a country's census, in its list of citizens, required conforming to its beliefs. In the modern era, one must always be prepared to prove one's ideology. Are you a loyal American? Do you believe in science and evolution? Are you emotionally moderate and politically tolerant?

In the kingdom of God, such testing would be a sin. We would be united in the belief that our only judge is God. We would not seek to examine others, because we would not feel that we own the standards of good and evil. We would lead ourselves away from such assessments and deliver ourselves from this common evil.

9. Power to the Powerless

The actual political structure of the kingdom of God is not defined until we come to the last sentence of the Lord's Prayer. Prior to that,

Jesus has merely prescribed the kingdom's work-life, society, and culture. The divine kingdom is to have an economy of non-accumulation, social relations geared toward forgiveness, and a culture where beliefs and faith are accepted rather than tested. But how is the social order to be governed? Who will restrain those who choose hate rather than love? Who will call the congregation together so that it can make decisions? How are the spiritual and geographical borders of the kingdom to be protected? If the kingdom is indeed a kingdom, then who is the king?

Jesus was very subtle in the way that he used the Lord's Prayer to disclose the political constitution of the kingdom. Certainly, he had reason to be especially circumspect about this aspect of his teachings, because it was directly political, and the scribes, Pharisees, and Herodians were constantly looking for an explicit political statement with which they could condemn him before the Romans. Somehow, Jesus had to leave us with a political manifesto apparent to the faithful but invisible to everyone else.

Jesus managed to do this with the Lord's Prayer, but the message was hidden so well, it was almost lost forever. Jesus revealed the political structure of the kingdom in the two different ways that he taught the Lord's Prayer to the multitudes and to his disciples. Jesus disclosed the constitution of the kingdom in what he *failed* to say to the latter.

Jesus presented the Lord's Prayer to the uninitiated multitudes during his sermon on the mountain. He concluded the prayer with the line, "for thine is the kingdom and the power and the glory, for ever and ever."[65] This was the heart of his teaching about the kingdom of God; people are to give all power and glory to God.

When this is implemented—and this is indeed what Jesus intended for the multitudes—the social order as we know it will dissolve. Imagine a society where no one acknowledges any social rank, authority, or status at all, a society, in other words, where everyone grants status and power to God alone. Not only will the obvious power structures be dismantled—the power of bosses over employees, of rulers over subjects, of priests over laity, of parents over children—but also the subtle ones.

It will be a sin just to acknowledge differences in status between people, or to follow another's commands. We in the modern era say that it is wrong to be prejudiced against any races, ethnic groups, genders, and other categories of individuals when hiring, promoting, or training workers, or when renting or selling housing. We have also become sensitive to statements that disparage or stereotype certain people.

But the kingdom of God requires much more. It requires eliminating all status distinctions of any sort. We cannot treat children as subhumans. We cannot shun the poor, the sick, the ugly, the obese, or any one else. We cannot fawn over the wealthy, or create celebrities with our adulation, or show special respect to beautiful women or handsome men.

This radical rejection of status and authority is exactly what seemed to shock people most about Jesus. He did not disdain the poor or the sick, or the tax collectors, or harlots. Even those who did not know him well understood this about him. When the Pharisees and the Herodians tried to trick Jesus into revealing his anti-establishment philosophy by asking whether they should pay taxes, they first said to him, "We know that thou art true, and carest for no man: for thou regardest not the person of men."[66] Jesus did not care whether you were a prostitute or the Roman governor of Israel; he responded only person-to-person.

The apostle who understood this best was Jesus' brother James. James recognized that it is not a minor transgression against Jesus' teachings to respect earthly wealth and power, but a sin against the entire message.[67] When James sought to explain this to others, his example of improperly respecting earthly power and glory was not obeying the Romans or paying taxes—which were obvious transgressions against God's domain—but treating people differently in church depending on their wealth, which was no less common then than it is now. He said it is a sin to give a person a better seat than others at church just because he or she wears expensive clothes and a gold ring: "If ye fulfill the royal law according to the scripture, thou shalt love thy neighbor as thyself, ye do well: But if ye have respect to persons, ye commit sin."[68] James understood that giving power and glory to God entailed a complete transformation, not only or even primarily in government, but in the most basic relations between human beings.

When Jesus taught the multitudes to conclude the Lord's Prayer by asserting that all power and glory are God's, he was instructing them to throw out their natural prejudices. He wanted each of us to see one another as the image of God. He knew that this runs against our worldliness, our belief that we possess knowledge of who is good and who is evil. He knew that when people encounter one another, they automatically categorize one another in terms of age, sex, race, attractiveness, and other attributes; they scan one another's clothes and demeanor for indications of social status, and they respond to one another accordingly. Men fawn over a beautiful woman, or at the very least show special attention. People treat the poor as if they were invisible, sidestepping them both physically and emotionally. Adults frequently relate to other people's children like they are less than human; they interrupt them, break in front of them in lines, and boss them like animals. Ranking one another—giving power and glory to some while denying it to others—is as natural to human beings as breathing. But Jesus wanted us to shed this eternal judgement; he asked us to step outside this self-created hell and experience not the fleeting moments of happiness we have been getting from our occasional moments of glory, but lasting enjoyment—constant or eternal life.

Jesus instructed the multitudes to set aside their judgements. Give power and glory to God, and love all people. Recognize that your judgements of one another are presumptuous, that you do not have knowledge of good and evil, that God alone is capable of such judgements, and you will be born again.

10. Jesus Was the First King in the New Kingdom

Still, Jesus was not calling for his followers to become a nation of sheep. He knew that faith alone could not defeat Satan any more than passive resistance could overturn the Roman Empire. If earthly power and glory were to be dissolved, people would need to have leaders. To establish a kingdom of God, there must be a godly king.

Jesus intended for this king to be himself and his spiritual descendants. This is why the prayer he taught to his disciples differed from the one he gave to the multitudes. He told the multitudes to conclude the Lord's Prayer by vowing to bestow all power and glory on God, but he gave no such instruction to his disciples. Instead, he simply had them stop the Lord's Prayer a sentence earlier with the statement about being delivered from temptation.[69] Jesus expected his disciples to give power and glory to the messiah, who would speak for God.

The gospels are very clear that it was Jesus' intention to be recognized as a king; the founders of the Church as well as the Bible's modern readers have simply refused to believe the obvious. The early leaders of the Church suppressed this teaching of Jesus, because advocating a king other than Caesar or Herod, a king anointed by God, would have put them in direct conflict with the Roman authorities. Subsequent Christians have averted their eyes from this teaching because they have been indoctrinated to look for the kingdom of God descending from the heavens.

The Bible says clearly that the disciples of Jesus referred to him as a king, and Jesus did not object. When Jesus came down from the Mount of Olives, his disciples shouted, "Blessed be the King that cometh in the name of the Lord."[70] The Pharisees told Jesus that he should tell his disciples not to say such things, but Jesus replied, "I tell you that, if these should hold their peace, the stones would immediately cry out."[71]

When Jesus entered Jerusalem, he rode on a donkey so that he would invoke the prophecy of Zechariah about the coming king. Zechariah had declared, "Rejoice greatly, O daughter of Zion; shout, O daughter of Jerusalem: behold, thy King cometh unto thee: he is just, and having salvation; lowly, and riding upon an ass, and upon a colt the foal of an ass."[72] Jesus told his disciples to be sure to find an ass with a colt.[73] And the imagery had its intended effect; as Jesus rode into town, the crowds cheered, "Blessed is the King of Israel that cometh in the name of the Lord."[74]

Jesus also told his disciples that he was establishing a political order. He said, "I appoint unto you a kingdom, as my Father hath appointed unto me."[75] This is why the disciples began to compete to become Jesus' heir. The mother of Zebedee's children (James and John) actually came to Jesus and asked him to let her two sons be Jesus' captains in the kingdom. It was no secret that Jesus was establishing an eternal dynasty.

For that matter, the Bible is abundantly clear that the trial of Jesus focused on his claims to kingship. Jesus was asked by Pontius Pilate, "Art thou the King of the Jews?"[76] When Pilate asked the crowd which offender to release for Passover, he referred to Jesus as their king.[77] The sign that was placed on Jesus' cross said, "THE KING OF THE JEWS."[78] The soldiers who mocked Jesus as he was crucified called him "King of the Jews."[79] Even those who were crucified with him referenced Jesus' claims to being a king.[80]

Jesus declared himself to be the first king of the new kingdom of God. He expected others to follow him. All they had to do was be willing to drink of the same cup, that is, to suffer persecution in the name of God. False messiahs might arise, but they would be known by their fruits. The congregation, the multitude who said the Lord's Prayer and who thereby pledged its allegiance to the divine kingdom of the spirit rather than to the worldly kingdoms of men and women, would follow the messiah and would eventually transform all power and glory.

11. The Worldly Argument for Political Power

The role of Jesus and his successors in the new kingdom was to guide the development of humanity, that is, to nurture the spirit of holiness, so that eventually all laws and restrictions would be unnecessary. Worldly legal and political systems rest on the assumption that people are unalterably selfish and conflictual, and that therefore political power and social stratification are essential to human life. But Jesus claimed, and sought to demonstrate through his own works, that people can actually transform themselves, fundamentally and in a moment, simply through faith. With the help of the holy spirit, Jesus said, government was not necessary. In fact, the whole aim of civilization should be getting rid of power and glory altogether, except for the power and glory given to God.

This is a remarkably different stance toward politics. In the ancient world as well as our own times, the main political question was, How should government be structured so as best to assure order, prosperity, security, fairness, and other widely shared values? The aim was not to eliminate government, but to find the best government possible.

As previously mentioned, Greek political philosophy reached a conclusion on this issue very similar to what we believe today. Plato argued that the character of a nation was determined by which class dominated its government. When the masses are in control, he claimed, the social order is very licentious and tumultuous. When the wealthy dominate, the community is oppressive and corrupt. When the military holds sway, everyone seeks glory and honor. Aristotle elaborated Plato's theory by studying the many political constitutions of the ancient world. He was especially interested in how different governmental institutions and procedures affected the balance of power between the social classes. On the basis of extensive research, he concluded that the best social order is one with a "mixed" consti-tution, that is, one with a combination of democratic, judicial, and monarchical elements. Aristotle believed that different social classes controlled different kinds of governmental institutions: the masses dominated the leaders who were elected, the wealthy controlled judicial systems, and the military along with the historic nobility monopolized the highest positions of power. Aristotle favored the mixed system, which combined each of these kinds of governmental bodies, because he said it gave each social class a role in the political process and kept the classes in balance.

The way Plato and Aristotle conceptualized forms of government continues to be used to this very day. They differentiated social orders on the basis of who rules. The rule of the common people, the *demos*, was called "democracy." The rule of the wealthy, the *oligi*, was termed "oligarchy." And the rule of the leading or best families, the *aristoi*, was referred to as "aristocracy."

The choice, as the ancients saw, was not between having a govern-ment or not having a government, but simply which of these various forms of government was selected. Further, they believed that most social orders went round and round on the issue, choosing first the rule of elites, then the wealthy, then the masses, and back again. This is why the root of the word *revolution* is *revolve*, from the Latin *revolvere*, which means "to go around," as in a circle. During the Roman Empire, people began to believe that all revolutions led eventually back to the same point.

The only form of government that the Greek philosophers thought was stable was the mixed form. This is the kind of government established in both ancient Athens and Rome. As the Greek philosopher Polybius explained, the mixed state was stable rather than "revolutionary" because it combined all three social classes into a single government and counterbalanced the ambitions of each class and its branch of government with those of the other two.

> Whenever one of the three elements swells in importance and tends to encroach upon the others . . . the designs of any one can be blocked or impeded by the rest, with the result that none will unduly dominate the others or treat them with contempt.[81]

Almost the exact same defense of political power prevails today. We, too, believe that government is a necessity and that the only question is what form government should take. We also believe that the best form of government is one with a mixture of elements, or what we now call a system of "checks and balances."

The one difference today is that we no longer believe revolutions are futile or circular. Instead, our new faith is that power and glory develop along an upward spiral, like a stairway to heaven. We think that our own social order is both the culmination of history and the platform from which all future history will emerge. We are the end of history and the beginning. Prior to our era, all of history is thought to have been rooted in superstition and blindness, and consequently to have been stuck at the same spot, changing in dress, fashion, and ideas, but never really moving forward. Conversely, our own era is envisioned as an era based on truth and reason, from which an unlimited potential can and will unfold, taking human beings to the deepest seas and the furthest planets, exposing all the mysteries of the universe, and even giving us power over all of nature's forces. We call our new social and political ideal "progress."

However, Jesus turned this view of politics and government on its head. He implied that all worldly governments are essentially the same, regardless of who is in charge or whether the systems of decision-making are mixed or singular in structure. All worldly governments rest on the belief that human beings possess knowledge of good and evil, and they set up or support a system of ranks and social status that preempts the judgement of God. The only legitimate government is a kingdom that rules in God's name, which means that it enforces only God's commandments; its aim is not to maintain order, but to eliminate the need for law and order altogether. Progress is measured by the extent to which coercion becomes unnecessary; status disappears, and people look directly to God or to God's representative as their king.

12. Origins of the Divine Constitution

Although certainly he stated it more forcefully than anyone before or since, Jesus did not invent this anti-political thesis; to the contrary, he drew his ideas from a long line of biblical prophets who preceded him. The Old Testament clearly rejects the principles from Greek philosophy and modern social science that social orders must have rulers and that the key political question is therefore who is best suited to govern. The belief and experience from the Judaic tradition was that people have divine law written in their souls and hence can govern themselves without government, so long as they are not seduced by Satan or led into pagan nature-worship. This view of authority redefines the political problem from who governs, to how to establish a community of faith.

The government called for by the Old Testament conception of authority can be gleaned from the constitution established by Moses. The Mosaic social order was governed largely by discussion and consensus, but it was not a democracy, because it did not rest on the belief that authority comes from the congregation. Rather, the social order of Moses was premised on the faith that God alone is the judge of right and wrong; the purpose of debate and collective reasoning was to discern God's will. Moses, the spokesman of God, had no official title and led entirely through persuasion.

During the years the Jews wandered in the wilderness and then subsequently up to the time of Samuel, the people of Israel lived without a king. When the Israelites fled Egypt, their social order included the congregation, the priesthood, and the host or army. Moses added two new classes. Following the congregation's brief flirtation with idolatry, he appointed his own tribe, the tribe of Levi, as helpers for the priests, as teachers, and perhaps in some circumstances as a police force to deal with unruly elements in the congregation.[82] He also established a system of judges to rule on disputes and matters of divine law.

The congregation functioned as a loose assembly. There are many examples in the book of Exodus where the congregation questioned Moses, "murmured" against him or the chief priest Aaron, and arrived at a will contrary to Moses' recommendations.[83] The best known example of the congregation contravening Moses was its decision not to enter the promised land. Moses sent men to investigate the land, and upon their return only Caleb and Joshua urged the people to go in. The congregation accepted the majority report even though Moses and Aaron "fell on their faces" and beseeched them otherwise.[84]

Moses himself was neither a priest nor a general. He was a prophet and a judge, two functions which were also part of the discussion-based character of the congregation. To be accepted as a prophet, that is, as a spokesman for God, a man had to convince the congregation that he was indeed speaking God's words. By the same token, judges were selected by the people themselves, in the sense that the people chose to whom to take their disputes. In fact, Moses was compelled to establish a system of judges because he was so overwhelmed by his own popularity.

The role of the prophet was to warn and admonish the congregation, but not to rule it. The prophets would predict that calamities would occur if certain actions were taken, and the congregation would learn from experience that the prophet spoke for God as his prophecies were fulfilled. An example during the time of Moses was the rebellion by Korah, a Levite who sought to become the people's king or leader. Moses told Korah to light fire and incense before God, and God would show the people his will. Korah took Moses' challenge and gathered the congregation together at the tabernacle. When he and his followers lit the incense, God became angry, "and the earth opened her mouth and swallowed them up, and their houses, and the men that appertained unto Korah, and all their goods."[85] Moses did not cause this or demand that the people listen to him, but certainly the event made a point. In short, prophets did not rule by argument and propaganda, but instead by a blunt "I told you so" form of leadership. This may explain why many prophets were stoned to death.

The Israelites did not appoint a king until several generations after Moses died, and even then they were opposed by the prophet and priest Samuel, who told the congregation that *God* was their king. If they selected a worldly king, he warned, the king "will take your sons and appoint them for himself, for his chariots, and to be his horsemen; and some will run before his chariots";[86] the king will make your daughters cooks and bakers; he will take your fields and give them to others; he will take a tenth of your sheep; and you will be his servants. Samuel said all of this and more, but the people responded, "Nay; but we will have a king over us; that we also may be like all the nations; and that our king may judge us, and go before us, and fight our battles."[87] Samuel opposed the people's desire for a king because he understood that kingship is contrary to biblical teachings and is unnecessary because of the soul's access to divine law.

13. The Political Structure of the Kingdom of God

From the standpoint of a social movement, Jesus' proposal was to alter the spirituality of the population so that political institutions would change or dissolve as a matter of course. If the Greeks and Romans wanted to believe that power and glory are necessary because people are selfish and combative, let them. But in the meantime the world would change right out from under them, for as people became perfect, the evil in worldly institutions would become increasingly apparent.

The kingdom of God he envisioned was one where human beings are fully aware of the divine order of things above them. They live in the world and amidst the temptation to evil with which the world surrounds them, but they behave, think, will, and intend in accord with the divine order. They live in the world but are divinely inspired. They rise to God spiritually and have faith that God will descend to them and reveal his presence even while they have their mind imbedded in flesh and their flesh tied to the world around them.

The king of this kingdom is a messiah or prophet, who is selected by the congregation and whose authority rests solely on the congregation's willingness to listen. The king and those who want to assist him do not lord over the people, nor do they judge individual disputes. The role of the leaders of the kingdom is to minister to the people, teaching them forgiveness, encouraging them not to worry about the future, showing them how to take pleasure in small things, revealing to them, in short, how to enjoy life and how not to be sucked into the hell of worldly judgements, fears, and ambitions. The king is a king of the spirit, whose aim is to nurture the spirit of holiness.

CHAPTER SIX

The Day of Judgement Will Be a Global Political Crisis

W̶E HAVE finally reached the point where we can take up in some detail the issue of the so-called "second coming" of Jesus. I hope it is clear by now that my objective is not to debunk Christianity but rather to find the deeper meaning in Jesus' teachings and to bring this meaning into the modern era, the era for which it was actually intended. I know that my account of Jesus will be troublesome to many Christians, who have been taught for generations to expect the messiah to return physically and establish the kingdom of God. But there are many forms in which the spirit of Jesus might be reborn, and we, who are supposed to be meek in our faith, should remain open to every possibility.

Compared to the many other political messages he was trying to deliver, including his themes of disavowing authority, refusing to acknowledge social status, and replacing human laws with divine commandments, Jesus had to speak most obliquely about how to cause the kingdom of God to come. Because of the oppressive character of the society in which he lived, he could not go forth advocating a revolution of disobedience, and yet this was precisely what he was prophesying. He wanted people to drop their allegiance to the rulers of the earth and declare their citizenship in a voluntary covenant with God. They would become paupers, govern themselves with complete mercy and forgiveness, and allow no testing or ridiculing of one another's faith or spirit. They would not seek out authority to defy it, but neither would they bow to power when they encountered it, or acknowledge distinctions of status among persons. They would subvert earthly kingdoms by ignoring them and by establishing a spiritual counter-kingdom alongside them.

I believe that Jesus presented his expectation about the coming kingdom as a prophecy about his own return because he expected the spirit he embodied, the spirit of holiness, to be driven under by the Satan of worldly kingdoms and then to return in an even stronger form. Although it is always offset and challenged by doubt and by the worldly concerns doubt inspires, the holy spirit has been and will continue to stir in humanity, for it is the spirit that makes civilization possible, even when that civilization is itself anti-spiritual. The modern world order, with its scientific effort to control nature and eliminate chance, is rooted in a preoccupation with the world, and it is becoming more oppressive every day, constantly judging, subtly demanding that each person's rank be displayed by the expense of his or her clothing, making some people idols while treating others as if they were scum in a rancid pond. But dawning in the background, like the sun rising behind a decaying and dirty city, is an emergent world opinion that seeks peace, love, and mercy for all.

In speaking of the rebirth of his spirit and the coming day of judgement, Jesus was predicting the very crisis we are beginning to see today as this transcendent spirit begins to come into conflict with structures of power and status. The awakening of the holy spirit is causing a reaction among the worldly, who ridicule faith, cling to power, and prop up the pyramidal systems of glory that give them their privileges and their sense of self. But Jesus also said that this oppression of faith would cause the spirit of holiness to spread further, which is indeed what we are witnessing. The world reacts with horror at tyranny and cruelty—even the suffering of a single individual, or of a single animal. A huge crisis, a global conflict between faith in God and faith in the world, has been building since Jesus came into the world.

1. The Mistake that Became Organized Christianity

At this point, it should be clear that Christianity tragically misunderstood what Jesus said about establishing the kingdom of God. Peter and the others who founded Christianity began to preach that Jesus would come again and would raise his spiritual followers from the grave. They said Jesus would have God's power and, through God and with the resurrected Christians, would rule the world. The coming of the kingdom depended on the "second coming" of Jesus.

This teaching was not the only, or even the primary teaching of the Church in its earliest years. Anyone can see this by carefully reading the first eight chapters of the Acts.

Certainly Stephen, the first Christian martyr after the crucifixion, did not believe in a second coming. He clearly thought of himself as motivated by the spirit of Jesus, who he said had been moved by the spirit of God. As he ministered to the poor, Stephen did not tell his listeners to wait for a second coming; he declared openly that earthly power and glory must be overturned, that both the law and the temple must be pulled down and spiritually rebuilt. This is why he was brought before the Sanhedrin. Further, at his trial, he did not say a single thing about Jesus coming again in the sense that we think of today. Instead, after recounting how the holy spirit had appeared many times in the history of the Jews, he said that the patriarchs of Israel had never listened to the spirit of holiness before, and that they were not listening to it then, when it had been brought to them by Jesus and now by Stephen. Stephen did not preach the second coming of Jesus but the recurring return of the holy spirit.

However, skip ahead in the Acts to Paul's meeting with the scholars of Athens, and the teaching of the second coming is central. In fact, this was the only thing in Paul's lecture that the Greeks found at all interesting; since they themselves believed in a worldly god they called "nature," they were intrigued by Paul's mysterious claim that the law of nature, which is death, might be overcome.

The thesis of organized Christianity that Jesus would return personally to resurrect the dead and rule in God's name was formulated by Peter. Whether Peter intended it as a creed to aid in marketing the Church is not clear, but it undoubtedly had this effect. People were told that if they joined this group, they would later be, literally, resuscitated from the grave. It was as if the Church began to sell a procedure where people's bodies would be frozen at their passing and later thawed out, except in this case the procedure was totally costless, painless, and risk-free. Further, Peter offered, with no additional requirements, a taste of the "Holy Ghost" through the laying on of hands. The idea of the second coming of Jesus and the resurrection of the dead quickly became the dominant view within the Jesus movement, and eventually defined Christianity in its entirety, because this belief was extremely appealing to the multitudes.

Of course, Jesus himself had always been leery of the public. He warned against a broad-based ministry because he said that the multitudes could not accept his secret teaching. To speak to them about an end to power and glory would be like casting pearls before swine, and if they ever saw through the parables and really understood the message, they would turn and rend the prophet in front of them. That the teachings of Jesus as reinterpreted by Peter were popular among large numbers of people shows that the essential meanings of the teachings had been lost, for the true teachings of Jesus said that people must save themselves rather than wait on God; Jesus called on them to rebel by martyring themselves, and promised them only continued poverty and meekness.

Still, it is easy to understand how Peter arrived at his doctrine of the second coming. Many of Jesus' political messages were encoded in parables that lent themselves to this interpretation. Indeed, this was the idea; Jesus spoke metaphorically to fool the Romans, the Herodians, and the Pharisees into thinking that he was talking about a kingdom in heaven rather than a social order on earth.

2. The True Meaning of the Resurrection

When Jesus said that he would come again, he meant that his spirit, the spirit of holiness, would constantly be reborn until it enveloped the world. He was not referring to a reincarnation, where the actual mind of a particular individual is said to have been reborn in another body, with all of that mind's memories and intentions. Rather, he was talking about people being born with his same basic attitudes and personality, that is, with his "spirit."

This way of thinking is visible in some of Jesus' other teachings. For example, he said that John the Baptist was a reborn Elijah.[1] Now, by this, Jesus obviously did not intend to suggest that the conscious subjectivity of Elijah had been injected into John's body. In fact, Jesus must have known that John himself explicitly rejected the idea that he was Elijah. John said, instead, that he was "the voice of one crying in the wilderness," who had been prophesied by Isaiah.[2] When Jesus asserted that John was a reborn Elijah, he meant it precisely in the sense intended by the angel who told John's father about his mission before John was born. The angel had said that John would announce the messiah "in the spirit and power" of Elijah,[3] that is, with the same zeal, fearlessness, and asceticism. When Jesus spoke of people being reborn, he was speaking figuratively, not literally.

This is a very common way of presenting ideas in politics; it is used to this day. Supporters of certain candidates for the U.S. Presidency often say that their person is the new Harry Truman, or the next John Kennedy. With these simple statements, they can deliver an enormous amount of information. If someone is like Harry Truman, then he is tough, direct, and willing to make difficult decisions and accept responsibility. If he is like JFK, then he is charismatic, desirous of social change, and capable of bringing people together around noble ideals. One of the main idioms in the language of politics is characterizing one person as "in the spirit and power" of another.

When Jesus said that John the Baptist was Elijah, he was not claiming to know John's mind better than John; he was paying John a compliment and also saying something about himself. Jesus was implying that John was being modest. John thought that he was just a voice in the wilderness, as predicted by Isaiah, but Jesus suggested that John should read the prophecies of Malachi instead. Malachi was the very last prophet of Israel before prophecy ended about 400 years prior to the days of Jesus. Malachi said, "Behold, I will send you Elijah the prophet before the coming of the great and dreadful day of the Lord."[4] Like a modern-day historian revising assessments of our leaders, Jesus was elevating John the Baptist in his account of history. According to Jesus, John was no mere announcer in the desert; John stood in the footsteps of one of the greatest of all prophets.

The implication for Jesus was that Jesus was more than a prince of peace. Isaiah's and Malachi's prophecies about the messiah differed significantly. Isaiah said that the sacrifice of the messiah, the deliverance of the "lamb to the slaughter,"[5] would launch an era of world harmony. Swords would be "beaten into plowshares"[6] and the calf would "lie with the young lion."[7] But Malachi foretold that the messiah would also bring a day "that shall burn as an oven,"[8] when God shall return and "discern between the righteous and the wicked, between him that serveth God and him that serveth him not."[9] So when Jesus said that John was Elijah, he was also revealing that he himself was bringing not merely peace, but also divine judgement.

Speaking about the spiritual rebirth of earlier prophets was a political code and a shorthand for delivering important messages.

Considerable disagreement swirled around Jesus as to what sort of prophet he was, and these disagreements, like those concerning John the Baptist, took the same form. The disciples of Jesus asked him if he was John, Elijah, or Jeremiah.[10] Obviously, they knew he was not a reborn John, because he and John lived at the same time and they in fact were cousins; clearly, they were asking Jesus whether his mission was like John's, Elijah's, or Jeremiah's. The disagreement over Jesus was so widespread that it even reached Herod, who also did not think it implied a transmigration of souls from one person to another but rather centered on the nature of Jesus' ministry. Herod became interested in seeing Jesus to learn more about him; if Herod had believed Jesus was an ancient prophet reincarnated in a new body, he would have been afraid to seek him out.[11]

Of course, Jesus was clear that he was none of these earlier prophets,[12] for he was bringing an entirely new message. The prophets had brought the law, which they had made very detailed even if they had propounded it with a righteous spirit. But Jesus was bringing an end to earthly law and the beginning of divine law, the end of the kingdoms of men and women and the beginning of the kingdom of God. This is the reasoning behind Jesus' seemingly bizarre statement that "Among those that are born of women there is not a greater prophet than John the Baptist: but he that is least in the kingdom of God is greater than he."[13] Jesus was different, and all those who would follow Jesus would be different—and greater—because the kingdom of God would implement the spirit of God rather than the doctrines of people, including the doctrines of prophets.

Jesus explained his relationship to God and the prophets with a vision that was experienced by Peter, James, and John. Jesus took them atop a high mountain, where they saw Jesus transfigured and in the company of Moses and Elijah.[14] The gospels do not explain how the three disciples recognized the latter, since none of them would have known what Moses and Elijah looked like, so there must have been more to the vision than what was reported. But the important point was that the vision showed where Jesus stood in the history of God's revelation of himself to humanity. Moses brought the law, which was far more extensive than God's commandments but which was required to break the people of their idolatry. Elijah brought the prophecy of the day of judgement and prepared the way for the messiah. And Jesus brought the kingdom of God, which fulfilled the work of both Moses and Elijah by initiating the rule on earth, not of law, but of the spirit of holiness.

3. The Second Coming has Already Come; Others Will Follow

When Jesus prophesied that he would return, he meant that his spirit would spread. He hoped that he was instilling his spirit in his disciples, and he said precisely that. Once, when James and John asked if they should "command fire to come down from heaven" and consume the wicked, as Elijah had done to the soldiers that had been sent to capture him,[15] Jesus "rebuked them, and said, Ye know not what manner of spirit ye are of."[16] The spirit Jesus was bringing was love, mercy, and forgiveness.

The gospels never use the phrase "second coming." This phrase is an invention of organized Christianity.

The only time that Jesus is quoted as speaking of "coming again" is in the Gospel of John, and even here the reference is unclear. Jesus is giving his last sermon to his disciples. He tells them that he will be executed, but he urges them not to worry, because he is going to his Father. He also says that he will prepare a place in heaven for them, and that "I will come again, and receive you unto myself; that where I am, there ye may be also."[17] Given that Jesus is saying this shortly before his arrest, which he knew was imminent, it appears to mean that Jesus expects his spirit to inspire them after his death, not that he intends to come back from the dead to establish the kingdom of God. He wants the disciples to be where he is, in a spiritual sense.

The idea within organized Christianity that Jesus would return, not spiritually to establish a real-world social order based on love and forgiveness, but physically to rule a supernatural kingdom of reembodied souls, comes from Jesus' prophecies about the times of "tribulation" and "vengeance."[18] He predicted that the world would descend into a terrible period of faithlessness and destruction, and that after these times people would witness "the son of man coming in a cloud with power and great glory."[19]

But, as we have seen, Jesus was referring not to a supernatural period of destruction and a physical second coming, but to the destiny of worldly power and glory. He expected precisely what we are now experiencing, that is, the emergence of a monstrous system of political power and social ranking, which is being held in check by a faint but irrepressible spirit of holiness. Civilization is entering into the Valley of Hinnom, and the air is becoming dryer and hotter every day. But at the same time, human consciousness is also expanding; people are becoming increasingly aware that they are all part of a single world and that they all deserve love, forgiveness, and mercy. The new spirit of holiness is not especially visible; it does indeed seem to be coming "in a cloud." But the more depraved the social order gets, the stronger this spirit seems to grow. The times of tribulation are upon us; let us pray that the spiritual child of our humanity, which appeared first in Jesus, is being reborn.

Rather than saying that he himself will return to establish the kingdom of God, Jesus said that the coming of the kingdom will be brought about by a huge increase in spirituality. He suggested that there will be numerous prophets and messiahs. The difficulty will not be a dearth of spiritual leaders, which had been the terrible tragedy in Israel when no prophets appeared from the time of Malachi until John the Baptist. Rather, the challenge will be to tell those who truly have the spirit of holiness from those who do not. "For there shall arise false Christs, and false prophets, and shall shew great signs and wonders; insomuch that, if it were possible, they shall deceive the very elect."[20]

Jesus said that some of the false prophets would come even from among the disciples. During a conversation with his disciples, Jesus put a twist on the analogy that he often drew between his teachings and a growing plant or seed. "I am the vine," he explained to his disciples, "ye are the branches."[21] He asked them to hold close to his teachings, because, "as the branch cannot bear fruit of itself, except it abide in the vine; no more can ye, except ye abide in me."[22] And yet Jesus knew that some of his students would stray. This is why he also told them that God, his Father, was the "husbandman," and that "every branch in me that beareth not fruit he taketh away."[23] Jesus recognized that some of his disciples would be fruitless branches, and that some might even break off completely and yield a bitter crop.

As usual, while Jesus claimed that God would take care of the problem, he revealed with other statements that God's work would have to be done through inspired people. This is why Jesus gave instructions about how to discern who are the true prophets and Christs—the true sons and daughters of humanity—and who are not. He said to look at the consequences of their teachings: "Ye shall know them by their fruits."[24]

We have not seen the explosion of messianism and prophecy that Jesus said would usher in the kingdom of God, because the organized Christian Church has held the holy spirit hostage since the days of Peter, who replaced Jesus' spiritual account of the world with a ghostly account. Unlike Thomas, Philip, Mary, and Stephen the martyr, Peter proclaimed that the spirit of holiness was an actual power or force like electricity, a force that could be transmitted through touch, through the laying on of hands. By the same token, he interpreted Jesus' teachings about the return of the son of man to mean literally the return of the mind and body of Jesus. In both cases, Jesus' idea of a spreading inspiration against earthly power and glory was garbled into a religion of phantoms. One must wonder if Jesus called Peter a rock because he was so dense and so materialistic in his understanding of Jesus' teachings.

In any event, once Peter's ghostly vision took possession of the Jesus movement, the gift of prophecy was lost. For people were taught to seek God, not in the reaction of their own spirit to the demands of the world, but in mystical encounters with phantoms and specters. The reality is that God does not appear so apparently; he dwells in a mist or a cloud,[25] that is, in the recesses of our souls. Peter told the world to look for God in the wrong place, in the bottle that he called the Church, and when they did what he said, they turned their eyes away from the place where God actually resides.

The Protestant Reformation weakened the Church's misguided theology, which imprisons the holy spirit, but it did not break it. Protestants said that God could inspire people directly, rather than through the intermediary of the Church, and they did look for the reemergence of prophecy. The Bible was translated from Latin into the languages of ordinary people precisely because it was assumed that the spirit of God could be experienced by every individual. Protestantism is associated, to this day, with revivals and "born again" spirituality because the Reformation reclaimed the common person's access to his or her own conscience.

But Protestantism has unfortunately retained a ghostly account of Christianity. Most Protestants still look for a second coming, think that Satan is a red demon with horns, and expect the kingdom of God to be delivered to them on a platter. They do not see Satan, or atheism and doubt, in worldly power and glory, nor do they look within themselves for inspiration to stand up to those who command them and who give them only crumbs of dignity. Protestants continue to wait for the kingdom of God rather than establishing it themselves.

4. The Immaculate Revolution

Nevertheless, Jesus said that the kingdom would eventually come. One of the best images he presented of how this spiritual revolution would overtake and transform the world's political orders was his analogy of the mustard seed. Most people who have considered this analogy have focused on Jesus' point about how such a large tree grows from such a small seed, and this was certainly part of the idea. But the parable ended with another image entirely. Jesus said the mustard tree would "shooteth out great branches so that the fowls of the air may lodge under the shadow of it."[26] The point is not merely that the new faith will grow from small to large, but that it will become a gathering place for the world's powers, and will overshadow them.

This vision of social change is totally different from people's usual way of thinking, both now and in the days of Jesus. During the time in which Jesus lived, the theory was that social orders shift from one form to another through direct political actions, such as wars, revolutions, and coups. In the modern era, we continue to believe this, but we have added to it the thesis that change can also occur through the introduction of new technologies.

In both cases, the religion and culture of a people are thought to be effects rather than causes. We can see this easily when we look not at the general beliefs of the ancient and modern eras, but at specific theories from each period. The ancient belief that politics is the central cause of social life, structuring everything else, is spelled out in detail in the works of Plato. *The Republic* is rightly known as his classic work, because it explains how each social order of the day—aristocracy, monarchy, tyranny, democracy, etc.—leads to a particular type of culture and creates a certain personality among the populace. For example, Plato said that democracy leads to a culture of liberty, where all ideas and lifestyles are considered to be equally valuable. The personality type associated with democracy—what Plato called the "democratic man"—is an individualist, who strives to express his or her uniqueness through dress, attitudes, and activities. Today, we use Plato's idea that politics causes culture and personality whenever we speak of "national character" or say that a change in government policy has caused a shift in the public's philosophy or in individuals' attitudes.

Similarly, the modern conviction that social change is prompted by economic innovation is detailed in the works of Karl Marx. The Western industrial democracies may have rejected Marxism as a political ideology, but most people accept fully the Marxist theory that economic change causes cultural change, and not vice versa. Marx referred to government, culture, and legal systems as society's "superstructure," which, he said, is determined in its entirety by economic relations. In analyzing the ancient era, he did not see much difference between the monarchies, aristocracies, democracies, and other governments. Rather, he said that the economies of the ancient empires were based on slavery and large scale agriculture, and that the political and cultural systems were geared to maintaining the economy. In theory, the shift to capitalism, where much production took place in factories, caused a political movement to mass democracy and a cultural transformation to individualism, because factory production created a large mass of isolated individuals who could be plugged into the production process like interchangeable parts. Today, we follow Marx when we expect industrialization in developing nations to spawn democratic political systems and tolerant cultures.

The ancient and modern belief that social change occurs, so to speak, behind society's back—in economic innovation or political ventures by a small group of activists—explains why our modern accounts of society and history give so much emphasis to individuals and small social groups rather than to a social order's overall spirit. Plato thought that the key to any social formation was held by "the lawgiver," the individual who was looked to during political crises to reform the system. Likewise, Marx said that meaningful social change could be undertaken only by the "proletariate," the oppressed mass of workers who he thought had an interest in nationalizing all the factories. If culture and spirit are a consequence rather than a cause of social change, then there is no reason to address humanity as a whole. Instead, the focus is on the particular individuals and groups who hold the levers of change and who can be motivated to push the levers in desired directions.

Today, with all of our attachments to the world, it seems impossible to us that society could change through the spirit. We look for explanations of history in some sort of cause, some factor or force external to the collective will of humanity. It is obvious why we hold such a vision, for to think otherwise would be to put the blame for society's abuses on ourselves. It is always easier to condemn the economy or the government, and to wait for a lawgiver or a certain social class to correct things, than to recognize the source of our suffering in our own lack of spirituality.

But Jesus put the responsibility for establishing a godly kingdom directly on us. He implied with his parable about the mustard seed that if we let our faith grow large—if we express it in our daily lives by refusing to acknowledge earthly power, seeking only our necessary property, and not testing our faith; if, in other words, we join the kingdom of God—we will eventually hold the governments of the world in our branches like birds. Note, though, that political power will not be eliminated; there will still be eagles. Nor will the spiritual tree hold the world's governments by force; they will sit in our tree, not in a cage. But they will be small in comparison to the greatest of our spirit; in fact, they will come to us voluntarily, to sit in our branches, because we will provide shade from the hot sun of judgement, class conflict, and war.

The question remains as to whether the spirit that will produce this cultural transformation comes from God or from human formulators of religious beliefs. Is the spiritual revolution that Jesus envisioned going to be a product of divine inspiration or human preaching and teaching? This question was posed by Mary Magdalene when Jesus told her the parable of the mustard seed. She asked, "Of what sort is that mustard seed? Is it something from heaven or is it something from earth?"[27] Jesus did not answer.

5. The World and the Word

As discussed in Chapter 4, Jesus prophesied in his indirect manner that the kingdom of God would come in three days, or stages. He did not say how long each stage would take. Perhaps the most serious mistake made by those who took Jesus' words at face value without seeking to penetrate their inner meaning was to assume that the kingdom was just around the corner. But Jesus said many things to indicate that he envisioned a protracted, and perhaps multi-millennial period of conflict between the established kingdoms of the world and the emergent kingdom of God.

The first stage of the kingdom coming was the initial preaching of the gospel. The word is spread, but not through missionary proselytizing. Rather, preachers of the new faith must speak very carefully. Jesus said he taught in parables specifically because he did not want the unfaithful to understand what he was saying. "All these things are done in parables: That seeing they may see, and not perceive; and hearing they may hear, and not understand; lest at any time they should be converted, and their sins should be forgiven them."[28]

Why would Jesus not want people to be converted and their sins forgiven? Because he knew that many of those who were easily converted, who heard about the kingdom and immediately wanted to join, might not really understand the radical implications of his message and in any event would have difficulty living a life of forgiveness, poverty, and license. If told by a Christ that the law is undone, that the world is now to be governed only by the simplest of God's commandments, that the many rules and conventions of society are not just unnecessary but are actually sins of humankind; if told all this, many people might just focus on their new freedom from sin— from the strictures of arbitrary legal and social limitations—while ignoring their new responsibility to love God and neighbor. In this case, their very weakness would cast doubt on the viability of the kingdom.

Jesus knew, in other words, that many of his ideas would fall among rocks or in poor soil and would not grow, but this did not trouble him in the least. To the contrary, he worried that the word might spread too quickly. The initial stage of bringing God's rule to earth had to involve a very select group.

Furthermore, the spiritual movement was to be recruited not from among the priests or the educated classes, but from workers, tax collectors, and harlots. Jesus said the kingdom of God was like a wedding, where the guests who should have come—the guests who had been invited first—had said they were too busy, so guests were recruited from the countryside.[29] Of course, this did not mean that those who continued to live in hate, greed, and judgement would be allowed in; the recruited guests who showed up improperly dressed would be turned away.[30] But the initial founders of the new kingdom were definitely to come from marginal social classes.

This was not because Jesus did not want rich and powerful converts. His parable of the wedding said that they had been invited first. The problem was that they had sold their souls to Satan, to the world, for trinkets and passing glory.

Jesus implied that the faith was to be spread exclusively through face to face contact. It is no happenstance that he did not leave any written works for posterity. The only time he is said to have written anything was when the people brought him a woman to be stoned; he turned away from them and wrote something in the sand, which he then brushed away. Written words, he seemed to be saying, could be a distraction from real-life decisions, and did not really last because they can always be wiped away or reinterpreted, while spoken words live forever in the influence they produce in others. We know what Jesus said to those who would have stoned the adulteress, but not what he wrote.

Jesus also did other things that revealed that his intention was to spark faith through direct contact with other human beings. When he chose his disciples, it was always a one-to-one appeal. He did not stand in the synagogue or call from his Sermon on the Mount for people to follow him. He looked individuals directly in the eyes and said that if they truly had faith in the kingdom of heaven and in the connection between heaven and earth—faith in the afterlife and in the divine judgement of God—they would join him in establishing a kingdom of God on earth. Not everyone thus approached was convinced or inspired. We are told of the wealthy man who wanted to be as good and spiritual as possible; but when urged by Jesus to sell all he had, give the proceeds to the poor, and then join the disciples in their quest, he felt that Jesus asked too much, and declined.[31]

This emphasis on direct personal contact follows from Jesus' message of personal responsibility and accountability. Mass communication, whether it is through books, broadcast television, or just speaking before a crowd, breaks the bonds of accountability to the messenger. One can always close a book, turn off a television, or walk away from a speaker. The one who prepares the way for the messiah can address crowds, crying in the wilderness, but the bearer of the message must deliver it in person.

The emphasis on personal communication also explains the emergence of the gnostic tradition. Jesus did indeed speak to crowds, but he was clearly *not* intending to convert those to whom he preached. This is an important point and has been missed by almost the whole of Christianity. Jesus did not believe the kingdom of God was to be established through a mass movement. He expected the multitudes to be skeptical and condemning, and indeed he wanted them to be, for it was the interaction between the holy spirit of his followers and the satanic spirit of the world that would cause the bread of society to rise.

Jesus' commitment to direct contact accounts for the peculiar way in which the New Testament documents the messiah's experiences. As we have observed, despite the fact that it was written decades after the events surrounding Jesus' preaching and crucifixion, it is full of names. This is very much unlike the Old Testament and certainly unlike other religious movements. Even in the Old Testament, many of the most important characters are not specified. For example, we do not know the name of Noah's wife, even though she was the second mother, after Eve, of the entire human species.

In short, Jesus started the spiritual movement for the kingdom of God through his own appeal to our souls, and this is how he expected the movement to spread. When we truly connect as persons, when we set aside the distinctions of rank and power, when we leap across the "media" that separate us, we experience the holy spirit and initiate the kingdom. As Jesus told his disciples, "If two of you shall agree on earth as touching any thing that they shall ask, it shall be done for them of my Father which is in heaven. For where two or three are gathered together in my name, there am I in the midst of them."[32] The kingdom of God is not a form of government or a state of mind, it is a relationship between people.

6. The Political Meaning of the Book of Revelation

I believe that we are in the transition between the second and third stages of the world spiritual revolution Jesus prophesied. The second stage of the kingdom coming is the clash between the two kingdoms, between the kingdom of Satan and the kingdom of God. The third stage is the day of judgement. The latter will be a worldwide political crisis in which the holy spirit of humanity will emerge to hold all the world's powers, from the power of the smallest family to that of the largest nation, in its branches. The judgement or crisis will be an apocalypse in the traditional sense of the word, that is, an awakening. It will be brought on when people around the world finally come to recognize collectively that political power and social status destroy the godly spirit in humanity and break our bonds of love.

Jesus did not devote much attention to explaining how the spiritual conflict between the kingdoms of the world and the kingdom of God would unfold, but his parables suggested that this would be the longest stage of the world spiritual revolution he envisioned. His parables of the mustard tree and the leaven in the bread both focused on the revolution's beginning and end while ignoring the long period of change in the middle. The example of the mustard tree starts with the small seed and then jumps immediately to the mature plant, which becomes a gathering place for birds. Similarly, the analogy of the leaven in the bread begins with the leaven and the dough and then shifts more or less directly to the risen loaf. Each parable clearly implies a lengthy period of spiritual growth or development, but neither one says what this period will be like or how to best get through it. Jesus showed us how to start the change, and he described our final destination, but when it came to actually reaching the kingdom, he left it for us to make our own way.

This may be why John experienced the spirit of Jesus at the Island of Patmos. Many people have interpreted John's vision to be mainly about the judgement day, but I believe otherwise. In my view, the Book of Revelation deals principally with the long period of spiritual growth between John's day and our own.

John reports that he was told he was seeing "things that must be hereafter."[33] The vision included many strange events in heaven and on earth, involving angels, beasts, spirits, and people.

Nearly all analysts of the Book of Revelation have seen it as a prediction concerning the second coming. Although the meaning attached to different symbols may vary, the general conclusion among biblical scholars has been that John was given a glimpse of the events leading up to the return of Jesus to earth and the institution of divine rule, with Satan cast into a lake of fire and the faithful resurrected in body and soul. Many have looked to this vision to try to understand and predict the future, seeing, for example, in the battle between Gog and Magog at Armageddon a prediction of the end of the world through nuclear conflagration. Interpretations for almost every little part of John's vision have been offered. If there were ever a vision that has been used to support a wait-for-the-kingdom theology, it is certainly John's.

I do not doubt that John had the vision he reported, nor do I question his conviction that it was divinely inspired. But I believe there is a very different meaning to the vision, a meaning that calls for us to act rather than to retreat into the hope for a second coming.

A correct interpretation of John's vision first requires that we hold John's own analysis of his experience in some doubt. He reported a fantastic image of the future, and its very grandeur and scale give us confidence that it was deeply inspired. In an age that had never seen the epic palate of cinematography, in a time that had not even produced much real analysis of history beyond stories about the lives of kings and tyrants, and in an epoch of unchallenged Roman rule, John saw and described for future generations an unparalleled landscape stretching across the earth and into the heavens, with creatures never before dreamt of battling in ways never before imagined.

But the scale, complexity, and symbolic nature of John's vision make it virtually impossible to fully comprehend. We do not understand it today, and John did not understand it himself. In fact, the way John described his vision showed that he was fully aware of his ignorance about its meaning; he wrote down what he saw as he had the vision, and he took great care not to insert his own conclusions about what it meant. Although at times he explains the meaning of a certain symbol, generally he avoids this unless he is reporting the explanation offered by one of the angels in the vision itself. John left us with a record of the wondrous sights he was allowed to glimpse, but he was as ignorant as we are as to its real meaning.

If we accept that the meaning of John's vision is not self-evident and if we recognize its mysterious character, we are led, I believe, to a cautious or circumspect strategy of interpretation. Rather than trying to decipher every nuance and symbol, we should stand back from the vision and seek to capture its basic structure. We should not ask, for example, what the four horses or their riders stand for, but we should wonder about the overall cast of actors, the movement of the drama, and the setting. John saw an allegory of the future, and its meaning is in the plot and the characters, not the cut of their costumes or the nuances of a given moment of action.

7. Kingdoms Colliding

When John's vision is viewed at this distance, there is no need to reach for an otherworldly interpretation. The vision can be seen as a statement of the lengthy, terrible, and at times uncertain conflict that is going to occur as those who believe in God and the afterlife try to bring about the kingdom of God on earth. John had at least a partial understanding of what Jesus called on his followers to do; John may have been one of the first to take a wait-for-the-kingdom stance, but he understood better than most do today, and certainly better than most of the organized churches, that Jesus had prophesied a divine order on earth. As John was moved by the holy spirit, as he thought about the enormous task this presented to humanity but also that this was the one goal humanity would inevitably embrace or would inevitably perish from neglecting, John came to see that the coming of the kingdom would involve a horrendous spiritual battle: a battle, moreover, that would lead to the destruction of entire kingdoms, peoples, and languages.

That this is the meaning of the vision can be seen in three of its essential characteristics. One is the pervasive theme of the interaction between heaven and earth. As we have discussed, Jesus constantly preached that heavenly justice and love had been brought to earth through him and could be actualized in an earthly kingdom of God. The Lord's prayer was a declaration by the faithful of their commitment to live in the faith that heaven and earth are intimately related— that goodness and evil receive their appropriate rewards or punishments in the afterlife, and that God was working through his followers to defeat evil on earth and establish an order based on love and mercy. But this latter order was not to be instituted supernaturally, except through the supernatural force of faith emerging in history.

The connection between heaven and earth in John's vision is basically one of heavenly spirits descending to earth and increasingly becoming a force in civilization. The Book of Revelation contains repeated references to the effects caused on earth from heaven. God is going to be intimately involved in human affairs on earth through the spiritual forces first brought to earth by Jesus. Whereas in the past the most important forces on earth were natural disasters and the seemingly uncontrollable influence of kingly power and glory, Jesus tried to assure that in the future the most important influence would be divine motives. The spiritual forces would move through the world like a power greater than nature and greater than nations. The clash between the forces of the world and the forces of heaven would be so large they would make nature appear small and would bear down on entire nations, so that both natural and historical events would be seen as only small pieces of landscape in the superordinant struggle.

We can recognize that this is indeed how the world has become. In the days of Jesus, political power, in the form of the Roman Empire and its predecessors, extended beyond religious beliefs and indeed saw itself as a protector of religious rights. People were also awed by natural disasters, and much of life was devoted to dealing with famines, floods, and other calamities. But today the reverse is true: not only are we becoming capable of dealing collectively with almost every sort of natural threat, a global public opinion is emerging which transcends nations and which values peace and love.

The second characteristic of John's vision is that the forces he saw in the revolution for the kingdom of God were very diverse. He did not envision two combatants on a single field of conflict, or even two armies engaged at different places or times. The vision was definitely of a very convoluted struggle. At one point, the spirit of God might emerge as love, the creature who conquers with a bow that shoots straight to the heart.[34] At another point, humanity might experience the reality of God negatively, as people turn away from God and see peace removed from the world. At still other times, the spirit of God may arrive as a demand for earthly justice, that is, as a demand for equity and fairness, or as a demand for vengeance. John's vision implied that the spirit of holiness takes various forms and rides many horses.

Truly, the complexity and convolutedness of the spirits in John's revelation seem to capture the history of the human yearning for divine order. Our desire for the kingdom of God has been felt in many different ways. In the early Church, and especially in the writings of Paul, it was experienced as a search for love. Later, after the Church became terribly corrupt, people began to thirst for liberty and justice—the fairness of a scale rather than the love and mercy of a creator—a longing that led to the democratic revolutions of the eighteenth century and launched what we now call the "modern" era. Today, the spirit of God seems to be appearing to us as an obvious silence;[35] God and the powers of God are nowhere to be found, and suddenly we see satanic forces unleashed in our cities, our families, and ourselves. Further, just as John's vision suggests, these different spiritual sensations have swept through the world like huge winds, with effects much larger than nations and more enduring than natural disasters or wars.

The third characteristic of John's vision, which is perhaps the most important, counterbalances the apparent complexity and precariousness of the struggle. It is that ultimately—despite the various forms taken by the combatants—there are only two real forces at work, God and Satan, and ultimately God will prevail. Again, as we have learned, this is one of the essential points Jesus made in his preaching. The force that rules the earth; the spirit that moves people to collaborate unconsciously to acheive selfish ends, as did Herod and his wife and

daughter when they killed John the Baptist; the force behind individual and collective evil, constitutes a kingdom, and the kingdom has
a king, and that king is called Satan. Just as the holy spirit takes many
forms, Satan is manifest in many spirits.

The diversity is so great, on both sides, that people easily miss the
underlying unity of good on the one hand and evil on the other. They
see all the bad that is done on the earth, and they attribute it to a
thousand reasons. People do wrong, they say, because they are
oppressed, or greedy, or weak, or ignorant, or hopeless, while, conversely, people do good because they want to feel good about themselves, or they hope that it will bring them riches, or they are afraid of
punishment, or they have simply been taught to do so. We perceive the
moral world as if we were looking through a fly's eye; a thousand kinds
of wrongs are matched by a thousand goods, and the world appears to
be a marbled mix of good and evil.

Each color and shade of the mix is described by a different specialist.
Historians tell us of historic battles between oppression and liberation. Psychologists offer isolated explanations for the humanity in
humankind, and for the beast. Even the different Christian churches
stress different things: the fallen Adam and Eve, the promise of
redemption in a covenant with God, the holy spirit in everyone, the
presence of Jesus in the poor.

John's vision seems to imply that these various images of good and
evil will eventually be replaced by a true understanding, which is that
the conflict is between human power and glory on the one hand and
divine power and glory on the other. Even though the world may be
plagued at times by terrible disorder, as if evil were triumphing; even
though the spiritual movements for love, justice, and freedom may
turn out to be of a limited duration; and even though heaven may be
silent for what seems like a long time, eventually all of the various
angels will worship the same throne, or humanity will see that all of its
various conceptions of goodness are fragments of a single ideal, the
ideal that Jesus brought into the world and asked us to govern
ourselves under. At this point, too, people will recognize the basic
unity of evil. As they come together with a single understanding of how
humanity should be governed and how they can live responsibly, their
understanding of evil will be clarified and focused. They will see that

all the various kinds of evil are really just the same thing: the effort to escape their own humanity, to be as God and not subject to God, an aim that drives them into the arms of the world and the satanic force that governs it.

8. Characteristics of the Emerging World Spirit

Still, Jesus did not leave us completely unenlightened about the form that our spiritual development would take. We have examined his two analogies for the canon gospels: the parables of the mustard seed and the leaven in the bread. He also offered two other analogies in the *Gospel of Thomas*, and in all of the gospels he presented a number of prophecies in the so called "beatitudes," where he says what is "blessed." Further, Jesus prescribed a set of spiritual axioms or principles for establishing the kingdom of God by spiritualizing our view of God's commandments. If we examine all of these carefully, we can see that Jesus anticipated many of the characteristics of the modern era, and we can get an idea of the particular developments that are taking us toward the kingdom and those that are not.

The two parables from Thomas call for us to withdraw, mentally and physically, from the worldly systems of power and glory in which we find ourselves. In one of the stories, Jesus compares the coming of the kingdom to "a certain woman who was carrying a jar full of meal."[36] On the way home, "the handle of the jar broke and the meal emptied out behind her on the road." She did not notice the accident until she arrived home and found the jar empty.

This parable is the opposite of the parable of the mustard seed and the leaven in the bread. In both of the latter, the spirit is described as being planted in the social order and growing up within it, to the point that eventually it subsumes and transforms worldly systems of power and glory. In the story of the broken jar, the idea is that worldly power and glory will continue on, but our allegiance to them will drain out into the larger world, and eventually earthly kingdoms will be empty. The idea is that we will transfer our allegiance to the kingdom of God, and before the world-powers even know what has happened, they will be without support.

In the other parable from the *Gospel of Thomas*, Jesus says, "The kingdom of the father is like a certain man who wanted to kill a powerful man."[37] The killer first practiced in his own home by drawing his sword and stabbing it into the wall "in order to find whether his hand could carry through." Once he knew that he could do it, "he slew the powerful man."

Again, there is a reversal of the imagery from the parables of the mustard seed and the leaven in the bread. The overthrow of power occurs not from within, but from without. The kingdom of God is to be established as a counter-kingdom alongside the kingdoms of the world. We are to learn to live without power and glory; we are to kill or to practice killing power in our own home, our own society within the larger social formation. Once we know that we can do it, we are to go to the home of the powerful man, to the world's centers of power and glory, and put an end to power and glory altogether.

We have been witnessing the growth of this counter-kingdom since the days when Jesus first brought the idea into the world. Despite its misunderstandings, the Church established itself as a cultural force over and above individual nations. The Reformation reaffirmed within Western civilization that claims of conscience and bonds of faith are superior, both politically and ethically, to the demands of the state. The democratic movements of the eighteenth century; the abolitionist movements of the nineteenth century; and the twentieth-century movements for women's rights, labor organization, environmental protection, children's rights, and the like, while misguided in their acceptance of existing systems of power, nevertheless confront even the largest governments with an even larger spiritual force.

The parables of the broken jar and the murder of a powerful man point to the importance of continuing the effort to establish a cohesive, worldwide counter-culture. The emphases by at least some elements of the social movements of the 1960s on dropping out of society, shedding property rather than accumulating wealth, and looking for personal love rather than violent, collective revolution, show that Jesus correctly foresaw the form that the holy spirit would take at the end of the second day and the beginning of the third. We must each drop from the jar of power and just let civilization proceed along the road toward its home, where, when it arrives, it will find the jar empty. Together, we can kill power in our own homes and communities, and then we will be able to deal with power-centers elsewhere. The key is to join hands globally in recognition that earthly power and glory must be dis-acknowledged.

The 1960s offered a mere taste of what might be achieved if people truly exalted themselves above the petty judgements of modern society. What this decade of change lacked was a foundation in the holy spirit. Unlike most of the leaders of the civil rights movement, the students, both in America and Europe, veered off into the worst form of atheism. They began to search for a spiritual foundation in the pseudo-spirituality of drugs, sex, and other forms of mindless expression and indulgence. To be sure, people felt the spirit of holiness in the sixties, the spirit that lifts you above the judgements of the world and that connects one person to another and to God, but they failed to understand its source and its aim. Those who truly desire to lead us against, as the students said then, "the system," must understand that the only alternative to worldly power and glory is a divine order rooted in faith. Leaders must minister to the spark of faith that everyone carries; they must be the soft breath that blows this spark into a flame, explaining faith's invisible foundations and revealing the reality of God, so that people may rid themselves of their incessant judging and ranking.

9. The Beatitudes Fulfilled

The beatitudes are often mistaken to be expressions merely of characteristics that Jesus valued, but they are also prophecies about the kingdom of God. We can see this in the alternating structure of the beatitudes in the Gospel of Matthew. When describing "the poor in spirit" and those who are "persecuted for righteousness' sake," Jesus speaks in the present tense, saying that theirs *is* the kingdom of heaven. He does this because they indeed are already in the kingdom, in the sense that, spiritually, they have broken off from worldly systems of power and glory. In contrast, Jesus uses the future tense when referring to those who mourn, those who hunger for righteousness, the meek, the merciful, the pure in heart, and the peacemakers. In each case, he says that people with these motivations *shall* be exalted at some future date, presumably when the kingdom of God has been established. The meek *shall* inherit the earth. The merciful *shall* obtain mercy. The pure in heart *shall* see God, and so on. In effect, establishing the kingdom of God means implementing these values, and, conversely, when the meek have indeed inherited the earth and the merciful have obtained mercy, the kingdom of God will be a reality.

We are generally familiar with the beatitudes in the canon gospels, and we can easily see that the values espoused in these beatitudes are, as Jesus prophesied, becoming increasingly central to world civilization, even if religious doubt and scientific ideologies weaken their effects. In the days of the Roman Empire, meekness, peacefulness, mournfulness, and willingness to suffer for the sake of principles would have been considered the opposite of goodness. Many Romans and the Greeks extolled pride, fierceness, cunning, trickery, pragmatism, and religious relativism. Some people may believe that the influence of Jesus has waned, but in actuality it is becoming stronger all the time when considered in terms of these values. The instances where cultures have opposed them in the twentieth century—the Roman revivalism of the Nazis, who sought to return their nation to a warrior code, and the similar efforts of the Japanese—resulted in wars that led to their defeat. At the end of the second millennium after Jesus, the values of Jesus have become the values of the world.

Of course, one could argue that this is just a remnant of a Christianity, which is itself waning, and that these values will eventually dissolve once the influence of the Middle Ages is no longer felt. Jesus, it might be argued, shaped Western civilization through the institution of the Church, not by awakening the holy spirit in humanity, in which case his influence will be only as strong as the organized religion proselytizing in his name.

But the beatitudes in the gnostic gospels—which were lost for well over a thousand years and could not be self-fulfilling prophecies since their obscurity prevented them from having any direct effect on our culture—show that Jesus truly understood where the spirit of holiness is taking us. One of the beatitudes from the *Gospel of Thomas* deals with solitariness. "Jesus said, 'Blessed are the solitary and elect, for you will find the kingdom. For you are from it, and to it you will return.'"[38] Jesus made many similar statements in the canon gospels, especially to the effect that people would forsake the bonds of family: "The father shall be divided against the son, and the son against the father; the mother against the daughter, and the daughter against the mother; the mother-in-law against the daughter-in-law, and the daughter-in-law against the mother-in-law."[39] The kingdom of God is to be built entirely on individuals, not on any other unit—not races, nations, cities, groups, or even families.

A related prophecy was that male and female will become alike. Jesus said that we would enter the kingdom of God "when you make the male and the female one and the same, so that the male not be male and the female not be female."[40] The idea that being male or female necessarily entails certain characteristics will disappear. We will see ourselves, and we will truly be, unique individuals.

Certainly, the increasing importance of the individual and the gradual withering away of other social categories is one of the defining trends of civilization. As we come to love one another—that is, as we come to recognize that all human beings are equally valuable, regardless of their age, gender, race, family name, family position, sexual orientation, or whatever—the importance of these and other characteristics necessarily diminishes, and such features come to be seen as superficial. This is not, as Plato might have suggested, an outgrowth of democracy; nor is it, as Marx would have argued, a consequence of industrialization. Rather, it is the holy spirit becoming active in humankind. Love recognizes individuals, not groups, races, or nations. The world is beginning to condemn bigotry in any form because world civilization is starting to demand that each person be considered as a solitary creature, an individual, rather than as a member of a group or the holder of a position. Eventually, all inclinations to label people in any way whatsoever will be recognized as the deep sins which they are.

10. Blessed Are the Immodest

Another characteristic of the emerging kingdom of God discussed several times by Jesus in the gnostic gospels deserves to be mentioned at this point even though Jesus never stated it as a beatitude. It has to do with immodesty:

His disc1iples said, "When will you become revealed to us and when shall we see you?"

Jesus said, "When you disrobe without being ashamed and take up your garments and place them under your feet like little children and tread on them, then will you see the son of the living one, and you will not be afraid."[41]

Elsewhere, in *The Dialogue of the Savior*, Jesus explains that "when you rid yourselves of jealousy, then you will clothe yourselves in light."[42]

We are familiar with the idea of becoming a child from the canon gospels. Jesus says that the kingdom of God is made of people who are like little children, and he warns that "Whosoever shall not receive the kingdom of God as a little child, he shall not enter therein."[43] The *Gospel of Thomas* explains that one thing Jesus meant by saying that we should become like children is that we should not be so modest.

Little children have no modesty because they have not been taught to be ashamed of their bodies. They are in the state that Adam and Eve were in before they ate from the tree of knowledge of good and evil, that is, before they concluded that they, rather than God, had ultimate knowledge of right and wrong. To be as a little child means to shed human conventions about, among other things, clothing. Being ashamed of our bodies was the first form taken by our original sin against God; we concluded that we knew better than God how we should look. God created us in nakedness, but we adopted our own morals, and then we covered his creation. Clothes are a sin.

At first blush, Jesus' claim that the holy spirit is moving us toward immodesty may seem farfetched, but observation suggests that this prophecy, too, is being fulfilled. In fact, one of the defining features of the past century has been a rapid decline in concern about clothing. Women used to be ashamed to show their ankles, and men covered their necks with scarves, bandannas, or ties. But today, revealing clothing, even at work, is more the norm than the exception. Certainly, at a beach or swimming pool, no one thinks anything about bathing suits that expose virtually everything but the breasts and genitals.

Further, this trend is continuing. Women have sued to strike down laws that prevent them, but not men, from going topless. Nude beaches are common in Europe and becoming common in the United States. In just another fifty or a hundred years, if the trend does not end, nakedness should be accepted everywhere.

To be sure, this assumes that other civilizing tendencies also proceed commensurately. We will not be able to go nude if we are still attacking one another physically, nor will we want to reveal ourselves if we remain caught up in our incessant judging and ranking. The extent to which we are prepared to shed our clothing will be an indication not only of how far we have come in dismantling our presumptuous and petty beliefs about good and evil, but also of our related progress in other areas, such as our peacefulness, self-respect, and personal sense of security.

But this is precisely what Jesus predicted. He said that we would see the son of humanity, the spirit of God in each of us, as soon as we become like children, accepting ourselves as we are and recognizing one another's deep tenderness. We must learn to be carefree, "to take no thought for your life,"[44] to become "passers-by,"[45] and to find pleasures in such small things as breaking bread, playing with our youngsters, bathing, and simply being with people.

11. Spiritualizing the Law

One other point Jesus made about the coming of the kingdom of God during the second stage (or second day) was that it would involve the spiritualization of the law. Although he came to save us from judgement and demanding regulations, he made it clear he was not a prophet of license, at least not in the ordinary sense. "Think not that I am come to destroy the law, or the prophets: I am not come to destroy, but to fulfill."[46] Jesus wanted to replace the "doctrines of men" with the commandments of God.

Jesus gave numerous examples of how God's commandments are at once both easier and more demanding than the conventional rules of humanity. They are more demanding because they focus on intention and spirit, rather than on outcomes or effects. Not only is it a great sin to commit murder or adultery, it is a sin even to be angry with another without cause, or to look at another lustfully.[47] By the same token, worship is to be for one's own soul, not for the glory it may secure from others; people should give alms in secret, and pray in their closets.[48]

Jesus expected us to expunge every evil thought from our minds. "If thy right eye offend thee, pluck it out, and cast it from thee: for it is profitable for thee that one of thy members should perish, and not that thy whole body should be cast into hell."[49] We are to tolerate no evil in ourselves and are to try to become as good as God in heaven.

On the other hand, the definition of good and evil is much simpler and easier under God than under humanity. For God has only two basic commandments: to love God and neighbor. We can forget about dressing properly, speaking correctly, following rules of etiquette, trying to be "with it," adopting the opinions of others, cutting our hair in the conventional fashion, and so on, at least insofar as we continue to treat one another with dignity and love. We can abandon the countless rules, laws, habits, conventions, and customs that form the iron bars of human society.

This is why Jesus said, in both the Gospel of Matthew and the *Gospel of Thomas*, that "my yoke is easy, and my burden is light."[50] The analogy between political power and a yoke is an old one in the Bible. It can be found in Genesis, Leviticus, 1 Kings, 2 Chronicles, Isaiah, Jeremiah, Lamentations, Ezekiel, Hosea, and Nahum.[51] The Old Testament gives example after example of how oppressive political power has been placed on people like a collar and harness. When Jesus says that his teachings are a light and easy yoke, he is not saying that all order and rule will be eliminated; there will still be a yoke. But the rule will be simple. It will aim at assuring that people show love to God and one another.

In many ways, we can see this spiritualization of the law in our history. In the days of Jesus, what mattered was not what one intended, but what happened. Plato tells the story of the master who accidentally killed a slave who had murdered someone else. The master was to be prosecuted, despite the facts that the killing was unintentional and had occurred when he was trying to bring the victim to justice. In contrast, today we make very fine distinctions based on states of mind. We would say that the master in Plato's story was guilty, not of murder, but of involuntary manslaughter. Further, we require persons to have been in control of their faculties, and to have known the difference between right and wrong, before we will prosecute them for crimes. If sanity and moral knowledge are lacking, we commit offenders to mental institutions instead of trying them for their actions. We have done this even for people who have tried to kill our highest leaders.

In short, we can see in modern society many of the characteristics Jesus attributed to the kingdom of God. We expect people to be pleasant and caring. We are gradually shedding our clothes and our modesty. We are coming to understand that it is wrong to view others as anything but solitary individuals. Our ties to groups, races, regions, nations, and genders are weakening. Women and men are becoming more alike. And the law is oriented increasingly toward intentions and away from effects. In Jesus' words, the bread is rising and the mustard tree is growing large.

12. Harvest of Souls

The third stage of the kingdom coming to fruition is the harvest. Eventually, the kingdom of God will become strong enough to destroy the kingdoms of the world. At this point, all the past wrongs will be known. Then, in the minds of people, all the early voices of the holy spirit will be resurrected and given a new place in the accepted view of history.

But this final stage will come neither quickly nor steadily. Certainly it has not come yet.

Jesus prophesied that faith would almost disappear at times before the kingdom was finally ushered in. He told the parable of the man who planted a vineyard and left it to be tended by a servant. He also said the spirit of humanity, or the son of humankind, was like a man who leaves his home in the care of his servants while he takes a long journey; one never knows when he is going to return. Surely we in the modern era feel as if the spirit has left us, but Jesus predicted these times of abandonment and said they would not last forever.

Jesus warned, too, that there would be many false prophets, and that their falseness would be revealed only by their fruits, which is to say, only after a long time. One might think of Peter and the culmination of the Papacy in the Spanish Inquisition; or of Mohammed, and the

Jihad of modern terrorism; or of Karl Marx and the oppression of Soviet communism. Truly, Jesus was correct when he said that it is impossible to know in advance who is a true prophet. The coming of the kingdom is slow and uncertain.

But Jesus made it very clear that he expected the movement produced by the holy spirit ultimately to culminate in a period of judgement. The analogies of the leaven in the bread, the mustard seed, the broken jar, and the murder of a powerful man all pointed to a time of maturation and transformation. The bread would eventually rise; the mustard seed would become a tree to shelter the birds; the woman carrying the jar would arrive home and find it empty; the powerful man would be killed. An even more pointed analogy was likening the kingdom of God to a harvest. Jesus plants the seed of faith in many soils, and the spiritual wheat grows up amidst weeds and tares. Eventually, though, there is a harvest, and the wheat is kept while the tares are burned.

Did this mean that Jesus intended Christianity to culminate in a revolutionary bloodbath? No, he never described it as a time of killing and persecution; he referred to it as a time of judgement. Although the idea of the judgement day was interpreted by Jesus' followers as a time when God would give a reincarnated Jesus power over the earth and would resurrect the bodies and souls of the faithful, this other-worldly interpretation was a misunderstanding. In fact, a more commonsensible interpretation would take the form Jesus described; that is, the judgement day will be a time when God-oriented judgements will prevail, the wicked will be revealed in their wickedness, the deeds of the faithful will be recognized, and good and evil will be sorted out.

This is in fact the nature of all spiritual revolutions. Consider as an example the nonviolent civil rights movement in America in the 1960s. When this movement began, many segregationists were viewed by large numbers of Americans to be on the right side of the issue, while civil rights leaders, including Dr. Martin Luther King, Jr., were thought to be "outside agitators." But as the movement unfolded and the white supremacists revealed themselves to be cruel oppressors, the judgement of the multitude shifted. It is now generally agreed that racism is abhorrent, and those who practice racism are punished in all manner of ways. Furthermore, history has been reinterpreted; the memory of Dr. King has been resurrected and placed high in the people's spiritual ordering of leaders, while the collective recollections of segregationists have been consigned to oblivion.

There is no reason to assume that Jesus depended on God to intervene supernaturally. As the spirit of righteousness weaves its way through the social order, it will inevitably highlight the oppression and force by which the worldly powers maintain their control. As evil is confronted by good, it will sense the danger and will consolidate its power, and will thus display its devilish inner nature by baring its fangs. Once goodness prevails, values will be reversed, the first will be last, and the last will be first.

13. How To Bring On the Kingdom

In conclusion, I believe we may be about to begin the third and final day of a protracted apocalypse, a protracted tension between the temptations of the world and the spirit of holiness. The kingdom of God will come when faith in God and heaven is spread throughout the planet and humanity unites as a single will, a global spirit of holiness. We see this spirit stirring today, but we can also recognize the tremendous powers arrayed against it.

The movement for the kingdom turns each day on each person, as the personal choice is made between joining the kingdom of God or staying in the kingdoms of men and women. We have misunderstood our history. The kingdom of God will not come in a flash shortly after Jesus' crucifixion. Nor is it coming in the future with trumpets blowing and clouds floating down from the sky above. It will come only with a long spiritual struggle.

The danger that we face is not that we will lose in our battle with the world and its temptations, but that we will fail to recognize that we are in the battle that we are in. The pride of the modern era has led us to misunderstand our own history. We are like a man who, in his adolescence, wanted to be strong and loving, but who became caught up in his work and turned cruel and harsh. He thinks he has grown up, but he has really just grown away from his own goodness. He does not understand that his soul depends on resurrecting the ideals of his youth and reforming his life around them.

The very idea of the "modern" era, the notion that all prior history is antiquated and culturally juvenile, has presented us with a terrible temptation. Our willingness to accept this image must be attributed to the great deceptiveness of Satan. It has blinded us to the fact that this era is exactly like all others in its idolatry, its tendency to worship things and human creations, its incessant judging and ranking, and its inclination to run from responsibility and accountability. We have much to be thankful for, but it is not that we are modern. Quite the reverse, we are blessed in having much that is holy still in us, and still moving our civilization. Like the man who needs to return to his youthful idealism, we need to galvanize our civilization around the spirit of holiness.

We must begin to look once again for the signs of God and Jesus in our own lives, and to announce these messages. I am speaking here not of miracles but of the spiritual insights that God grants everyone. Because of the profound influence of science, which takes the world to be the alpha and the omega of existence, people today are embarrassed to speak of the visible signs of God in their own lives. Indeed, to do so could lead to their being seen as psychotic. But we must stop being intimidated by the sophisticated atheism of our universities. What God whispers in our ears, we must shout from the rooftops.[52] We cannot establish a powerful kingdom on a mountain and keep it concealed.[53]

Jesus has taught us how to bring about the kingdom of God. We must cry in the wilderness. We must first speak out that we know God, that we believe in God, that we see his presence in signs all around us. True, most will not listen; most will go on with the ways of the world, following the currents of the world. By obeying the world's inclinations, they will give up their freedom and the responsibility it entails. But some will heed the witnesses. And others who see God in their lives, the spirit that Jesus brought to us, will begin to speak up, too: prophecy will return, and so will another gust of the spirit of holiness, perhaps the last one, the Armageddon, before the kingdom of God is finally and completely established.

This is not an anti-Christian or a superstitious expectation. We have seen these eras of prophecy at other times, in the times when Moses and Isaiah lived, and Jesus, and more recently during the Reformation, when men such as Thomas Muntzer and Jacob Boehme had great visions. Jesus was very direct in telling us there would have to be new prophets and new prophecies, and that indeed his spirit would have to return. He warned us against false prophets so that we could know the true prophets.

Now is the time for God's silence to end. Those who hear God must speak. As Jesus said, "There is light within a man of light, and he lights up the whole world. If he does not shine, he is darkness."[54]

Notes

Notes to the Preface

1. See Leo Strauss, *Persecution and the Art of Writing* (Chicago: University of Chicago Press, 1952, 1980).

2. Matthew 6:6.

3. Matthew 6:7.

4. Matthew 4:5–7; Luke 4:9–12.

5. This was reported at Jesus' trial. See Mark 14:58.

6. Matthew 19:27; 20:20–26.

7. I use James M. Robinson, general editor, *The Nag Hammadi Library in English* (San Francisco: HarperSanFrancisco, 1978, 1988, 1990).

Notes to Chapter One

1. Non-Christians agree with this account of the creed, but for them such meekness is less a virtue than a vice. The humility of most Christians led Frederich Nietzsche and Karl Marx, both of whom were atheists, to say that Christianity reflects a "herd instinct" and that it is "the opiate of the masses."

2. John 12:47. Unless otherwise indicated, all references are to the King James Version of the Bible.

3. Matthew 11:25. See also Luke 10:21.

4. Matthew 12:39, 16:4; Luke 11:29–30.

5. See Mark 6:52.

6. Matthew 1:20; Luke 1:31–80.

7. Luke 2:49.

8. Karl Barth, *A Karl Barth Reader*, ed. and trans. Geoffrey W. Bromiley (Grand Rapids: Eerdmans, 1986), p. 6.

9. The Catholic Church signed a concordat with Hitler in July, 1933. Likewise, it signed the Lateran Treaty of 1929 with Mussolini, making Roman Catholicism the state religion of Italy. For a brief history of these events, see Owen Chadwick, "Great Britain and Europe," in *The Oxford Illustrated History of Christianity*, John McManners, ed. (Oxford: Oxford University Press, 1990), pp. 341–383.

10. For a review of liberation theology, see John R. Pottenger, *The Political Theory of Liberation Theology: Toward a Reconvergence of Social*

Values and Social Science (Albany: State University of New York Press, 1989).

11. For an excellent review of this literature, see George E. Ladd, *Crucial Questions about the Kingdom of God* (Grand Rapids: Eerdmans, 1952). For an effort to go beyond these two positions, see Thomas Sheehan, *The First Coming: How the Kingdom of God Became Christianity* (New York: Random House, 1986).

12. William Barclay, *New Testament Words* (Philadelphia: Westminster, 1964), pp. 30–32.

13. Luke 23:26.

14. For a discussion of how iconoclasts have frequently been forced to write in this manner, see Strauss, *Persecution and the Art of Writing*.

15. Matthew 12:14–15.

16. Matthew 26:3–4.

17. Mark 3:6. See also Mark 11:8.

18. Mark 14:1. See also Luke 6:7, 19:47, 22:2; John 5:18, 7:1.

19. Matthew 12:15.

20. John 7:2–10.

21. Mark 14:13.

22. On the posting of Peter, James, and John, see Mark 14:33. On Peter being armed, see John 18:11.

23. Luke 20:20. See also Luke 11:53–54.

24. Matthew 22:15–22; Mark 12:14; Luke 20:25.

25. Matthew 21:24–25; Mark 11:29–30.

26. Matthew 26:61–62; Mark 14:58.

27. Even the gnostic texts discussed below are in Coptic, that is, Egyptian using the Greek alphabet.

28. Mark 4:11–12. See also Matthew 13:11.

29. Matthew 13:35.

30. Matthew 16:6–12; Mark 8:15–17.

31. Matthew 13:18; Mark 4:10; Luke 8:9.

32. Matthew 15:11; Mark 4:36.

33. Matthew 15:15.

34. Mark 4:34. See a similar statement at Matthew 13:34.

35. *Gospel of Thomas* 62. Throughout this book, I cite the gnostic gospels. Unless otherwise indicated, the source is Robinson, ed., *The Nag Hammadi Library*.

36. *Gospel of Philip* 80.30–34, 81.1.

37. Matthew 7:6.

38. Evidence has also been unearthed recently to show that the gospels contain important, encoded messages using the symbolic language of gematria, which assigns hidden meaning to words and phrases by attaching numerical values to letters. See David Fideler, *Jesus Christ, Sun of God: Ancient Cosmology and Early Christian Symbolism* (Wheaton: Quest Books, 1993).

39. I say "some" of the first disciples rather than all, because I believe Philip, Thomas, and Mary Magdalene may have understood the political message. Their gospels contain a number of indications to suggest they did, but we cannot be certain, because they wrote, like Jesus spoke, to conceal. I also think Judas understood it, and that that is why he could betray Jesus to the authorities.

40. See Luke 4:18. The words Luke says that Jesus read are from Isaiah 61:1, but Luke misquotes them slightly, perhaps to conceal Jesus' political agenda. The quote from Isaiah is, "The Spirit of the Lord GOD is upon me; because the LORD hath anointed me to preach good tidings unto the meek; he hath sent me to bind up the brokenhearted, to proclaim liberty to the captives, and the opening of the prison to them that are bound." Luke has Jesus speaking of the "deliverance" of the captives rather than their "liberty," and he omits the last phrase about opening the prison. However, the careful reader would have known to look up the verse in Isaiah, and there the reader would have seen that this whole section in Isaiah is about a faith-inspired revolution against oppression.

41. Moses Maimonides, *The Guide for the Perplexed* (New York: Dover, 1904, 1956). See especially chapter 29 and foreword.

42. Josephus Flavius, *The Jewish War*, trans. William Whiston (Israel: Steimatzky, no date), bk. 2, chap. 9.

43. Samuel 28:7–19. In fact, Samuel's ghost was said to be living inside the earth.

44. *Gospel of Thomas* 109.

45. See George Eldon Ladd, *Crucial Questions About the Kingdom of God* (Grand Rapids: Eerdmans, 1952). See also George Eldon Ladd, *The Presence of the Future: The Eschatology of Biblical Realism* (Grand Rapids: Eerdmans, 1946, 1952).

46. Mark 12:28–31. See also Matthew 22:36.

47. Quoted in Jaroslav Pelikan, *The Excellent Empire: The Fall of Rome and the Triumph of the Church* (San Francisco: Harper and Row, 1987), p. 24.

48. See Luke 23:1–4 and John 18:30–33.

49. Matthew 27:11; Mark 15:2; Luke 23:3; John 18:33.

50. John 18:36.

51. John 19:12. See also Luke 23:2.

52. Matthew 27:37; Luke 23:38; Mark 15:16.

53. Socrates was the teacher of Plato, who in turn taught Aristotle.

54. The first person in the modern era to recognize the totalitarian implications of this philosophy was Karl R. Popper. His work on the topic is a classic: *The Open Society and Its Enemies.* (Princeton: Princeton University Press, 1943, 1962, 1966).

55. *Gospel of Thomas* 79.

56. The eagle was the symbol of Rome, just as it is the symbol today of Rome's spiritual heir, the United States.

57. This "quote" is a conjunction of two statements by Nietzsche. One is that "God is dead." The other is that "If nothing is true, everything is permitted." Although I have taken license with Nietzsche's words, I believe that the "quote" captures his philosophy.

58. Matthew 26:52.

59. Matthew 6:24; Luke 16:3.

60. *Gospel of Thomas* 35. For the same teaching, see Matthew 12:29 and Mark 3:27. In the latter, Jesus is quoted as saying, "No man can enter into a strong man's house, and spoil his goods, except he will first bind the strong man; and then he will spoil his house."

61. *Gospel of Thomas* 3.

62. Matthew 9:17; Mark 2:22; Luke 5:38.

63. Mark 2:21.

64. Jacques Ellul, *The Subversion of Christianity*, trans. Geoffrey W. Bromiley (Grand Rapids: Eerdmans, 1986). Ellul says that Christianity was subverted in more ways than one. In addition to the church's accommodation of the empire were such other influences as Islam, nihilism, and science.

65. See Acts 17.

66. Matthew 20:16, 22:14.

67. Matthew 13:33; Luke 13:21.

68. *Gospel of Thomas* 10.

69. Matthew 4:4–10; Luke 4:3–6.

70. Matthew 10; Mark 6.

71. Acts 2:44–47.

72. Richard A. Horsley, *Jesus and the Spiral of Violence: Popular Jewish Resistance in Roman Palestine* (San Francisco: Harper and Row, 1987), p. 192.

73. Matthew 18:3, 19:14; Mark 10:15; Luke 18:17.

74. Matthew 19:24; Mark 10:23, 25; Luke 18:25.

75. Matthew 20:25–28.

76. For a graphic description from the actual time period when these tortures were being inflicted, see "The Passion of Perpetua and Felicity," in *The Other Bible*, Willis Barnstone, ed. (San Francisco: Harper and Row, 1984), pp. 174–181. For an overview of the period, see Elaine Pagels, *The Gnostic Gospels* (New York: Vintage Books, 1979, 1989), pp. 70–101.

77. Solomon J. Schepps, "Foreword to the 1979 Edition," *The Lost Books of the Bible* (New York: Bell, 1979), p. 9.

78. Matthew 15:9; Mark 7:7.

79. Genesis 12–15.

80. Exodus 2–3.

81. Matthew 3:16–17; Mark 1:9–10; Luke 3:21–22.

82. Matthew 7:7; Luke 11:9.

83. *Gospel of Thomas* 113.

Notes to Chapter Two

1. Walter A. Elwell, *Evangelical Dictionary of Theology* (Grand Rapids: Baker, 1984). See the section under "The Trinity."

2. Ibid., under "Monarchianism."

3. For a history of this period, see Henry Chadwick, "The Early Christian Community," in *Oxford Illustrated History of Christianity*, McManners, ed., pp. 48–59.

4. Matthew 19:17; Mark 10:18.

5. Mark 12:28. See also Matthew 22:36–39.

6. Matthew 10:18; Mark 13:11; Luke 12:11. In the latter, Jesus says they will bring you "unto the synagogues, and unto magistrates, and powers."

7. Matthew 10:19–20. See also Mark 13:11; Luke 12:11–12.

8. John 14:17, 15:16, 16:13.

9. *Gospel of Truth* 29.2, 30.5.

10. Matthew 23:30–31. See also Matthew 23:35; Luke 11:50–51.

11. John 6:53.

12. *Gospel of Philip* 57.7–8.

13. Matthew 12:31–32. See also Mark 3:29 and Luke 12:10.

14. Jesus specifically said that people could ridicule him and be forgiven. "And whosoever shall speak a word against the Son of man, it shall be forgiven him: but unto him that blasphemeth against the Holy Ghost it shall not be forgiven" (Luke 12:10).

15. Luke 11:13; John 14:26.

16. John 14:26.

17. John 10:30.

18. John 10:33.

19. John 10:34.

20. John 10:35.

21. For statements that Jesus loved Mary most, see *Gospel of Philip* 64.2–10 and *Gospel of Mary* 10.1–2.

22. *Gospel of Mary* 8.20.

23. *Gospel of Philip* 73.20–22.

24. On the "anointment," see Luke 4:18.

25. *Treatise on the Resurrection* 49.15–17.

26. *Gospel of Philip* 73.1–5.

27. *The Book of Thomas the Contender* 143.35–36, 32–33.

28. Barclay, *New Testament Words*, p. 150.

29. Genesis 2:7. The Hebrew word for "breath" (as in "breath of life") used in this verse means "wind," but it is not the same Hebrew word for "wind" used in the "Spirit of God." However, later (at Genesis 6:17), the phrase "breath of life" does use the same Hebrew word for "wind" as is employed in the phrase "Holy Spirit" and "Spirit of God." See James Strong, *Strong's Exhaustive Concordance of the Bible, with Dictionaries of the Hebrew and Greek Words* (Lake Wylie, SC: Christian Heritage, 1988).

30. Genesis 1:2.

31. *Dialogue of the Savior* 141.7–12.

32. *Gospel of Thomas* 15.

33. *Gospel of Philip* 64.11–13.

34. *Gospel of Thomas* 51.

35. John 14:20.

36. J. D. Douglas and Merrill C. Tenney, *NIV Compact Dictionary of the Bible* (Grand Rapids: Zondervan, 1989), p. 39.

37. *Dialogue of the Savior* 146.8–11.

38. The prophecy of Isaiah can be found at Isaiah 40:3. That John was fulfilling this prophecy is stated at Matthew 3:3; Mark 1:3; Luke 3:4; and John 1:23.

39. Genesis 37:7.

40. Genesis 37:5.

41. Luke 10:18.

42. On the warning, see Matthew 26:33–35; Mark 14:29–31; Luke 22:33–34; John 13:37–38.

43. Mark 14:68.

44. Matthew 26:69–74; Mark 14:66–72; Luke 22:56–62; John 18:25–27.

45. There are other examples of Peter's fearfulness. One was when Jesus was walking on water in a stormy sea. He asked Peter to join him, but once Peter was on the water, Peter grew afraid and began to sink. See Matthew 14:28–31.

46. Matthew 19:27.

47. Matthew 5–7.

48. Matthew 13:1–52.

49. John 13:9.

50. Matthew 16:23.

51. John 18:10.

52. John 18:11. See also Matthew 26:51–54; Mark 14:47–48; Luke 22:50–51.

53. Luke 22:31–32.

54. Acts 2:41.

55. Acts 4:4.

56. See Acts, chapter 8. He instructed Simon the "sorcerer" and also a powerful eunuch in the court of the Queen of Ethiopia.

57. Acts 8:12.

58. Matthew 20:16.

59. Acts 2:38; 3:19; 4:2.

60. Acts 2:39.

61. Jesus warns of false prophets in Matthew 7:15, 24:11, 24:24, and Mark 13:22.

62. Matthew 26:34; Mark 14:30; Luke 22:34; John 13:38.

63. Mark 8:33.

64. Matthew 7:16, 7:20.

65. John 8:15.

66. Matthew 7:1; Luke 6:37.

67. John 8:7.

68. Luke 12:13–14.

69. John 5:18, 8:11.

70. Jesus included himself in this assessment. As mentioned above, at one point he said, "Why callest thou me good? there is none good but one, that is God." Matthew 19:17; Mark 10:18.

71. Matthew 18:23–35.

72. Matthew 23:23. See also Luke 11:42.

73. Matthew 12:11–12.

74. *Gospel of Thomas* 6.

75. *Gospel of Mary* 7.13–17.

76. Acts 6:2

77. Acts 6:3–4.

78. Acts 6:5.

79. Acts 6:14.

80. Acts 7:27–28.

81. Exodus does not mention the planet, but Stephen said they worshiped "the star of your god Remphan" (Acts 7:43).

82. Acts 7:48.

83. Acts 7:49.

84. Acts 7:51.

85. Matthew 27:40.

86. Matthew 27:42.

87. Matthew 27:44.

88. *Gospel of Philip* 55.15–23.

89. Acts 8:1.

90. The "laying on of hands" is first mentioned in Acts 8:18.

91. John 20:21–22.

92. Matthew 9:18; Mark 16:18.

93. Luke 10:31.

94. Maurice Casey, *From Jewish Prophet to Gentile God: The Origins of Testament Christology* (Louisville: Westminster/John Knox, 1991), p. 63.

95. Matthew 21:46; Mark 12:12. See also Luke 21:12.

96. Acts 8:10.

97. See G. R. S. Mead, *Simon Magus* (London, 1892).

98. See Romans 8:16, where "spiritually minded" is contrasted with "carnally minded."

99. Matthew 11:19.

100. *Gospel of Thomas* 112.

101. John 18:36.

Notes to Chapter Three

1. I am assuming that Jesus told his disciples this about Satan, for no one was with Jesus when the temptation occurred.

2. Although the Book of Job suggests they may be Satan's to take away.

3. Luke 4:3. See also Matthew 4:3.

4. Matthew 4:4; Luke 4:4.

5. This is the ordering of temptations in Matthew. Luke puts this temptation last.

6. Luke 4:5–6. Emphasis added.

7. Although everyone would acknowledge that the Christianity of Peter and Paul provided the cultural foundation for the Holy Roman Empire, they might disagree about the Christian origins of the empire of Islam. But I would urge them to read the Koran. The religion of Mohammed depends thoroughly on Jesus's teachings about the afterlife, the judgment, and Satan.

8. Isaiah 40:17

9. Maimonides, *The Guide for the Perplexed*, chap. 22

10. Ephesians 6:12

11. *Gospel of Philip* 74.6–8, 11–13.

12. Genesis 3:18.

13. Genesis 4:3.

14. Genesis 4:4.

15. Genesis 4:17 and following.

16. Matthew 13:35. See also Isaiah 45:1–3.

17. Matthew 14:3–12; Mark 6:14–29; Luke 3:19–20.

18. Mark 14:64, 15:1; Luke 22:71.

19. John 18:31.

20. Luke 23:4, 23:8–11.

21. Matthew 27:15–23; Mark 15:7–16; Luke 23:16–18; John 18:39–40.

22. Matthew 27:24.

23. Matthew 26:24. See also Mark 14:21 and Luke 22:22.

24. Leo Strauss, "History of Political Philosophy," in *An Introduction to Political Philosophy* (Detroit: Wayne State University Press, 1989), pp. 159–246.

25. Genesis 3:6.

26. Deuteronomy 4:19.

27. Genesis 3:11.

28. Genesis 4:10.

29. Genesis 11:5.

30. Matthew 10:16.

31. Genesis 2:9. The tree of knowledge of good and evil was located at the center of the garden.

32. Aside from the Book of Job, the only other places where Satan is mentioned by name is 1 Chronicles 21:1; Psalm 109:6; and Zechariah 3:1–2.

33. Job 1:7, 2:2.

34. Job 2:6.

35. This point is made in Jacques Ellul, *Apocalypse: The Book of Revelation* (New York: Seabury Press, 1977).

36. I. F. Stone, *The Trial of Socrates* (New York: Anchor Books, 1989), pp. 200–201.

37. Xenophon, *Socrates' Defense* 4–12.

38. See Plato's dialogue, *The Apology*.

39. See Plato's dialogue, *The Crito*.

40. John 1:29.

41. Matthew 26:28.

42. John 18:20–21.

43. John 18:22.

44. John 18:23.

45. Matthew 5:39; Luke 6:29.

46. John 18:34.

47. This is a paraphrase of Luke 8:44.

Notes to Chapter Four

1. Mark 9:43.

2. *The Book of Thomas the Contender* 143.14.

3. *The Book of Thomas the Contender* 142.1–2.

4. Unfortunately, the King James Version of the Bible translates "Hades" as "hell," so in this translation it is not possible to see where different words are being used. The references to Hades are (1) when Jesus tells Peter that "the gates of Hades shall not prevail" against the church (Matthew 16:18); (2) when Jesus prophesied that the city of Capernaum "shalt be brought down to Hades" (Matthew 11:23; Luke 10:15); and in the parable of Lazarus described below, when Jesus says of the rich man that "in Hades he lift up his eyes" (Luke 16:21–26). On the unfortunate rendering of "Hades" as "hell," see the listing for Hades in *Vine's Expository Dictionary of New Testament Words* (Oklahoma City: Ellis, 1988).

5. The King James Version of the Bible translates this as "hell," but the original in Greek is Hades. See *Strong's Concordance*.

6. *Strong's Concordance*, number 1067. See also *Vine's Expository Dictionary of the New Testament* under the listing for "hell."

7. R. Laird Harris, *Theological Workbook of the Old Testament* (Chicago: Moody Bible Institute, 1980). See the listing under "malak," Strong's number 4427.

8. Luke 12:5. See *Strong's Concordance* for the reference back to "Ge-Hinnom" or "Geena." Strong's number is 1067.

9. Matthew 5:29, 18:19; Mark 9:43, 9:47.

10. Matthew 23:15.

11. Matthew 5:22.

12. See the section on "malak" in Harris, *Theological Workbook of the Old Testament*.

13. Jeremiah 2:13 is the first and only Old Testament usage of the phrase "living water." Jeremiah refers to God as "the fountain of living waters." Jesus calls his teaching the "living water" at John 4:10 and John 7:38.

14. Isaiah 1:30.

15. Jeremiah 7:32.

16. Luke 23:31.

17. Mark 3:29.

18. Psalm 9:15.

19. John 2:18–19 quotes Jesus as saying, "Destroy this temple, and in three days I will raise it up." I am using the quote by Jesus' accuser at his trial, as reported in Mark 14:58. There are at least two reasons for thinking

that the latter is the more accurate quote. First, the quote in John suggests that Jesus challenged his listeners to tear down the temple themselves, but Jesus clearly saw himself as tearing down the temple or, more precisely, the temple law. Second, Stephen was tried for saying that Jesus would "destroy this place" and "change the customs which Moses delivered us" (Acts 6:14). For political reasons, the Gospel of John may have played down the fact that Jesus was wanting to eliminate the authority of organized religion.

20. See Matthew 26:61–62 and Mark 14:58.

21. Matthew 27:39–40; Mark 15:29–30.

22. John 2:20.

23. Matthew 26:61; Mark 14:60.

24. See John 2:21.

25. Acts 6:14.

26. Acts 7:48.

27. *Gospel of Thomas* 82.

28. Matthew 12:43–45.

29. Oswald Spengler, *The Decline of the West: Volume I, Form and Actuality* (New York: Alfred A. Knopf, 1926), p. 21. The current influence of Spengler's philosophy can be seen in the push to treat all cultures and civilizations equally in high school and university curricula. If all cultures live and die; if, in other words, there is not a competition between cultures in which some survive and others collapse, then there can be no higher and no lower cultures. All cultures are like flowers—each different, each interesting, each equally valuable. A culture built on nature-worship and human sacrifice is just as good as one founded on love and piety.

30. Each began with a religion, which united and inspired the people to pursue a high purpose, but eventually the social order's religious foundations were supplanted by the secular religion called "patriotism," at which point the civilization became decadent and eventually collapsed, either because of internal conflicts between economic classes or because the society grew too weak to defend itself against outside aggressors.

31. Arnold J. Toynbee, *A Study of History*, abridgement of volumes 7–10 by D.C. Somervel (Oxford: Oxford University Press, 1957, 1985), p. 312.

32. Leo Strauss, "The Mutual Influence of Theology and Philosophy," *The Independent Journal of Philosophy* 3 (1979): 114.

33. On the global reach of Western civilization, see Theodore H. Vo. Laue, *The World Revolution of Westernization: The Twentieth Century in Global Perspective* (New York: Oxford University Press, 1987).

34. The quote is from Matthew 24:24. The reference to places away from the world is from Matthew 24:26, which refers to "the desert" and "the secret chambers." The latter might be misconstrued as veiled references to gnosticism, but the original Greek suggests otherwise. The word for "secret chambers" was *tameion*, "a dispensary or magazine, i.e. a chamber on the ground floor or interior of an Oriental house (generally used for storage or privacy, a spot for retirement)." See Strong's reference number 5009. The idea is clearly one of people assuming, incorrectly, that Jesus can be found in some social subculture or monastic sect.

35. Matthew 24:28.

36. Matthew 16:1–4.

37. *Gospel of Thomas* 92.

38. Psalm 115:4.

39. Mark 5:15 says that after he was healed, he came into his "right mind," so it can assumed that earlier he was deranged.

40. Mark 5:9.

41. Mark 6:56, 10:52.

42. Mark 12:29.

43. Graham Parker, *The Mona Lisa's Sister* (New York: RCA, 1988).

44. David Bowie, *The Rise and Fall of Ziggy Stardust and the Spiders from Mars* (Salem: Rykodisc, Jones Music America, 1972).

45. Isaiah 3:5.

46. Isaiah 1:23.

47. Modern environmentalists call this the steady-state or no-growth society. The objective is to keep humans and nature in a delicate balance. A no-growth society was advocated in one of the most influential environmental tracts of the twentieth century, *The Limits to Growth*, which used a computer model to argue that, unless they were reduced, current trends of population growth and industrialization would lead quickly to an environmental catastrophe. In the no-growth society, "the relative levels of population and capital, and their relationships to fixed constraints such as land, fresh water, and mineral resources, would have to be set so that there would be enough food and material production to maintain everyone at (at least) a subsistence level." Donella H. Meadows, Dennis L.

Meadows, Jorgen Randers, and William W. Behrens, *The Limits to Growth* (New York: New American Library, 1972), p. 183.

Notes to Chapter Five

1. John 11:41–43.
2. Luke 10:21.
3. Matthew 26:39,42; Mark 14:36; Luke 22:42; John 12:27, 17:1–26.
4. Luke 23:34, 36.
5. Jesus taught the prayer (1) at his sermon on the mountain, which was attended both by the disciples and huge crowd (see Matthew 5–7; the prayer is at Matthew 6:9–13; the disciples are mentioned at Matthew 5:1; the crowds are described at Matthew 7:28–29, 8:1) and (2) at separate meeting with his disciples after they had been to the home of Mary and Martha (see Luke 11:1–13).
6. See, for example, Sheehan, *The First Coming*.
7. The first instance was by David (1 Chronicles 29:10). The other references are Psalms 68:5, 89:26, and 103:13; Proverbs 3:12; Isaiah 63:16 and 64:8; and Jeremiah 31:9.
8. Matthew 6:5–6.
9. Matthew 6:7–8.
10. John 16:23.
11. On the meaning in Hebrew, see Maimonides, *The Guide for the Perplexed*, chapters 61–64. On the Greek, Strong's reference number is 3686.
12. Matthew 6:6.
13. Matthew 6:9.
14. John 11:41.
15. Matthew 5:44; Luke 6:28.
16. Matthew 26:41; Mark 14:38.
17. Mark 9:29.
18. Luke 22:40.
19. *Gospel of Thomas* 14.
20. *Gospel of Philip* 52.29–30.
21. Matthew 6:11.
22. See Strong's reference numbers 1967 and 740.
23. Genesis 3:18–19.
24. Genesis 8:17, 21–22.

25. Matthew 19:21; Mark 10:21; Luke 18:22.

26. Matthew 14:16–20; Mark 6:38–42; Luke 9:13–17; John 6:9–13.

27. Matthew 15:31–37; Mark 8:5–8. The number of 4,000 is cited at Matthew 16:9. Jesus later says that there were only four loaves.

28. Mark 6:52.

29. John 6:26–27.

30. Matthew 26:11; Mark 14:7; John 12:8.

31. Matthew 11:5; Mark 14:7; Luke 4:18, 7:22.

32. Luke 6:20.

33. Matthew 5:39; Luke 6:27.

34. Matthew 5:40; Luke 6:30.

35. Matthew 5:44; Luke 6:27.

36. Matthew 7:2. See also Mark 4:24: "And he said unto them, Take heed what ye hear: with what measure ye mete, it shall be measured to you: and unto you that hear shall more be given." And Luke 6:38: "Give, and it shall be given unto you; good measure, pressed down, and shaken together, and running over, shall men give into your bosom. For with the same measure that ye mete withal it shall be measured to you again."

37. John 8:15.

38. John 12:47.

39. Matthew 22:17; Mark 12:14; Luke 20:22.

40. Luke 12:13.

41. Matthew 19:7.

42. Matthew 12:10; Mark 3:2; Luke 6:7.

43. Matthew 5:21–48.

44. Luke 22:4.

45. John 18:31.

46. John 8:5.

47. John 8:6.

48. John 8:7.

49. Luke 17:3–4.

50. *Gospel of Thomas* 25–26. See also Matthew 7:1–5.

51. Matthew 5:48.

52. *Gospel of Thomas* 57.

53. See *Gospel of Mary* 7.13–17.

54. Exodus 18:16–22.

55. Matthew 18:15.

56. Matthew 18:16.

57. Matthew 18:17.

58. See Strong's reference number 3986.

59. Matthew 22:17–18; Mark 12:15; Luke 20:22–23.

60. Matthew 19:3; Mark 10:2.

61. Matthew 22:35; Luke 10:25.

62. John 8:6.

63. Matthew 16:1; Mark 8:11; Luke 11:16.

64. *Gospel of Thomas* 42.

65. Matthew 6:13. That Jesus was speaking to a crowd when he taught this version of the prayer can be seen at Matthew 7:28–29 and 8:1.

66. Matthew 22:16; Mark 12:14.

67. Epistle of James 2:10.

68. James 2:8–9

69. Luke 11:2–4.

70. Luke 19:38.

71. Luke 19:40.

72. Zechariah 9:9.

73. Matthew 21:2–3; John 12:14.

74. John 12:13.

75. Luke 22:29.

76. Matthew 27:11; Mark 15:2; Luke 23:3; John 18:33.

77. Mark 15:9; John 18:39.

78. Matthew 27:37; Mark 15:26; Luke 22:38; John 19:19.

79. Matthew 27:29; Mark 15:18; John 19:3.

80. Matthew 27:44; Mark 15:32.

81. Polybius, *The Rise of the Roman Empire* (New York: Penguin Books), p. 318.

82. Exodus 32:26–30; Numbers 1:50.

83. Exodus 15:24, 16:12, 17:3; Numbers 14:2; 14:36; 16:11, 41.

84. Numbers 13:30–14:9.

85. Numbers 16:32.

86. 1 Samuel 8:11.

87. 1 Samuel 8:19–20.

Notes to Chapter Six

1. Matthew 11:14, 17:10–13; Mark 9:11–13.

2. John 1:21–23.

3. Luke 1:17.

4. Malachi 4:5.

5. Isaiah 53:7.

6. Isaiah 2:4.

7. Isaiah 11:6.

8. Malachi 4:1.

9. Malachi 3:18.

10. Matthew 16:14–15; Mark 8:28.

11. Luke 9:7–9.

12. Mark 8:29–30.

13. Luke 7:28.

14. Mark 9:2–10; Luke 9:28–36.

15. 2 Kings 1:10.

16. Luke 9:55.

17. John 14:3.

18. Matthew 24:29; Mark 13:24; Luke 21:22.

19. Matthew 24:30; Mark 13:26; Luke 21:27.

20. Matthew 24:24. See also Matthew 7:15, 24:11; Mark 13:22.

21. John 15:5.

22. John 15:4.

23. John 15:1–2.

24. Matthew 7:16.

25. See Exodus 13:21, 14:19, 16:10, 19:9, 24:15.

26. Mark 4:32.

27. *The Dialogue of the Savior* 144.6–9.

28. Mark 4:11–12.

29. Matthew 22:1–11.

30. Matthew 22:11–14.

31. Matthew 19:21–22; Mark 10:21–22.

32. Matthew 18:19–20.

33. Revelation 4:1.

34. This is an interpretation of Revelation 6.

35. See Revelation 8.

36. *Gospel of Thomas* 97.

37. *Gospel of Thomas* 98.

38. *Gospel of Thomas* 49. See also *Gospel of Thomas* 55 and 75.

39. Luke 12:53. See also Matthew 10:29, 10:35–37, 12:49, 19:29; and Luke 14:26.

40. *Gospel of Thomas* 22.

41. *Gospel of Thomas* 7. See also *Gospel of Thomas* 21.

42. *Dialogue of the Savior* 138.17–19.

43. Mark 10:15. See also Matthew 18:2–6, 19:14; Mark 9:37; Luke 9:48, 18:16–17.

44. Matthew 6:25. See verses 25–33 and also Mark 8:35; Luke 9:24, 12:22–35; John 12:25.

45. *Gospel of Thomas* 42.

46. Matthew 5:17.

47. On murder, see Matthew 5:21–26. On adultery, see Matthew 5:27–32.

48. Matthew 6:1–8.

49. Matthew 5:29.

50. Matthew 11:30; *Gospel of Thomas* 91.

51. Genesis 27:40; Leviticus 26:13, 28:48; 1 Kings 12:4, 9, 10, 11, 14; 2 Chronicles 10:4, 9–11; Isaiah 9:4, 10:27, 14:25, 47:6, 58:6, 9; Jeremiah 2:20, 5:5, 27:8, 11, 12, 28:2, 4, 10–12, 14, 31:18; Lamentations 1:14; Ezekiel 34:27; Hosea 11:4; Nahum 1:13.

52. Matthew 10:26.

53. *Gospel of Thomas* 32.

54. *Gospel of Thomas* 24.

Bibliography

Barclay, William. *New Testament Words.* Philadelphia: Westminster, 1964.

Barth, Karl. *A Karl Barth Reader.* Ed. and trans. Geoffrey W. Bromiley. Grand Rapids: Eerdmans, 1986.

Book of Thomas the Contender in *The Nag Hammadi Library in English.* Trans. John D. Turner; James M. Robinson, general editor. San Francisco: HarperSanFrancisco, 1978, 1988, 1990.

Bowie, David. *The Rise and Fall of Ziggy Stardust and the Spiders from Mars.* Salem, Massachusetts: Rykodisc, Jones Music America, 1972, 1990.

Casey, Maurice. *From Jewish Prophet to Gentile God: The Origins of New Testament Christology.* Louisville: Westminster/John Knox, 1991.

Chadwick, Henry. "The Early Christian Community," in *The Oxford Illustrated History of Christianity.* Ed. John McManners. Oxford: Oxford University Press, 1990.

Chadwick, Owen. "Great Britain and Europe," In *The Oxford Illustrated History of Christianity.* Ed. John McManners. Oxford: Oxford University Press, 1990.

Dialogue of the Savior in *The Nag Hammadi Library in English.* Trans. Stephen Emmel; James M. Robinson, general editor. San Francisco: HarperSanFrancisco, 1978, 1988, 1990.

Douglas, J. D., and Merrill C. Tenney. *NIV Compact Dictionary of the Bible.* Grand Rapids: Zondervan, 1989.

Drury, Shadia B. *The Political Ideas of Leo Strauss.* New York: St. Martin's, 1988.

Ellul, Jacques. *Apocalypse: The Book of Revelation.* Trans. George W. Schreiner. New York: Seabury, 1977.

———. *The Humiliation of the Word.* Trans. Joyce M. Hanks. Grand Rapids: Eerdmans, 1985.

———. *The Subversion of Christianity.* Trans. Geoffrey W. Bromiley. Grand Rapids: Eerdmans, 1986.

———. *Anarchy and Christianity.* Trans. Geoffrey W. Bromiley. Grand Rapids: Eerdmans, 1988.

———. *What I Believe.* Trans. Geoffrey W. Bromiley. Grand Rapids:

Eerdmans, 1989.

———. *Reason for Being: A Meditation on Ecclesiastes.* Trans. Joyce Main Hanks. Grand Rapids: Eerdmans, 1990.

Elwell, Walter A. *Evangelical Dictionary of Theology.* Grand Rapids: Baker, 1984.

Fideler, David. *Jesus Christ, Sun of God: Ancient Cosmology and Early Christian Symbolism.* Wheaton: Quest Books, 1993.

Flavius, Josephus. *The Jewish War.* Trans. William Whiston. Israel: Steimatzky, n.d.

Gospel of Mary in *The Nag Hammadi Library in English.* Trans. George W. MacRae and R. McL. Wilson; James M. Robinson, general editor. San Francisco: HarperSanFrancisco, 1978, 1988, 1990.

Gospel of Philip in *The Nag Hammadi Library in English.* Trans. Wesley W. Isenberg; James M. Robinson, general editor. San Francisco: HarperSanFrancisco, 1978, 1988, 1990.

Gospel of Thomas in *The Nag Hammadi Library in English.* Trans. Thomas O. Lambdin; James M. Robinson, general editor. San Francisco: HarperSanFrancisco, 1978, 1988, 1990.

Gospel of Truth in *The Nag Hammadi Library in English.* Trans. Harold W. Attridge and George W. MacRae; James M. Robinson, general editor. San Francisco: HarperSanFrancisco, 1978, 1988, 1990.

Ladd, George Eldon. *The Presence of the Future: The Eschatology of Biblical Realism.* Grand Rapids: Eerdmans, 1946, 1952.

———. *Crucial Questions about the Kingdom of God.* Grand Rapids: Eerdmans, 1952.

Harris, R. Laird. *Theological Workbook of the Old Testament.* Chicago: The Moody Bible Institute of Chicago, 1980.

Horsley, Richard A. *Jesus and the Spiral of Violence: Popular Jewish Resistance in Roman Palestine.* San Francisco: Harper and Row, 1987.

Mead, G. R. S. *Simon Magus.* London, 1892.

Meadows, Donella H., Dennis L. Meadows, Jorgen Randers, and William W. Behrens. *The Limits to Growth.* New York: E.P. Dutton, 1972.

Maimonides, Moses. *The Guide for the Perplexed.* Trans. M. Friedlander. New York: Dover, 1904, 1956.

Pagels, Elaine. *The Gnostic Gospels.* New York: Vintage Books, 1979, 1989.

Parker, Graham. *The Mona Lisa's Sister.* New York: RCA, 1988.

The Passion of Perpetua and Felicity. in *The Other Bible.* Ed. Willis Barnstone.

San Francisco: Harper and Row, 1984.

Pelikan, Jaroslav. *The Excellent Empire: The Fall of Rome and the Triumph of the Church.* San Francisco: Harper and Row, 1987.

Plato. *The Apology.*

———. *The Crito.*

Polybius. *The Rise of the Roman Empire.* New York: Penguin Books, 1979.

Popper, Karl R. *The Open Society and Its Enemies.* Princeton: Princeton University Press, 1943.

Pottenger, John R. *The Political Theory of Liberation Theology: Toward a Reconvergence of Social Values and Social Science.* Albany: State University of New York Press, 1989.

Schepps, Solomon J. Foreword to *The Lost Books of the Bible.* New York: Bell, 1979.

Sheehan, Thomas. *The First Coming: How the Kingdom of God Became Christianity.* New York: Random House, 1986.

Spengler, Oswald. *The Decline of the West: Volume I, Form and Actuality.* Trans. Charles Francis Atkinson. New York: Alfred A. Knopf, 1926.

Spinoza, Benedict de. *A Theologico-Political Treatise.* Trans. R. H. M. Elwes. New York: Dover, 1951.

Stone, I. F. *The Trial of Socrates.* New York: Anchor, 1989.

Strauss, Leo. *Natural Right and History.* Chicago: University of Chicago Press, 1950.

———. *Persecution and the Art of Writing.* Chicago: The University of Chicago Press, 1952, 1980.

———. *Thoughts on Machiavelli.* Chicago: University of Chicago Press, 1958.

———. *What is Political Philosophy?* Chicago: University of Chicago Press, 1959.

———. "The Mutual Influence of Theology and Philosophy" in *The Independent Journal of Philosophy* 3 (1979): 111–118.

———. Introduction to *History of Political Philosophy* in *An Introduction to Political Philosophy: Ten Essays by Leo Strauss.* Ed. Hilail Gildin. Detroit: Wayne State University Press, 1989.

Strong, James. *Strong's Exhaustive Concordance of the Bible, with Dictionaries of the Hebrew and Greek Words.* Lake Wylie, South Carolina: Christian Heritage, 1988.

Tinder, Glenn. *The Political Meaning of Christianity: The Prophetic Stance.*

San Francisco: HarperSanFrancisco, 1991.

Toynbee, Arnold. *A Study of History.* Abridgement of volumes 7–10 by D. C. Somervel. Oxford: Oxford University Press, 1957, 1985.

Treatise on the Resurrection in *The Nag Hammadi Library in English.* Trans. Malcolm L. Peel; James M. Robinson, general editor. San Francisco: HarperSanFrancisco, 1978, 1988, 1990.

Vine's Expository Dictionary of New Testament Words. Oklahoma City: Ellis Enterprises, 1988.

Von Laue, Theodore H. *The World Revolution of Westernization: The Twentieth Century in Global Perspective.* New York: Oxford University Press, 1987.

Xenophon. *Socrates' Defense.*

Index

Aaron, 175

Abel, God learning about death of, 99; and original sin, 91–92

Abraham, 19, 25; with Lazarus, 113

Acts of the Apostles, as an account of Christianity's subversion, 38–39, 180–181; differences between the gospels and, 46, 50. *See also* Hands, laying on of; Simon the magician; Stephen, trial of

Adam, 28, 56; ejection of, from Eden, 90–91, 154, 199; and the inclination to worship nature, 98; meaning of, for Western civilization, 122; replacement of God's commandments with human laws by, 90–91, 106. *See also* Sin, of the world

Afterlife, the, Abraham in, 113; faith in, 13, 51; Jesus' teachings about, 26, 113–114; Lazarus in, 113. *See also* Hades; Hell

Aggaraeia, 20, 28. *See also* Roman Empire, type of oppression under

AIDS, 17

Alexander the Great, empire of, 31

Amos, 19

Angel, as a spirit of holiness, 101

Apocalypse, 59. *See also* Armageddon

Apostles, 15

Aristophanes, 105

Aristotle, political theory of, 172; unleashing of political power by, 31. *See also* Government, Greek philosophers' theory of; Greek philosophy; Modern era, nature worship in; Modern era, politics in; Science, compared to Greco-Roman philosophy

Arius, excommunication of, 47; and the Nicene Council, 48

Armageddon, John's revelations about, 195; and organized Christianity, 39

Atheism, concentration of, in the upper classes, 95; and hedonism, 96; and the idea of "nature," 95; in modern universities, 211; presence of, in all social orders, 94; and the search for justice, 162. *See also* Faith, deconstruction of, by science; Science, atheism of

Baal, and derivation of "Beelzebub," 36; worship of, at Tophet, 113

Babel, Tower of, 122

Barabas, 93

Barth, Karl, 15

Beatitudes, as prophecies, 200, 202–204

Bible, the, and belief that God is outside of nature, 96; codification of, 10; interpreting, 9; translation of, during the Reformation, 123, 187–188; science's mirroring of, 125–126. *See also* Gospel of; Gospels; New Testament; Old Testament

Book of Job. *See* Job, Book of

Book of Thomas the Contender, 10, 111–112. *See also* Gospels, gnostic

Cain, God learning about murder by, 99; and original sin, 91–92

Canaanites, religious subversion of, 35–36

Capitalism, as a cause of mass democracy, 189; spirit of, 62

Christianity, 9, 10, 13; accounts by, of the kingdom of God, 15–16; corruption of, 16, 42, 123, 208; early form of society in, 40;

235

HE comes to us as One unknown, without a name, as of old by the lakeside He came to those who knew him not. HE speaks to us the same word, "follow thou Me," and sets us to the task which HE has to fulfill for our time. HE commands. To those who obey, whether they be wise or simple, HE will reveal himself in the toils, the conflicts, the sufferings which they shall pass through in His fellowship, and as ineffable mystery, they shall learn in Their Own experience who HE IS.